ATS-101   ADMISSION TEST SERIES

This is your
PASSBOOK for...

California Achievement Test (CAT)

Test Preparation Study Guide
Questions & Answers

COPYRIGHT NOTICE

This book is SOLELY intended for, is sold ONLY to, and its use is RESTRICTED to individual, bona fide applicants or candidates who qualify by virtue of having seriously filed applications for appropriate license, certificate, professional and/or promotional advancement, higher school matriculation, scholarship, or other legitimate requirements of education and/or governmental authorities.

This book is NOT intended for use, class instruction, tutoring, training, duplication, copying, reprinting, excerption, or adaptation, etc., by:

1) Other publishers
2) Proprietors and/or Instructors of "Coaching" and/or Preparatory Courses
3) Personnel and/or Training Divisions of commercial, industrial, and governmental organizations
4) Schools, colleges, or universities and/or their departments and staffs, including teachers and other personnel
5) Testing Agencies or Bureaus
6) Study groups which seek by the purchase of a single volume to copy and/or duplicate and/or adapt this material for use by the group as a whole without having purchased individual volumes for each of the members of the group
7) Et al.

Such persons would be in violation of appropriate Federal and State statutes.

PROVISION OF LICENSING AGREEMENTS – Recognized educational, commercial, industrial, and governmental institutions and organizations, and others legitimately engaged in educational pursuits, including training, testing, and measurement activities, may address request for a licensing agreement to the copyright owners, who will determine whether, and under what conditions, including fees and charges, the materials in this book may be used them. In other words, a licensing facility exists for the legitimate use of the material in this book on other than an individual basis. However, it is asseverated and affirmed here that the material in this book CANNOT be used without the receipt of the express permission of such a licensing agreement from the Publishers. Inquiries re licensing should be addressed to the company, attention rights and permissions department.

All rights reserved, including the right of reproduction in whole or in part, in any form or by any means, electronic or mechanical, including photocopying, recording, or by any information storage and retrieval system, without permission in writing from the Publisher.

Copyright © 2025 by
National Learning Corporation

212 Michael Drive, Syosset, NY 11791
(516) 921-8888 • www.passbooks.com
E-mail: info@passbooks.com

PASSBOOK® SERIES

THE *PASSBOOK® SERIES* has been created to prepare applicants and candidates for the ultimate academic battlefield – the examination room.

At some time in our lives, each and every one of us may be required to take an examination – for validation, matriculation, admission, qualification, registration, certification, or licensure.

Based on the assumption that every applicant or candidate has met the basic formal educational standards, has taken the required number of courses, and read the necessary texts, the *PASSBOOK® SERIES* furnishes the one special preparation which may assure passing with confidence, instead of failing with insecurity. Examination questions – together with answers – are furnished as the basic vehicle for study so that the mysteries of the examination and its compounding difficulties may be eliminated or diminished by a sure method.

This book is meant to help you pass your examination provided that you qualify and are serious in your objective.

The entire field is reviewed through the huge store of content information which is succinctly presented through a provocative and challenging approach – the question-and-answer method.

A climate of success is established by furnishing the correct answers at the end of each test.

You soon learn to recognize types of questions, forms of questions, and patterns of questioning. You may even begin to anticipate expected outcomes.

You perceive that many questions are repeated or adapted so that you can gain acute insights, which may enable you to score many sure points.

You learn how to confront new questions, or types of questions, and to attack them confidently and work out the correct answers.

You note objectives and emphases, and recognize pitfalls and dangers, so that you may make positive educational adjustments.

Moreover, you are kept fully informed in relation to new concepts, methods, practices, and directions in the field.

You discover that you are actually taking the examination all the time: you are preparing for the examination by "taking" an examination, not by reading extraneous and/or supererogatory textbooks.

In short, this PASSBOOK®, used directedly, should be an important factor in helping you to pass your test.

CALIFORNIA ACHIEVEMENT TEST

The California Achievement Test measures broad academic proficiency in verbal and quantitative disciplines including vocabulary, reading and mathematics.

First introduced in 1950, the CAT is a test for children from kindergarten through grade 12 that is designed to measure academic competency in a variety of areas. The test is available in many different forms: CAT Complete Battery, CAT Basic Battery, CAT Survey (grades two through 12 only), and CAT Plus, to name the most prominent.

The CAT Elementary School Passbook covers all forms and areas of the test including, but not limited to: basic vocabulary and verbal ability, spelling, reading, arithmetic, verbal and numerical relationships, thinking and reasoning.

The California Achievement Test for Middle and Secondary School Passbook prepares students for entrance examinations into college, graduate and professional school as well as candidates for professional certification and licensure. It provides hundreds of questions and answers in the areas that will likely be covered on your upcoming exam, including but not limited to: vocabulary; reading comprehension; basic arithmetic; algebra; and more.

HOW TO TAKE A TEST

I. YOU MUST PASS AN EXAMINATION

A. *WHAT EVERY CANDIDATE SHOULD KNOW*

Examination applicants often ask us for help in preparing for the written test. What can I study in advance? What kinds of questions will be asked? How will the test be given? How will the papers be graded?

As an applicant for a civil service examination, you may be wondering about some of these things. Our purpose here is to suggest effective methods of advance study and to describe civil service examinations.

Your chances for success on this examination can be increased if you know how to prepare. Those "pre-examination jitters" can be reduced if you know what to expect. You can even experience an adventure in good citizenship if you know why civil service exams are given.

B. *WHY ARE CIVIL SERVICE EXAMINATIONS GIVEN?*

Civil service examinations are important to you in two ways. As a citizen, you want public jobs filled by employees who know how to do their work. As a job seeker, you want a fair chance to compete for that job on an equal footing with other candidates. The best-known means of accomplishing this two-fold goal is the competitive examination.

Exams are widely publicized throughout the nation. They may be administered for jobs in federal, state, city, municipal, town or village governments or agencies.

Any citizen may apply, with some limitations, such as the age or residence of applicants. Your experience and education may be reviewed to see whether you meet the requirements for the particular examination. When these requirements exist, they are reasonable and applied consistently to all applicants. Thus, a competitive examination may cause you some uneasiness now, but it is your privilege and safeguard.

C. *HOW ARE CIVIL SERVICE EXAMS DEVELOPED?*

Examinations are carefully written by trained technicians who are specialists in the field known as "psychological measurement," in consultation with recognized authorities in the field of work that the test will cover. These experts recommend the subject matter areas or skills to be tested; only those knowledges or skills important to your success on the job are included. The most reliable books and source materials available are used as references. Together, the experts and technicians judge the difficulty level of the questions.

Test technicians know how to phrase questions so that the problem is clearly stated. Their ethics do not permit "trick" or "catch" questions. Questions may have been tried out on sample groups, or subjected to statistical analysis, to determine their usefulness.

Written tests are often used in combination with performance tests, ratings of training and experience, and oral interviews. All of these measures combine to form the best-known means of finding the right person for the right job.

II. HOW TO PASS THE WRITTEN TEST

A. NATURE OF THE EXAMINATION

To prepare intelligently for civil service examinations, you should know how they differ from school examinations you have taken. In school you were assigned certain definite pages to read or subjects to cover. The examination questions were quite detailed and usually emphasized memory. Civil service exams, on the other hand, try to discover your present ability to perform the duties of a position, plus your potentiality to learn these duties. In other words, a civil service exam attempts to predict how successful you will be. Questions cover such a broad area that they cannot be as minute and detailed as school exam questions.

In the public service similar kinds of work, or positions, are grouped together in one "class." This process is known as *position-classification*. All the positions in a class are paid according to the salary range for that class. One class title covers all of these positions, and they are all tested by the same examination.

B. FOUR BASIC STEPS

1) Study the announcement

How, then, can you know what subjects to study? Our best answer is: "Learn as much as possible about the class of positions for which you've applied." The exam will test the knowledge, skills and abilities needed to do the work.

Your most valuable source of information about the position you want is the official exam announcement. This announcement lists the training and experience qualifications. Check these standards and apply only if you come reasonably close to meeting them.

The brief description of the position in the examination announcement offers some clues to the subjects which will be tested. Think about the job itself. Review the duties in your mind. Can you perform them, or are there some in which you are rusty? Fill in the blank spots in your preparation.

Many jurisdictions preview the written test in the exam announcement by including a section called "Knowledge and Abilities Required," "Scope of the Examination," or some similar heading. Here you will find out specifically what fields will be tested.

2) Review your own background

Once you learn in general what the position is all about, and what you need to know to do the work, ask yourself which subjects you already know fairly well and which need improvement. You may wonder whether to concentrate on improving your strong areas or on building some background in your fields of weakness. When the announcement has specified "some knowledge" or "considerable knowledge," or has used adjectives like "beginning principles of..." or "advanced ... methods," you can get a clue as to the number and difficulty of questions to be asked in any given field. More questions, and hence broader coverage, would be included for those subjects which are more important in the work. Now weigh your strengths and weaknesses against the job requirements and prepare accordingly.

3) Determine the level of the position

Another way to tell how intensively you should prepare is to understand the level of the job for which you are applying. Is it the entering level? In other words, is this the position in which beginners in a field of work are hired? Or is it an intermediate or advanced level? Sometimes this is indicated by such words as "Junior" or "Senior" in the class title. Other jurisdictions use Roman numerals to designate the level – Clerk I, Clerk II, for example. The word "Supervisor" sometimes appears in the title. If the level is not indicated by the title, check the description of duties. Will you be working under very close supervision, or will you have responsibility for independent decisions in this work?

4) Choose appropriate study materials

Now that you know the subjects to be examined and the relative amount of each subject to be covered, you can choose suitable study materials. For beginning level jobs, or even advanced ones, if you have a pronounced weakness in some aspect of your training, read a modern, standard textbook in that field. Be sure it is up to date and has general coverage. Such books are normally available at your library, and the librarian will be glad to help you locate one. For entry-level positions, questions of appropriate difficulty are chosen – neither highly advanced questions, nor those too simple. Such questions require careful thought but not advanced training.

If the position for which you are applying is technical or advanced, you will read more advanced, specialized material. If you are already familiar with the basic principles of your field, elementary textbooks would waste your time. Concentrate on advanced textbooks and technical periodicals. Think through the concepts and review difficult problems in your field.

These are all general sources. You can get more ideas on your own initiative, following these leads. For example, training manuals and publications of the government agency which employs workers in your field can be useful, particularly for technical and professional positions. A letter or visit to the government department involved may result in more specific study suggestions, and certainly will provide you with a more definite idea of the exact nature of the position you are seeking.

III. KINDS OF TESTS

Tests are used for purposes other than measuring knowledge and ability to perform specified duties. For some positions, it is equally important to test ability to make adjustments to new situations or to profit from training. In others, basic mental abilities not dependent on information are essential. Questions which test these things may not appear as pertinent to the duties of the position as those which test for knowledge and information. Yet they are often highly important parts of a fair examination. For very general questions, it is almost impossible to help you direct your study efforts. What we can do is to point out some of the more common of these general abilities needed in public service positions and describe some typical questions.

1) General information

Broad, general information has been found useful for predicting job success in some kinds of work. This is tested in a variety of ways, from vocabulary lists to questions about current events. Basic background in some field of work, such as sociology or economics, may be sampled in a group of questions. Often these are principles which have become familiar to most persons through exposure rather than through formal training. It is difficult to advise you how to study for these questions; being alert to the world around you is our best suggestion.

2) Verbal ability

An example of an ability needed in many positions is verbal or language ability. Verbal ability is, in brief, the ability to use and understand words. Vocabulary and grammar tests are typical measures of this ability. Reading comprehension or paragraph interpretation questions are common in many kinds of civil service tests. You are given a paragraph of written material and asked to find its central meaning.

3) Numerical ability

Number skills can be tested by the familiar arithmetic problem, by checking paired lists of numbers to see which are alike and which are different, or by interpreting charts and graphs. In the latter test, a graph may be printed in the test booklet which you are asked to use as the basis for answering questions.

4) Observation

A popular test for law-enforcement positions is the observation test. A picture is shown to you for several minutes, then taken away. Questions about the picture test your ability to observe both details and larger elements.

5) Following directions

In many positions in the public service, the employee must be able to carry out written instructions dependably and accurately. You may be given a chart with several columns, each column listing a variety of information. The questions require you to carry out directions involving the information given in the chart.

6) Skills and aptitudes

Performance tests effectively measure some manual skills and aptitudes. When the skill is one in which you are trained, such as typing or shorthand, you can practice. These tests are often very much like those given in business school or high school courses. For many of the other skills and aptitudes, however, no short-time preparation can be made. Skills and abilities natural to you or that you have developed throughout your lifetime are being tested.

Many of the general questions just described provide all the data needed to answer the questions and ask you to use your reasoning ability to find the answers. Your best preparation for these tests, as well as for tests of facts and ideas, is to be at your physical and mental best. You, no doubt, have your own methods of getting into an exam-taking mood and keeping "in shape." The next section lists some ideas on this subject.

IV. KINDS OF QUESTIONS

Only rarely is the "essay" question, which you answer in narrative form, used in civil service tests. Civil service tests are usually of the short-answer type. Full instructions for answering these questions will be given to you at the examination. But in case this is your first experience with short-answer questions and separate answer sheets, here is what you need to know:

1) Multiple-choice Questions

Most popular of the short-answer questions is the "multiple choice" or "best answer" question. It can be used, for example, to test for factual knowledge, ability to solve problems or judgment in meeting situations found at work.

A multiple-choice question is normally one of three types—
- It can begin with an incomplete statement followed by several possible endings. You are to find the one ending which *best* completes the statement, although some of the others may not be entirely wrong.
- It can also be a complete statement in the form of a question which is answered by choosing one of the statements listed.

- It can be in the form of a problem – again you select the best answer.

Here is an example of a multiple-choice question with a discussion which should give you some clues as to the method for choosing the right answer:

When an employee has a complaint about his assignment, the action which will *best* help him overcome his difficulty is to
- A. discuss his difficulty with his coworkers
- B. take the problem to the head of the organization
- C. take the problem to the person who gave him the assignment
- D. say nothing to anyone about his complaint

In answering this question, you should study each of the choices to find which is best. Consider choice "A" – Certainly an employee may discuss his complaint with fellow employees, but no change or improvement can result, and the complaint remains unresolved. Choice "B" is a poor choice since the head of the organization probably does not know what assignment you have been given, and taking your problem to him is known as "going over the head" of the supervisor. The supervisor, or person who made the assignment, is the person who can clarify it or correct any injustice. Choice "C" is, therefore, correct. To say nothing, as in choice "D," is unwise. Supervisors have and interest in knowing the problems employees are facing, and the employee is seeking a solution to his problem.

2) True/False Questions

The "true/false" or "right/wrong" form of question is sometimes used. Here a complete statement is given. Your job is to decide whether the statement is right or wrong.

SAMPLE: A roaming cell-phone call to a nearby city costs less than a non-roaming call to a distant city.

This statement is wrong, or false, since roaming calls are more expensive.

This is not a complete list of all possible question forms, although most of the others are variations of these common types. You will always get complete directions for answering questions. Be sure you understand *how* to mark your answers – ask questions until you do.

V. RECORDING YOUR ANSWERS

Computer terminals are used more and more today for many different kinds of exams.

For an examination with very few applicants, you may be told to record your answers in the test booklet itself. Separate answer sheets are much more common. If this separate answer sheet is to be scored by machine – and this is often the case – it is highly important that you mark your answers correctly in order to get credit.

An electronic scoring machine is often used in civil service offices because of the speed with which papers can be scored. Machine-scored answer sheets must be marked with a pencil, which will be given to you. This pencil has a high graphite content which responds to the electronic scoring machine. As a matter of fact, stray dots may register as answers, so do not let your pencil rest on the answer sheet while you are pondering the correct answer. Also, if your pencil lead breaks or is otherwise defective, ask for another.

Since the answer sheet will be dropped in a slot in the scoring machine, be careful not to bend the corners or get the paper crumpled.

The answer sheet normally has five vertical columns of numbers, with 30 numbers to a column. These numbers correspond to the question numbers in your test booklet. After each number, going across the page are four or five pairs of dotted lines. These short dotted lines have small letters or numbers above them. The first two pairs may also have a "T" or "F" above the letters. This indicates that the first two pairs only are to be used if the questions are of the true-false type. If the questions are multiple choice, disregard the "T" and "F" and pay attention only to the small letters or numbers.

Answer your questions in the manner of the sample that follows:

32. The largest city in the United States is
     A. Washington, D.C.
     B. New York City
     C. Chicago
     D. Detroit
     E. San Francisco

1) Choose the answer you think is best. (New York City is the largest, so "B" is correct.)
2) Find the row of dotted lines numbered the same as the question you are answering. (Find row number 32)
3) Find the pair of dotted lines corresponding to the answer. (Find the pair of lines under the mark "B.")
4) Make a solid black mark between the dotted lines.

VI. BEFORE THE TEST

Common sense will help you find procedures to follow to get ready for an examination. Too many of us, however, overlook these sensible measures. Indeed, nervousness and fatigue have been found to be the most serious reasons why applicants fail to do their best on civil service tests. Here is a list of reminders:

- Begin your preparation early – Don't wait until the last minute to go scurrying around for books and materials or to find out what the position is all about.
- Prepare continuously – An hour a night for a week is better than an all-night cram session. This has been definitely established. What is more, a night a week for a month will return better dividends than crowding your study into a shorter period of time.
- Locate the place of the exam – You have been sent a notice telling you when and where to report for the examination. If the location is in a different town or otherwise unfamiliar to you, it would be well to inquire the best route and learn something about the building.
- Relax the night before the test – Allow your mind to rest. Do not study at all that night. Plan some mild recreation or diversion; then go to bed early and get a good night's sleep.
- Get up early enough to make a leisurely trip to the place for the test – This way unforeseen events, traffic snarls, unfamiliar buildings, etc. will not upset you.
- Dress comfortably – A written test is not a fashion show. You will be known by number and not by name, so wear something comfortable.

- Leave excess paraphernalia at home – Shopping bags and odd bundles will get in your way. You need bring only the items mentioned in the official notice you received; usually everything you need is provided. Do not bring reference books to the exam. They will only confuse those last minutes and be taken away from you when in the test room.
- Arrive somewhat ahead of time – If because of transportation schedules you must get there very early, bring a newspaper or magazine to take your mind off yourself while waiting.
- Locate the examination room – When you have found the proper room, you will be directed to the seat or part of the room where you will sit. Sometimes you are given a sheet of instructions to read while you are waiting. Do not fill out any forms until you are told to do so; just read them and be prepared.
- Relax and prepare to listen to the instructions
- If you have any physical problem that may keep you from doing your best, be sure to tell the test administrator. If you are sick or in poor health, you really cannot do your best on the exam. You can come back and take the test some other time.

VII. AT THE TEST

The day of the test is here and you have the test booklet in your hand. The temptation to get going is very strong. Caution! There is more to success than knowing the right answers. You must know how to identify your papers and understand variations in the type of short-answer question used in this particular examination. Follow these suggestions for maximum results from your efforts:

1) Cooperate with the monitor

The test administrator has a duty to create a situation in which you can be as much at ease as possible. He will give instructions, tell you when to begin, check to see that you are marking your answer sheet correctly, and so on. He is not there to guard you, although he will see that your competitors do not take unfair advantage. He wants to help you do your best.

2) Listen to all instructions

Don't jump the gun! Wait until you understand all directions. In most civil service tests you get more time than you need to answer the questions. So don't be in a hurry. Read each word of instructions until you clearly understand the meaning. Study the examples, listen to all announcements and follow directions. Ask questions if you do not understand what to do.

3) Identify your papers

Civil service exams are usually identified by number only. You will be assigned a number; you must not put your name on your test papers. Be sure to copy your number correctly. Since more than one exam may be given, copy your exact examination title.

4) Plan your time

Unless you are told that a test is a "speed" or "rate of work" test, speed itself is usually not important. Time enough to answer all the questions will be provided, but this does not mean that you have all day. An overall time limit has been set. Divide the total time (in minutes) by the number of questions to determine the approximate time you have for each question.

5) Do not linger over difficult questions

If you come across a difficult question, mark it with a paper clip (useful to have along) and come back to it when you have been through the booklet. One caution if you do this – be sure to skip a number on your answer sheet as well. Check often to be sure that you have not lost your place and that you are marking in the row numbered the same as the question you are answering.

6) Read the questions

Be sure you know what the question asks! Many capable people are unsuccessful because they failed to *read* the questions correctly.

7) Answer all questions

Unless you have been instructed that a penalty will be deducted for incorrect answers, it is better to guess than to omit a question.

8) Speed tests

It is often better NOT to guess on speed tests. It has been found that on timed tests people are tempted to spend the last few seconds before time is called in marking answers at random – without even reading them – in the hope of picking up a few extra points. To discourage this practice, the instructions may warn you that your score will be "corrected" for guessing. That is, a penalty will be applied. The incorrect answers will be deducted from the correct ones, or some other penalty formula will be used.

9) Review your answers

If you finish before time is called, go back to the questions you guessed or omitted to give them further thought. Review other answers if you have time.

10) Return your test materials

If you are ready to leave before others have finished or time is called, take ALL your materials to the monitor and leave quietly. Never take any test material with you. The monitor can discover whose papers are not complete, and taking a test booklet may be grounds for disqualification.

VIII. EXAMINATION TECHNIQUES

1) Read the general instructions carefully. These are usually printed on the first page of the exam booklet. As a rule, these instructions refer to the timing of the examination; the fact that you should not start work until the signal and must stop work at a signal, etc. If there are any *special* instructions, such as a choice of questions to be answered, make sure that you note this instruction carefully.

2) When you are ready to start work on the examination, that is as soon as the signal has been given, read the instructions to each question booklet, underline any key words or phrases, such as *least, best, outline, describe* and the like. In this way you will tend to answer as requested rather than discover on reviewing your paper that you *listed without describing*, that you selected the *worst* choice rather than the *best* choice, etc.

3) If the examination is of the objective or multiple-choice type – that is, each question will also give a series of possible answers: A, B, C or D, and you are called upon to select the best answer and write the letter next to that answer on your answer paper – it is advisable to start answering each question in turn. There may be anywhere from 50 to 100 such questions in the three or four hours allotted and you can see how much time would be taken if you read through all the questions before beginning to answer any. Furthermore, if you come across a question or group of questions which you know would be difficult to answer, it would undoubtedly affect your handling of all the other questions.

4) If the examination is of the essay type and contains but a few questions, it is a moot point as to whether you should read all the questions before starting to answer any one. Of course, if you are given a choice – say five out of seven and the like – then it is essential to read all the questions so you can eliminate the two that are most difficult. If, however, you are asked to answer all the questions, there may be danger in trying to answer the easiest one first because you may find that you will spend too much time on it. The best technique is to answer the first question, then proceed to the second, etc.

5) Time your answers. Before the exam begins, write down the time it started, then add the time allowed for the examination and write down the time it must be completed, then divide the time available somewhat as follows:
    - If 3-1/2 hours are allowed, that would be 210 minutes. If you have 80 objective-type questions, that would be an average of 2-1/2 minutes per question. Allow yourself no more than 2 minutes per question, or a total of 160 minutes, which will permit about 50 minutes to review.
    - If for the time allotment of 210 minutes there are 7 essay questions to answer, that would average about 30 minutes a question. Give yourself only 25 minutes per question so that you have about 35 minutes to review.

6) The most important instruction is to *read each question* and make sure you know what is wanted. The second most important instruction is to *time yourself properly* so that you answer every question. The third most important instruction is to *answer every question*. Guess if you have to but include something for each question. Remember that you will receive no credit for a blank and will probably receive some credit if you write something in answer to an essay question. If you guess a letter – say "B" for a multiple-choice question – you may have guessed right. If you leave a blank as an answer to a multiple-choice question, the examiners may respect your feelings but it will not add a point to your score. Some exams may penalize you for wrong answers, so in such cases *only*, you may not want to guess unless you have some basis for your answer.

7) Suggestions
    a. Objective-type questions
        1. Examine the question booklet for proper sequence of pages and questions
        2. Read all instructions carefully
        3. Skip any question which seems too difficult; return to it after all other questions have been answered
        4. Apportion your time properly; do not spend too much time on any single question or group of questions

5. Note and underline key words – *all, most, fewest, least, best, worst, same, opposite,* etc.
6. Pay particular attention to negatives
7. Note unusual option, e.g., unduly long, short, complex, different or similar in content to the body of the question
8. Observe the use of "hedging" words – *probably, may, most likely,* etc.
9. Make sure that your answer is put next to the same number as the question
10. Do not second-guess unless you have good reason to believe the second answer is definitely more correct
11. Cross out original answer if you decide another answer is more accurate; do not erase until you are ready to hand your paper in
12. Answer all questions; guess unless instructed otherwise
13. Leave time for review

   b. Essay questions
     1. Read each question carefully
     2. Determine exactly what is wanted. Underline key words or phrases.
     3. Decide on outline or paragraph answer
     4. Include many different points and elements unless asked to develop any one or two points or elements
     5. Show impartiality by giving pros and cons unless directed to select one side only
     6. Make and write down any assumptions you find necessary to answer the questions
     7. Watch your English, grammar, punctuation and choice of words
     8. Time your answers; don't crowd material

8) Answering the essay question

Most essay questions can be answered by framing the specific response around several key words or ideas. Here are a few such key words or ideas:

M's: manpower, materials, methods, money, management
P's: purpose, program, policy, plan, procedure, practice, problems, pitfalls, personnel, public relations

   a. Six basic steps in handling problems:
     1. Preliminary plan and background development
     2. Collect information, data and facts
     3. Analyze and interpret information, data and facts
     4. Analyze and develop solutions as well as make recommendations
     5. Prepare report and sell recommendations
     6. Install recommendations and follow up effectiveness

   b. Pitfalls to avoid
     1. *Taking things for granted* – A statement of the situation does not necessarily imply that each of the elements is necessarily true; for example, a complaint may be invalid and biased so that all that can be taken for granted is that a complaint has been registered

2. *Considering only one side of a situation* – Wherever possible, indicate several alternatives and then point out the reasons you selected the best one
3. *Failing to indicate follow up* – Whenever your answer indicates action on your part, make certain that you will take proper follow-up action to see how successful your recommendations, procedures or actions turn out to be
4. *Taking too long in answering any single question* – Remember to time your answers properly

IX. AFTER THE TEST

Scoring procedures differ in detail among civil service jurisdictions although the general principles are the same. Whether the papers are hand-scored or graded by machine we have described, they are nearly always graded by number. That is, the person who marks the paper knows only the number – never the name – of the applicant. Not until all the papers have been graded will they be matched with names. If other tests, such as training and experience or oral interview ratings have been given, scores will be combined. Different parts of the examination usually have different weights. For example, the written test might count 60 percent of the final grade, and a rating of training and experience 40 percent. In many jurisdictions, veterans will have a certain number of points added to their grades.

After the final grade has been determined, the names are placed in grade order and an eligible list is established. There are various methods for resolving ties between those who get the same final grade – probably the most common is to place first the name of the person whose application was received first. Job offers are made from the eligible list in the order the names appear on it. You will be notified of your grade and your rank as soon as all these computations have been made. This will be done as rapidly as possible.

People who are found to meet the requirements in the announcement are called "eligibles." Their names are put on a list of eligible candidates. An eligible's chances of getting a job depend on how high he stands on this list and how fast agencies are filling jobs from the list.

When a job is to be filled from a list of eligibles, the agency asks for the names of people on the list of eligibles for that job. When the civil service commission receives this request, it sends to the agency the names of the three people highest on this list. Or, if the job to be filled has specialized requirements, the office sends the agency the names of the top three persons who meet these requirements from the general list.

The appointing officer makes a choice from among the three people whose names were sent to him. If the selected person accepts the appointment, the names of the others are put back on the list to be considered for future openings.

That is the rule in hiring from all kinds of eligible lists, whether they are for typist, carpenter, chemist, or something else. For every vacancy, the appointing officer has his choice of any one of the top three eligibles on the list. This explains why the person whose name is on top of the list sometimes does not get an appointment when some of the persons lower on the list do. If the appointing officer chooses the second or third eligible, the No. 1 eligible does not get a job at once, but stays on the list until he is appointed or the list is terminated.

X. HOW TO PASS THE INTERVIEW TEST

The examination for which you applied requires an oral interview test. You have already taken the written test and you are now being called for the interview test – the final part of the formal examination.

You may think that it is not possible to prepare for an interview test and that there are no procedures to follow during an interview. Our purpose is to point out some things you can do in advance that will help you and some good rules to follow and pitfalls to avoid while you are being interviewed.

What is an interview supposed to test?

The written examination is designed to test the technical knowledge and competence of the candidate; the oral is designed to evaluate intangible qualities, not readily measured otherwise, and to establish a list showing the relative fitness of each candidate – as measured against his competitors – for the position sought. Scoring is not on the basis of "right" and "wrong," but on a sliding scale of values ranging from "not passable" to "outstanding." As a matter of fact, it is possible to achieve a relatively low score without a single "incorrect" answer because of evident weakness in the qualities being measured.

Occasionally, an examination may consist entirely of an oral test – either an individual or a group oral. In such cases, information is sought concerning the technical knowledges and abilities of the candidate, since there has been no written examination for this purpose. More commonly, however, an oral test is used to supplement a written examination.

Who conducts interviews?

The composition of oral boards varies among different jurisdictions. In nearly all, a representative of the personnel department serves as chairman. One of the members of the board may be a representative of the department in which the candidate would work. In some cases, "outside experts" are used, and, frequently, a businessman or some other representative of the general public is asked to serve. Labor and management or other special groups may be represented. The aim is to secure the services of experts in the appropriate field.

However the board is composed, it is a good idea (and not at all improper or unethical) to ascertain in advance of the interview who the members are and what groups they represent. When you are introduced to them, you will have some idea of their backgrounds and interests, and at least you will not stutter and stammer over their names.

What should be done before the interview?

While knowledge about the board members is useful and takes some of the surprise element out of the interview, there is other preparation which is more substantive. It *is* possible to prepare for an oral interview – in several ways:

1) Keep a copy of your application and review it carefully before the interview

This may be the only document before the oral board, and the starting point of the interview. Know what education and experience you have listed there, and the sequence and dates of all of it. Sometimes the board will ask you to review the highlights of your experience for them; you should not have to hem and haw doing it.

2) Study the class specification and the examination announcement

Usually, the oral board has one or both of these to guide them. The qualities, characteristics or knowledges required by the position sought are stated in these documents. They offer valuable clues as to the nature of the oral interview. For example, if the job involves supervisory responsibilities, the announcement will usually indicate that knowledge of modern supervisory methods and the qualifications of the candidate as a supervisor will be tested. If so, you can expect such questions, frequently in the form of a hypothetical situation which you are expected to solve. NEVER go into an oral without knowledge of the duties and responsibilities of the job you seek.

3) Think through each qualification required

Try to visualize the kind of questions you would ask if you were a board member. How well could you answer them? Try especially to appraise your own knowledge and background in each area, *measured against the job sought*, and identify any areas in which you are weak. Be critical and realistic – do not flatter yourself.

4) Do some general reading in areas in which you feel you may be weak

For example, if the job involves supervision and your past experience has NOT, some general reading in supervisory methods and practices, particularly in the field of human relations, might be useful. Do NOT study agency procedures or detailed manuals. The oral board will be testing your understanding and capacity, not your memory.

5) Get a good night's sleep and watch your general health and mental attitude

You will want a clear head at the interview. Take care of a cold or any other minor ailment, and of course, no hangovers.

What should be done on the day of the interview?

Now comes the day of the interview itself. Give yourself plenty of time to get there. Plan to arrive somewhat ahead of the scheduled time, particularly if your appointment is in the fore part of the day. If a previous candidate fails to appear, the board might be ready for you a bit early. By early afternoon an oral board is almost invariably behind schedule if there are many candidates, and you may have to wait. Take along a book or magazine to read, or your application to review, but leave any extraneous material in the waiting room when you go in for your interview. In any event, relax and compose yourself.

The matter of dress is important. The board is forming impressions about you – from your experience, your manners, your attitude, and your appearance. Give your personal appearance careful attention. Dress your best, but not your flashiest. Choose conservative, appropriate clothing, and be sure it is immaculate. This is a business interview, and your appearance should indicate that you regard it as such. Besides, being well groomed and properly dressed will help boost your confidence.

Sooner or later, someone will call your name and escort you into the interview room. *This is it.* From here on you are on your own. It is too late for any more preparation. But remember, you asked for this opportunity to prove your fitness, and you are here because your request was granted.

What happens when you go in?

The usual sequence of events will be as follows: The clerk (who is often the board stenographer) will introduce you to the chairman of the oral board, who will introduce you to the other members of the board. Acknowledge the introductions before you sit down. Do not be surprised if you find a microphone facing you or a stenotypist sitting by. Oral interviews are usually recorded in the event of an appeal or other review.

Usually the chairman of the board will open the interview by reviewing the highlights of your education and work experience from your application – primarily for the benefit of the other members of the board, as well as to get the material into the record. Do not interrupt or comment unless there is an error or significant misinterpretation; if that is the case, do not hesitate. But do not quibble about insignificant matters. Also, he will usually ask you some question about your education, experience or your present job – partly to get you to start talking and to establish the interviewing "rapport." He may start the actual questioning, or turn it over to one of the other members. Frequently, each member undertakes the questioning on a particular area, one in which he is perhaps most competent, so you can expect each member to participate in the examination. Because time is limited, you may also expect some rather abrupt switches in the direction the questioning takes, so do not be upset by it. Normally, a board member will not pursue a single line of questioning unless he discovers a particular strength or weakness.

After each member has participated, the chairman will usually ask whether any member has any further questions, then will ask you if you have anything you wish to add. Unless you are expecting this question, it may floor you. Worse, it may start you off on an extended, extemporaneous speech. The board is not usually seeking more information. The question is principally to offer you a last opportunity to present further qualifications or to indicate that you have nothing to add. So, if you feel that a significant qualification or characteristic has been overlooked, it is proper to point it out in a sentence or so. Do not compliment the board on the thoroughness of their examination – they have been sketchy, and you know it. If you wish, merely say, "No thank you, I have nothing further to add." This is a point where you can "talk yourself out" of a good impression or fail to present an important bit of information. Remember, *you close the interview yourself.*

The chairman will then say, "That is all, Mr. _____, thank you." Do not be startled; the interview is over, and quicker than you think. Thank him, gather your belongings and take your leave. Save your sigh of relief for the other side of the door.

How to put your best foot forward

Throughout this entire process, you may feel that the board individually and collectively is trying to pierce your defenses, seek out your hidden weaknesses and embarrass and confuse you. Actually, this is not true. They are obliged to make an appraisal of your qualifications for the job you are seeking, and they want to see you in your best light. Remember, they must interview all candidates and a non-cooperative candidate may become a failure in spite of their best efforts to bring out his qualifications. Here are 15 suggestions that will help you:

1) Be natural – Keep your attitude confident, not cocky

If you are not confident that you can do the job, do not expect the board to be. Do not apologize for your weaknesses, try to bring out your strong points. The board is interested in a positive, not negative, presentation. Cockiness will antagonize any board member and make him wonder if you are covering up a weakness by a false show of strength.

2) Get comfortable, but don't lounge or sprawl

Sit erectly but not stiffly. A careless posture may lead the board to conclude that you are careless in other things, or at least that you are not impressed by the importance of the occasion. Either conclusion is natural, even if incorrect. Do not fuss with your clothing, a pencil or an ashtray. Your hands may occasionally be useful to emphasize a point; do not let them become a point of distraction.

3) Do not wisecrack or make small talk

This is a serious situation, and your attitude should show that you consider it as such. Further, the time of the board is limited – they do not want to waste it, and neither should you.

4) Do not exaggerate your experience or abilities
In the first place, from information in the application or other interviews and sources, the board may know more about you than you think. Secondly, you probably will not get away with it. An experienced board is rather adept at spotting such a situation, so do not take the chance.

5) If you know a board member, do not make a point of it, yet do not hide it
Certainly you are not fooling him, and probably not the other members of the board. Do not try to take advantage of your acquaintanceship – it will probably do you little good.

6) Do not dominate the interview
Let the board do that. They will give you the clues – do not assume that you have to do all the talking. Realize that the board has a number of questions to ask you, and do not try to take up all the interview time by showing off your extensive knowledge of the answer to the first one.

7) Be attentive
You only have 20 minutes or so, and you should keep your attention at its sharpest throughout. When a member is addressing a problem or question to you, give him your undivided attention. Address your reply principally to him, but do not exclude the other board members.

8) Do not interrupt
A board member may be stating a problem for you to analyze. He will ask you a question when the time comes. Let him state the problem, and wait for the question.

9) Make sure you understand the question
Do not try to answer until you are sure what the question is. If it is not clear, restate it in your own words or ask the board member to clarify it for you. However, do not haggle about minor elements.

10) Reply promptly but not hastily
A common entry on oral board rating sheets is "candidate responded readily," or "candidate hesitated in replies." Respond as promptly and quickly as you can, but do not jump to a hasty, ill-considered answer.

11) Do not be peremptory in your answers
A brief answer is proper – but do not fire your answer back. That is a losing game from your point of view. The board member can probably ask questions much faster than you can answer them.

12) Do not try to create the answer you think the board member wants
He is interested in what kind of mind you have and how it works – not in playing games. Furthermore, he can usually spot this practice and will actually grade you down on it.

13) Do not switch sides in your reply merely to agree with a board member
Frequently, a member will take a contrary position merely to draw you out and to see if you are willing and able to defend your point of view. Do not start a debate, yet do not surrender a good position. If a position is worth taking, it is worth defending.

14) Do not be afraid to admit an error in judgment if you are shown to be wrong

The board knows that you are forced to reply without any opportunity for careful consideration. Your answer may be demonstrably wrong. If so, admit it and get on with the interview.

15) Do not dwell at length on your present job

The opening question may relate to your present assignment. Answer the question but do not go into an extended discussion. You are being examined for a *new* job, not your present one. As a matter of fact, try to phrase ALL your answers in terms of the job for which you are being examined.

Basis of Rating

Probably you will forget most of these "do's" and "don'ts" when you walk into the oral interview room. Even remembering them all will not ensure you a passing grade. Perhaps you did not have the qualifications in the first place. But remembering them will help you to put your best foot forward, without treading on the toes of the board members.

Rumor and popular opinion to the contrary notwithstanding, an oral board wants you to make the best appearance possible. They know you are under pressure – but they also want to see how you respond to it as a guide to what your reaction would be under the pressures of the job you seek. They will be influenced by the degree of poise you display, the personal traits you show and the manner in which you respond.

ABOUT THIS BOOK

This book contains tests divided into Examination Sections. Go through each test, answering every question in the margin. We have also attached a sample answer sheet at the back of the book that can be removed and used. At the end of each test look at the answer key and check your answers. On the ones you got wrong, look at the right answer choice and learn. Do not fill in the answers first. Do not memorize the questions and answers, but understand the answer and principles involved. On your test, the questions will likely be different from the samples. Questions are changed and new ones added. If you understand these past questions you should have success with any changes that arise. Tests may consist of several types of questions. We have additional books on each subject should more study be advisable or necessary for you. Finally, the more you study, the better prepared you will be. This book is intended to be the last thing you study before you walk into the examination room. Prior study of relevant texts is also recommended. NLC publishes some of these in our Fundamental Series. Knowledge and good sense are important factors in passing your exam. Good luck also helps. So now study this Passbook, absorb the material contained within and take that knowledge into the examination. Then do your best to pass that exam.

EXAMINATION SECTION

VERBAL ABILITIES TEST

DIRECTIONS AND SAMPLE QUESTIONS

Study the sample questions carefully. Each question has four suggested answers. Decide which one is the best answer. Find the question number on the Sample Answer Sheet. Show your answer to the question by printing the letter of the correct answer in the space at the right. If you have to erase a mark, be sure to erase it completely. Mark only one answer for each question. Do NOT mark space E for any question.

SAMPLE VERBAL QUESTIONS

I. *Previous* means MOST NEARLY
    A. abandoned   B. former   C. timely   D. younger

I.____

II. (Reading) "Just as the procedure of a collection department must be clear cut and definite, the steps being taken with the sureness of a skilled chess player, so the various paragraphs of a collection letter must show clear organization, giving evidence of a mind that, from the beginning, has had a specific end in view."
The quotation BEST supports the statement that a collection letter should always
    A. show a spirit of sportsmanship   B. be divided into several paragraphs
    C. be brief, but courteous   D. be carefully planned

II.____

III. Decide which sentence is preferable with respect to grammar and usage suitable for a formal letter or report.
    A. They do not ordinarily present these kind of reports in detail like this.
    B. A report of this kind is not hardly ever given in such detail as this one.
    C. This report is more detailed than what such reports ordinarily are.
    D. A report of this kind is not ordinarily presented in as much detail as this one is.

III.____

IV. Find the correct spelling of the word and print the letter of the correct answer in the space at the right. If no suggested spelling is correct, print the letter D.
    A. athalete   B. athelete   C. athlete   D. none of these

IV.____

V. SPEEDOMETER is related to POINTER as WATCH is related to
    A. case   B. hands   C. dial   D. numerals

V.____

EXAMINATION SECTION
TEST 1

DIRECTIONS: Each question or incomplete statement is followed by several suggested answers or completions. Select the one that BEST answers the question or completes the statement. *PRINT THE LETTER OF THE CORRECT ANSWER IN THE SPACE AT THE RIGHT.*

1. *Flexible* means MOST NEARLY
    A. breakable   B. flammable   C. pliable   D. weak

    1.____

2. *Option* means MOST NEARLY
    A. use   B. choice   C. value   D. blame

    2.____

3. To *verify* means MOST NEARLY to
    A. examine   B. explain   C. confirm   D. guarantee

    3.____

4. *Indolent* means MOST NEARLY
    A. moderate   B. happiness   C. selfish   D. lazy

    4.____

5. *Respiration* means MOST NEARLY
    A. recovery   B. breathing   C. pulsation   D. sweating

    5.____

6. PLUMBER is related to WRENCH as PAINTER related to
    A. brush   B. pipe   C. shop   D. hammer

    6.____

7. LETTER is related to MESSAGE as PACKAGE is related to
    A. sender
    B. merchandise
    C. insurance
    D. business

    7.____

8. FOOD is related to HUNGER as SLEEP is related to
    A. night   B. dream   C. weariness   D. rest

    8.____

9. KEY is related to TYPEWRITER as DIAL is related to
    A. sun   B. number   C. circle   D. telephone

    9.____

GRAMMAR

10. A. I think that they will promote whoever has the best record.
    B. The firm would have liked to have promoted all employees with good records.
    C. Such of them that have the best records have excellent prospects of promotion.
    D. I feel sure they will give the promotion to whomever has the best record.

    10.____

11. A. The receptionist must answer courteously the questions of all them callers.
    B. The receptionist must answer courteously the questions what are asked by the callers.
    C. There would have been no trouble if the receptionist had have always answered courteously.
    D. The receptionist should answer courteously the questions of all callers.

11.____

SPELLING

12. A. collapsible   B. colapseble
    C. collapseble   D. none of the above

12.____

13. A. ambigeuous   B. ambigeous
    C. ambiguous   D. none of the above

13.____

14. A. predesessor   B. predecesar
    C. predecesser   D. none of the above

14.____

15. A. sanctioned   B. sancktioned
    C. sanctionned   D. none of the above

15.____

READING

16. "The secretarial profession is a very old one and has increased in importance with the passage of time. In modern times, the vast expansion of business and industry has greatly increased the need and opportunities for secretaries, and for the first time in history their number has become large."
    The above quotation BEST supports the statement that the secretarial profession
    A. is older than business and industry
    B. did not exist in ancient times
    C. has greatly increased in size
    D. demands higher training than it did formerly

16.____

17. "Civilization started to move ahead more rapidly when man freed himself of the shackles that restricted his search for the truth."
    The above quotation BEST supports the statement that the progress of civilization
    A. came as a result of man's dislike for obstacles
    B. did not begin until restrictions on learning were removed
    C. has been aided by man's efforts to find
    D. the truth is based on continually increasing efforts

17.____

18. *Vigilant* means MOST NEARLY
    A. sensible   B. watchful   C. suspicious   D. restless

18.____

19. *Incidental* means MOST NEARLY
    A. independent   B. needless   C. infrequent   D. casual

19.____

20. *Conciliatory* means MOST NEARLY
    A. pacific   B. contentious   C. obligatory   D. offensive

21. *Altercation* means MOST NEARLY
    A. defeat
    B. concurrence
    C. controversy
    D. vexation

22. *Irresolute* means MOST NEARLY
    A. wavering
    B. insubordinate
    C. impudent
    D. unobservant

23. DARKNESS is related to SUNLIGHT as STILLNESS is related to
    A. quiet   B. moonlight   C. sound   D. dark

24. DESIGNED is related to INTENTION as ACCIDENTAL is related to
    A. purpose   B. caution   C. damage   D. chance

25. ERROR is related to PRACTICE as SOUND is related to
    A. deafness   B. noise   C. muffler   D. horn

26. RESEARCH is related to FINDINGS as TRAINING is related to
    A. skill
    B. tests
    C. supervision
    D. teaching

27. A. If properly addressed, the letter will reach my mother and I.
    B. The letter had been addressed to myself and my mother.
    C. I believe the letter was addressed to either my mother or I.
    D. My mother's name, as well as mine, was on the letter.

28. A. The supervisor reprimanded the typist, whom she believed had made careless errors.
    B. The typist would have corrected the errors had she of known that the supervisor would see the report.
    C. The errors in the typed report were so numerous that they could hardly be overlooked.
    D. Many errors were found in the report which she typed and could not disregard them.

29. A. minieture   B. minneature
    C. mineature   D. none of the above

30. A. extemporaneous   B. extempuraneus
    C. extemporraneous   D. none of the above

31. A. problemmatical   B. problematical
    C. problematicle   D. none of the above

32. A. descendant   B. decendant
    C. desendant   D. none of the above

33. "The likelihood of America's exhausting her natural resources seems to be growing less. All kinds of waste are being reworked and new uses are constantly being found for almost everything. We are getting more use out of our goods and are making many new byproducts out of what was formerly thrown away."
The above quotation BEST supports the statement that we seem to be in less danger of exhausting our resources because
    A. economy is found to lie in the use of substitutes
    B. more service is obtained from a given amount of material
    C. we are allowing time for nature to restore them
    D. supply and demand are better controlled

34. "Memos should be clear, concise, and brief. Omit all unnecessary words. The parts of speech most often used in memos are nouns, verbs, adjectives, and adverbs. If possible, do without pronouns, prepositions, articles, and copulative verbs. Use simple sentences, rather than complex or compound ones.
The above quotation BEST supports the statement that in writing memos one should always use
    A. common and simple words
    B. only nouns, verbs, adjectives, and adverbs
    C. incomplete sentences
    D. only the word essential to the meaning

35. To *counteract* means MOST NEARLY to
    A. undermine   B. censure   C. preserve   D. neutralize

36. *Deferred* means MOST NEARLY
    A. reversed   B. delayed
    C. considered   D. forbidden

37. *Feasible* means MOST NEARLY
    A. capable   B. justifiable   C. practicable   D. beneficial

38. To *encounter* means MOST NEARLY to
    A. meet   B. recall   C. overcome   D. retreat

39. *Innate* means MOST NEARLY
    A. eternal   B. well-developed
    C. native   D. prospective

40. STUDENT is to TEACHER as DISCIPLE is related to
    A. follower   B. master   C. principal   D. pupil

41. LECTURE is related to AUDITORIUM as EXPERIMENT is related to
    A. scientist   B. chemistry   C. laboratory   D. discovery

42. BODY is related to FOOD as ENGINE is related to
    A. wheels   B. fuel   C. motion   D. smoke

43. SCHOOL is related to EDUCATION as THEATER is related to
    A. management
    B. stage
    C. recreation
    D. preparation

44. A. Most all these statements have been supported by persons who are reliable and can be depended upon.
    B. The persons which have guaranteed these statements are reliable.
    C. Reliable persons guarantee the facts with regards to the truth of these statements.
    D. These statements can be depended on, for their truth has been guaranteed by reliable persons.

45. A. The success of the book pleased both his publisher and he.
    B. Both his publisher and he was pleased with the success of the book.
    C. Neither he or his publisher was disappointed with the success of the book.
    D. His publisher was as pleased as he with the success of the book.

46. A. extercate
    B. extracate
    C. extricate
    D. none of the above

47. A. hereditory
    B. hereditary
    C. hereditairy
    D. none of the above

48. A. auspiceous
    B. auspiseous
    C. auspicious
    D. none of the above

49. A. sequance
    B. sequence
    C. sequense
    D. none of the above

50. "The prevention of accidents makes it necessary not only that safety devices be used to guard exposed machinery but also that mechanics be instructed in safety rules which they must follow for their own protection, and that the lighting in the plant be adequate."
    The above quotation BEST supports the statement that industrial accidents
    A. may be due to ignorance
    B. are always avoidable
    C. usually result from inadequate machinery
    D. cannot be entirely overcome

51. "The English language is peculiarly rich in synonyms, and there is scarcely a language spoken among men that has not some representative in English speech. The spirit of the Anglo-Saxon race has subjugate these various elements to one idiom, making not a patchwork, but a composite language."
    The above quotation BEST supports the statement that the English language
    A. has few idiomatic expressions
    B. is difficult to translate
    C. is used universally
    D. has absorbed words from other languages

52. To *acquiesce* means MOST NEARLY to
    A. assent   B. acquire   C. complete   D. participate

53. *Unanimity* means MOST NEARLY
    A. emphasis
    B. namelessness
    C. harmony
    D. impartiality

54. *Precedent* means MOST NEARLY
    A. example   B. theory   C. law   D. conformity

55. *Versatile* means MOST NEARLY
    A. broad-minded
    B. well-known
    C. up-to-date
    D. many-sided

56. *Authentic* means MOST NEARLY
    A. detailed   B. reliable   C. valuable   D. practical

57. BIOGRAPHY is related to FACT as NOVEL is related to
    A. fiction   B. literature   C. narration   D. book

58. COPY is related to CARBON PAPER as MOTION PICTURE is related to
    A. theater   B. film   C. duplicate   D. television

59. EFFICIENCY is related to REWARD as CARELESSNESS is related to
    A. improvement
    B. disobedience
    C. reprimand
    D. repetition

60. ABUNDANT is related to CHEAP as SCARCE is related to
    A. ample
    B. costly
    C. inexpensive
    D. unobtainable

61. A. Brown's & Company employees have recently received increases in salary.
    B. Brown & Company recently increased the salaries of all its employees.
    C. Recently, Brown & Company has increased their employees' salaries.
    D. Brown & Company have recently increased the salaries of all its employees.

62. A. In reviewing the typists' work reports, the job analyst found records of unusual typing speeds.
    B. It says in the job analyst's report that some employees type with great speed.
    C. The job analyst found that, in reviewing the typists' work reports, that some unusual typing speeds had been made.
    D. In the reports of typists' speeds, the job analyst found some records that are kind of unusual.

63. A. obliterate
    B. oblitterat
    C. obbliterate
    D. none of the above

64. A. diagnoesis B. diagnossis 64._____
    C. diagnosis D. none of the above

65. A. contenance B. countenance 65._____
    C. knowledge D. none of the above

66. A. conceivably B. concieveably 66._____
    C. conceiveably D. none of the above

67. "Through advertising, manufacturers exercise a high degree of control over 67._____
    consumers' desires. However, the manufacturer assumes enormous risks in
    attempting to predict what consumers will want and in producing goods in
    quantity and distributing them in advance of final selection by the consumers."
    The above quotation BEST supports the statement that manufacturers
    A. can eliminate the risk of overproduction by advertising
    B. distribute goods directly to the consumers
    C. must depend upon the final consumers for the success of their
       undertakings
    D. can predict with great accuracy the success of any product they put on
       the market

68. "In the relations of man to nature, the procuring of food and shelter is 68._____
    fundamental. With the migration of man to various climates, ever new
    adjustments to the food supply and to the climate became necessary."
    The above quotation BEST supports the statement that the means by which
    man supplies his material needs are
    A. accidental   B. varied   C. limited   D. inadequate

69. *Strident* means MOST NEARLY 69._____
    A. swaggering   B. domineering
    C. angry   D. harsh

70. To *confine* means MOST NEARLY to 70._____
    A. hide   B. restrict   C. eliminate   D. punish

71. To *accentuate* means MOST NEARLY to 71._____
    A. modify   B. hasten   C. sustain   D. intensify

72. *Banal* means MOST NEARLY 72._____
    A. commonplace   B. forceful
    C. tranquil   D. indifferent

73. *Incorrigible* means MOST NEARLY 73._____
    A. intolerable   B. retarded
    C. irreformable   D. brazen

74. POLICEMAN is related to ORDER as DOCTOR is related to 74._____
    A. physician   B. hospital   C. sickness   D. health

75. ARTIST is related to EASEL as WEAVER is related to
    A. loom   B. cloth   C. threads   D. spinner

76. CROWD is related to PERSONS as FLEET is related to
    A. expedition   B. officers   C. navy   D. ships

77. CALENDAR is related to DATE as MAP is related to
    A. geography   B. trip   C. mileage   D. vacation

78. A. Since the report lacked the needed information, it was of no use to him.
    B. This report was useless to him because there were no needed information in it.
    C. Since the report did not contain the needed information, it was not real useful to him.
    D. Being that the report lacked the needed information, he could not use it.

79. A. The company had hardly declared the dividend till the notices were prepared for mailing.
    B. They had no sooner declared the dividend when they sent the notices to the stockholders.
    C. No sooner had the dividend been declared than the notices were prepared for mailing.
    D. Scarcely had the dividend been declared than the notices were sent out.

80. A. compitition   B. competition
    C. competetion   D. none of the above

81. A. occassion   B. ocassion
    C. occasion   D. none of the above

82. A. knowlege   B. knowledge
    C. knolledge D. none of the above

83. A. deliborate   B. deliberate
    C. deliberate   D. none of the above

84. "What constitutes skill in any line of work is not always easy to determine; economy of time must be carefully distinguished from economy of energy, as the quickest method may require the greatest expenditure of muscular effort, and may not be essential or at all desirable."
    The above quotation BEST supports the statement that
    A. the most efficiently executed task is not always the one done in the shortest time
    B. energy and time cannot both be conserved in performing a single task
    C. a task is well done when it is performed in the shortest time
    D. skill in performing a task should not be acquired at the expense of time

85. "It is difficult to distinguish between bookkeeping and accounting. In attempts to do so, bookkeeping is called the art, and accounting the science, of recording business transactions. Bookkeeping gives the history of the business in a systematic manner; and accounting classifies, analyzes, and interpret the facts thus recorded."
The above quotation BEST supports the statement that
   A. accounting is less systematic than bookkeeping
   B. accounting and bookkeeping are closely related
   C. bookkeeping and accounting cannot be distinguished from one another
   D. bookkeeping has been superseded by accounting

KEY (CORRECT ANSWERS)

1.	C	16.	C	31.	B	46.	C	61.	B	76.	D
2.	B	17.	C	32.	A	47.	B	62.	A	77.	C
3.	C	18.	B	33.	B	48.	C	63.	A	78.	A
4.	D	19.	D	34.	D	49.	B	64.	C	79.	C
5.	B	20.	A	35.	D	50.	A	65.	B	80.	B
6.	A	21.	C	36.	B	51.	D	66.	A	81.	B
7.	B	22.	A	37.	C	52.	A	67.	C	82.	C
8.	C	23.	C	38.	A	53.	C	68.	B	83.	B
9.	D	24.	D	39.	C	54.	A	69.	D	84.	A
10.	A	25.	C	40.	B	55.	D	70.	B	85.	B
11.	D	26.	A	41.	C	56.	B	71.	D		
12.	A	27.	D	42.	B	57.	A	72.	A		
13.	C	28.	C	43.	C	58.	B	73.	C		
14.	D	29.	D	44.	D	59.	C	74.	D		
15.	A	30.	A	45.	D	60.	B	75.	A		

TEST 2

DIRECTIONS: Each question or incomplete statement is followed by several suggested answers or completions. Select the one that BEST answers the question or completes the statement. *PRINT THE LETTER OF THE CORRECT ANSWER IN THE SPACE AT THE RIGHT.*

1. *Option* means MOST NEARLY
   A. use
   B. choice
   C. value
   D. blame
   E. mistake

2. *Irresolute* means MOST NEARLY
   A. wavering
   B. insubordinate
   C. impudent
   D. determined
   E. unobservant

3. *Flexible* means MOST NEARLY
   A. breakable
   B. inflammable
   C. pliable
   D. weak
   E. impervious

4. To *counteract* means MOST NEARLY to
   A. undermine
   B. censure
   C. preserve
   D. sustain
   E. neutralize

5. To *verify* means MOST NEARLY to
   A. justify
   B. explain
   C. confirm
   D. guarantee
   E. examine

6. *Indolent* means MOST NEARLY
   A. moderate
   B. relentless
   C. selfish
   D. lazy
   E. hopeless

7. To say that an action is *deferred* means MOST NEARLY that it is
   A. delayed
   B. reversed
   C. considered
   D. forbidden
   E. followed

8. To *encounter* means MOST NEARLY to
   A. meet
   B. recall
   C. overcome
   D. weaken
   E. retreat

9. *Feasible* means MOST NEARLY
   A. capable
   B. practicable
   C. justifiable
   D. beneficial
   E. reliable

10. *Respiration* means MOST NEARLY
    A. dehydration
    B. breathing
    C. pulsation
    D. sweating
    E. recovery

11. *Vigilant* means MOST NEARLY
    A. sensible
    B. ambitious
    C. watchful
    D. suspicious
    E. restless

12. To say that an action is taken *before the proper time* means MOST NEARLY that it is taken
    A. prematurely
    B. furtively
    C. temporarily
    D. punctually
    E. presently

13. *Innate* means MOST NEARLY
    A. eternal
    B. learned
    C. native
    D. prospective
    E. well-developed

14. *Precedent* means MOST NEARLY
    A. duplicate
    B. theory
    C. law
    D. conformity
    E. example

15. To say that the flow of work into an office is *incessant* means MOST NEARLY that it is
    A. more than can be handled
    B. uninterrupted
    C. scanty
    D. decreasing in volume
    E. orderly

16. *Unanimity* means MOST NEARLY
    A. emphasis
    B. namelessness
    C. disagreement
    D. harmony
    E. impartiality

17. *Incidental* means MOST NEARLY
    A. independent
    B. needless
    C. infrequent
    D. necessary
    E. casual

18. *Versatile* means MOST NEARLY
    A. broad-minded
    B. well-known
    C. old-fashioned
    D. many-sided
    E. up-to-date

19. *Conciliatory* means MOST NEARLY
    A. pacific
    B. contentious
    C. disorderly
    D. obligatory
    E. offensive

20. *Altercation* means MOST NEARLY
    A. defeat
    B. concurrence
    C. controversy
    D. consensus
    E. vexation

21. "The secretarial profession is a very old one and has increased in importance with the passage of time. In modern times, the vast expansion of business and industry has greatly increased the need and opportunities for secretaries, and for the first time in history their number as become large."

The above quotation BEST supports the statement that the secretarial profession
- A. is older than business and industry
- B. did not exist in ancient times
- C. has greatly increased in size
- D. demands higher training than it did formerly
- E. has always had many members

22. "The modern system of production unites various kinds of workers into a well-organized body in which each has a definite place."
The above quotation BEST supports the statement that the modern system of production
- A. increases production
- B. trains workers
- C. simplifies tasks
- D. combines and places workers
- E. combines the various plants

23. "The prevention of accidents makes it necessary not only that safety devices be used to guard exposed machinery but also that mechanics be instructed in safety rules which they must follow for their own protection, and that the lighting in the plant be adequate.
The above quotation BEST supports the statement that industrial accidents
- A. may be due to ignorance
- B. are always avoidable
- C. usually result from inadequate machinery
- D. cannot be entirely overcome
- E. result in damage to machinery

24. "It is wise to choose a duplicating machine that will do the work required with the greatest efficiency and at the least cost. Users with a large volume of business need speedy machines that cost little to operate and are well made."
The above quotation BEST supports the statement that
- A. most users of duplicating machines prefer low operating cost to efficiency
- B. a well-built machine will outlast a cheap one
- C. a duplicating machine is not efficient unless it is sturdy
- D. a duplicating machine should be both efficient and economical
- E. in duplicating machines speed is more usual than low operating cost

25. "The likelihood of America's exhausting her natural resources seems to be growing less. All kinds of waste are being reworked and new uses are constantly being found for almost everything. We are getting more use out of our goods and are making many new byproducts out of what was formerly thrown away."
The above quotation BEST supports the statement that we seem to be in less danger of exhausting our resources because
- A. economy is found to lie in the use of substitutes
- B. more service is obtained from a given amount of material
- C. more raw materials are being produced
- D. supply and demand are better controlled
- E. we are allowing time for nature to restore them

26. "Probably few people realize, as they drive on a concrete road, that steel is used to keep the surface flat and even, in spite of the weight of busses and trucks. Steel bars, deeply imbedded in the concrete, provide sinews to take the stresses so that they cannot crack the slab or make it wavy."
The above quotation BEST supports the statement that a concrete road
   A. is expensive to build
   B. usually cracks under heavy weights
   C. looks like any other road
   D. is used exclusively for heavy traffic
   E. is reinforced with other material

27. "Through advertising, manufacturers exercise a high degree of control over consumers' desires. However, the manufacturer assumes enormous risks in attempting to predict what consumers will want and in producing goods in quantity and distributing them in advance of final selection by the consumers."
The above quotation BEST supports the statement that manufacturers
   A. can eliminate the risk of overproduction by advertising
   B. completely control buyers' needs and desires
   C. must depend upon the final consumers for the success of their undertakings
   D. distribute goods directly to the consumers
   E. can predict with great accuracy the success of any product they put on the market

28. "Success in shorthand, like success in any other study, depends upon the interest the student takes in it. In writing shorthand, it is not sufficient to know how to write a word correctly; one must also be able to write it quickly."
The above quotation BEST supports the statement that
   A. one must be able to read shorthand as well as to write it
   B. shorthand requires much study
   C. if a student can write correctly, he can also write quickly
   D. proficiency in shorthand requires both speed and accuracy
   E. interest in shorthand makes study unnecessary

29. "The countries in the Western Hemisphere were settled by people who were ready each day for new adventure. The peoples of North and South America have retained, in addition to expectant and forward-looking attitudes, the ability and the willingness that they have often shown in the past to adapt themselves to new conditions.
The above quotation BEST supports the statement that the peoples in the Western Hemisphere
   A. no longer have fresh adventures daily
   B. are capable of making changes as new situations arise
   C. are no more forward-looking than the peoples of other regions
   D. tend to resist regulations
   E. differ considerably among themselves

30. "Civilization started to move ahead more rapidly when man freed himself of the shackles that restricted his search for the truth."
The above quotation BEST supports the statement that the progress of civilization
   A. came as a result of man's dislike for obstacles
   B. did not begin until restrictions on learning were removed
   C. has been aided by man's efforts to find the truth
   D. is based on continually increasing efforts
   E. continues at a constantly increasing rate

31. "It is difficult to distinguish between bookkeeping and accounting. In attempts to do so, bookkeeping is called the art, and accounting the science, of recording business transactions. Bookkeeping gives the history of the business in a systematic manner, and accounting classifies, analyzes, and interprets the facts thus recorded."
The above quotation BEST supports the statement that
   A. accounting is less systematic than bookkeeping
   B. accounting and bookkeeping are closely related
   C. bookkeeping and accounting cannot be distinguish from one another
   D. bookkeeping has been superseded by accounting
   E. the facts recorded by bookkeeping may be interpreted in many ways

32. "Some specialists are willing to give their services to the Government entirely free of charge; some feel that a nominal salary, such as will cover traveling expenses, is sufficient for a position that is recognized as being somewhat honorary in nature; many other specialists value their time so highly that they will not devote any of it to public service that does not repay them at a rate commensurate with the fees that they can obtain from a good private clientele."
The above quotation BEST supports the statement that the use of specialists by the Government
   A. is rare because of the high cost of securing such persons
   B. may be influenced by the willingness of specialists to serve
   C. enables them to secure higher salaries in private fields
   D. has become increasingly common during the past few years
   E. always conflicts with private demands for their services

33. "The leader of an industrial enterprise has two principal functions. He must manufacture and distribute a product at a profit, and he must keep individuals and groups of individuals working effectively together."
The above quotation BEST supports the statement that an industrial leader should be able to
   A. increase the distribution of his plant's product
   B. introduce large-scale production methods
   C. coordinate the activities of his employees
   D. profit by the experience of other leaders
   E. expand the business rapidly

34. "The coloration of textile fabrics composed of cotton and wool generally requires two processes, as the process used in dyeing wool is seldom capable of fixing the color upon cotton. The usual method is to immerse the fabric in the requisite baths to dye the wool and then to treat the partially dyed material in the manner found suitable for cotton."
The above quotation BEST supports the statement that the dyeing of textile fabrics composed of cotton and wool
   A. is less complicated than the dyeing of wool alone
   B. is more successful when the material contains more cotton than wool
   C. is not satisfactory when solid colors are desired
   D. is restricted to two colors for any one fabric
   E. is usually based upon the methods required for dyeing the different materials

35. "The fact must not be overlooked that only about one-half of the international trade of the world crosses the oceans. The other half is merely exchanges of merchandise between countries lying alongside each other or at least within the same continent."
The above quotation BEST supports the statement that
   A. the most important part of any country's trade is transoceanic
   B. domestic trade is insignificant when compared with foreign trade
   C. the exchange of goods between neighboring countries is not considered international trade
   D. foreign commerce is not necessarily carried on by water
   E. about one-half of the trade of the world is international

36. "In the relations of man to nature, the procuring of food and shelter is fundamental. With the migration of man to various climate, ever new adjustments to the food supply and to the climate became necessary."
The above quotation BEST supports the statement that the means by which man supplies his material needs are
   A. accidental   B. varied   C. limited
   D. uniform   E. inadequate

37. "Every language has its peculiar word associations that have no basis in logic and cannot therefore be reasoned about. These idiomatic expressions are ordinarily acquired only by much reading and conversation although questions about such matters may sometimes be answered by the dictionary. Dictionaries large enough to include quotations from standard authors are especially serviceable in determining questions of idiom."
The above quotation BEST supports the statement that idiomatic expressions
   A. give rise to meaningless arguments because they have no logical basis
   B. are widely used by recognized authors
   C. are explained in most dictionaries
   D. are more common in some languages than in others
   E. are best learned by observation of the language as actually used

38. "Individual differences in mental traits assume importance in fitting workers to jobs because such personal characteristics are persistent and are relatively little influenced by training and experience."
The above quotation BEST supports the statement that training and experience
   A. are limited in their effectiveness in fitting workers to jobs
   B. do not increase a worker's fitness for a job
   C. have no effect upon a person's mental traits
   D. have relatively little effect upon the individual's chances for success
   E. should be based on the mental traits of an individual

39. "The telegraph networks of the country now constitute wonderfully operated institutions, affording for ordinary use of modern, business an important means of communication. The transmission of message by electricity has reached the goal for which the postal service has long been striving, namely, the elimination of distance as an effective barrier of communication."
The above quotation BEST supports the statement that
   A. a new standard of communication has been attained
   B. in the telegraph service, messages seldom go astray
   C. it is the distance between the parties which creates the need for communication
   D. modern business relies more upon the telegraph than upon the mails
   E. the telegraph is a form of postal service

40. "The competition of buyers tends to keep prices up, the competition of sellers to send them down. Normally, the pressure of competition among sellers is stronger than that amount by buyers since the seller has his article to sell and must get rid of it, whereas the buyer is not committed to anything."
The above quotation BEST supports the statement that low prices are caused by
   A. buyer competition
   B. competition of buyers with sellers fluctuations in demand
   C. greater competition among sellers than among buyers
   D. more sellers than buyers

Questions 41-60.

DIRECTIONS: In answering Questions 41 through 60, find the CORRECT spelling of the word. Sometimes there is no correct spelling; if none of the suggested spellings is correct, indicate the letter D in the space at the right.

41. A. compitition   B. competition
    C. competetion   D. none of the above

42. A. diagnoesis   B. diagnossis
    C. diagnosis   D. none of the above

43. A. contenance   B. countenance
    C. countinance   D. none of the above

8 (#2)

44. A. deliborate   B. deliberate   44._____
    C. delibrate   D. none of the above

45. A. knowlege   B. knolledge   45._____
    C. knowledge   D. none of the above

46. A. occassion   B. occasion   46._____
    C. ocassion   D. none of the above

47. A. sanctioned   B. sancktioned   47._____
    C. sanctionned   D. none of the above

48. A. predesessor   B. predecesar   48._____
    C. predecessor   D. none of the above

49. A. problemmatical   B. problematical   49._____
    C. problematicle   D. none of the above

50. A. descendant   B. decendant   50._____
    C. desendant   D. none of the above

51. A. collapsible   B. collapseable   51._____
    C. collapseble   D. none of the above

52. A. sequance   B. sequence   52._____
    C. sequense   D. none of the above

53. A. oblitorate   B. obbliterat   53._____
    C. obbliterate   D. none of the above

54. A. ambigeuous   B. ambigeous   54._____
    C. ambiguous   D. none of the above

55. A. minieture   B. minneature   55._____
    C. mineature   D. none of the above

56. A. extemporaneous   B. extempuraneus   56._____
    C. extemperaneous   D. none of the above

57. A. hereditory   B. hereditary   57._____
    C. hereditairy   D. none of the above

58. A. conceivably   B. concieveably   58._____
    C. conceiveably   D. none of the above

59. A. extercate   B. extracate   59._____
    C. extricate   D. none of the above

60. A. auspiceous B. auspiseous 60.____
    C. auspicious D. none of the above

Questions 61-80.

DIRECTIONS: In answering Questions 61 through 80, select the sentence that is preferable with respect to grammar and usage such as would be suitable in a formal letter or report.

61. A. The receptionist must answer courteously the questions of all them callers. 61.____
    B. The questions of all callers had ought to be answered courteously.
    C. The receptionist must answer courteously the questions what are asked by the callers.
    D. There would have been no trouble if the receptionist had have always answered courteously.
    E. The receptionist should answer courteously the questions of all callers.

62. A. I had to learn a great number of rules, causing me to dislike the course. 62.____
    B. I disliked that study because it required the learning of numerous rules.
    C. I disliked that course very much, caused by the numerous rules I had to memorize.
    D. The cause of my dislike was on account of the numerous rules I had to learn in that course.
    E. The reason I disliked this study was because there were numerous rules that had to be learned.

63. A. If properly addressed, the letter will reach my mother and I. 63.____
    B. The letter had been addressed to myself and mother.
    C. I believe the letter was addressed to either my mother or I.
    D. My mother's name, as well as mine, was on the letter.
    E. If properly addressed, the letter it will reach either my mother or me.

64. A. A knowledge of commercial subjects and a mastery of English are essential if one wishes to be a good secretary. 64.____
    B. Two things necessary to a good secretary are the she should speak good English and too know commercial subjects.
    C. One cannot be a good secretary without she knows commercial subjects and English grammar.
    D. Having had god training in commercial subjects, the rules of English grammar should also be followed.
    E. A secretary seldom or ever succeeds without training in English as well as in commercial subjects.

65. A. He suspicions that the service is not so satisfactory as it should be. 65.____
    B. He believes that we should try and find whether the service is satisfactory.
    C. He raises the objection that the way which the service is given is not satisfactory.
    D. He believes that the quality of our services are poor.
    E. He believes that the service that we are giving is unsatisfactory.

66. A. Most all these statements have been supported by persons who are reliable and can be depended upon. 66.____
    B. The persons which have guaranteed these statements are reliable.
    C. Reliable persons guarantee the facts with regard to the truth of these statements.
    D. These statements can be depended on, for their truth has been guaranteed by reliable persons.
    E. Persons as reliable as what these are can be depended upon to make accurate statements.

67. A. Brown's & Company's employees have all been given increases in salary. 67.____
    B. Brown & Company recently increased the salaries of all its employees.
    C. Recently Brown & Company has increased their employees' salaries.
    D. Brown's & Company employees have recently received increases in salary.
    E. Brown & Company have recently increased the salaries of all its employees.

68. A. The personnel office has charge of employment, dismissals, and employee's welfare. 68.____
    B. Employment, together with dismissals and employees' welfare, are handled by the personnel department.
    C. The personnel office takes charge of employment, dismissals, and etc.
    D. The personnel office hires and dismisses employees, and their welfare is also its responsibility.
    E. The personnel office is responsible for the employment, dismissal, and welfare of employees.

69. A. This kind of pen is some better than that kind. 69.____
    B. I prefer having these pens than any other.
    C. This kind of pen is the most satisfactory for my use.
    D. In comparison with that kind of pen, this kind is more preferable.
    E. If I were to select between them all, I should pick this pen.

70. A. He could not make use of the report, as it was lacking of the needed information. 70.____
    B. This report was useless to him because there were no needed information in it.
    C. Since the report lacked the needed information, it was of no use to him.
    D. Being that the report lacked the needed information, he could not use it.
    E. Since the report did not contain the needed information, it was not real useful to him.

71.   A. The paper we use for this purpose must be light, glossy, and stand hard usage as well.
      B. Only a light and a glossy, but durable, paper must be used for this purpose.
      C. For this purpose, we want a paper that is light, glossy, but that will stand hard wear.
      D. For this purpose, paper that is light, glossy, and durable is essential.
      E. Light and glossy paper, as well as standing hard usage, is necessary for this purpose.

71.____

72.   A. The company had hardly declared the dividend till the notices were prepared for mailing.
      B. They had no sooner declared the dividend when they sent the notices to the stockholders.
      C. No sooner had the dividend been declared than the notices were prepared for mailing.
      D. Scarcely had the dividend been declared than the notices were sent out.
      E. The dividend had not scarcely been declared when the notices were ready for mailing.

72.____

73.   A. Of all the employees, he spends the most time at the office.
      B. He spends more time at the office than that of his employees.
      C. His working hours are longer or at least equal to those of the other employees.
      D. He devotes as much, if not more, time to his work than the rest of the employees.
      E. He works the longest of any other employee in the office.

73.____

74.   A. In the reports of typists' speeds, the job analyst found some records that are kind of unusual.
      B. It says in the job analyst's report that some employees type with great speed.
      C. The job analyst found that, in reviewing the typists' work Reports, that some unusual typing speeds had been made.
      D. Work reports showing typing speeds include some typists who are unusual.
      E. In reviewing the typists' work reports, the job analyst found records of unusual typing speeds.

74.____

75.   A. It is quite possible that we shall reemploy anyone whose training fits them to do the work.
      B. It is probable that we shall reemploy those who have been trained to do the work.
      C. Such of our personnel that have been trained to do the work will be again employed.
      D. We expect to reemploy the ones who have had training enough that they can do the work.
      E. Some of these people have been trained.

75.____

76.
   A. He as well as his publisher were pleased with the success of the book.
   B. The success of the book pleased both his publisher and he.
   C. Both his publisher and he was pleased with the success of the book.
   D. Neither he or his publisher was disappointed with the success of the book.
   E. His publisher was as pleased as he with the success of the book.

76.____

77.
   A. You have got to get rid of some of these people if you expect to have the quality of the work improve
   B. The quality of the work would improve if they would leave fewer people do it.
   C. I believe it would be desirable to have fewer persons during this work.
   D. If you had planned on employing fewer people than this to do the work, this situation would not have arose.
   E. Seeing how you have all those people on that work, it is not surprising that you have a great deal of confusion.

77.____

78.
   A. She made lots of errors in her typed report, and which caused her to be reprimanded.
   B. The supervisor reprimanded the typist, whom she believed had made careless errors.
   C. Many errors were found in the report which she typed and could not disregard them.
   D. The typist would have corrected the errors, had she of known that the supervisor would see the report.
   E. The errors in the typed report were so numerous that they could hardly be overlooked.

78.____

79.
   A. This kind of a worker achieves success through patience.
   B. Success does not often come to men of this type except they who are patient.
   C. Because they are patient, these sort of workers usually achieve success.
   D. This worker has more patience than any man in his office.
   E. This kind of worker achieves success through patience.

79.____

80.
   A. I think that they will promote whoever has the best record.
   B. The firm would have liked to have promoted all employees with good records.
   C. Such of them that have the best records have excellent prospects of promotion.
   D. I feel sure they will give the promotion to whomever has the best record.
   E. Whoever they find to have the best record will, I think, be promoted.

80.____

KEY (CORRECT ANSWERS)

1.	B	21.	C	41.	B	61.	E
2.	A	22.	D	42.	C	62.	B
3.	C	23.	A	43.	B	63.	D
4.	E	24.	D	44.	B	64.	A
5.	C	25.	B	45.	C	65.	E
6.	D	26.	E	46.	B	66.	D
7.	A	27.	C	47.	A	67.	B
8.	A	28.	D	48.	D	68.	E
9.	B	29.	B	49.	B	69.	C
10.	B	30.	C	50.	A	70.	C
11.	C	31.	B	51.	A	71.	D
12.	A	32.	B	52.	B	72.	C
13.	C	33.	C	53.	D	73.	A
14.	E	34.	E	54.	C	74.	E
15.	B	35.	D	55.	D	75.	B
16.	D	36.	B	56.	A	76.	E
17.	E	37.	E	57.	B	77.	C
18.	D	38.	A	58.	A	78.	E
19.	A	39.	A	59.	C	79.	E
20.	C	40.	D	60.	C	80.	A

EXAMINATION SECTION
TEST 1

DIRECTIONS: Each question or incomplete statement is followed by several suggested answers or completions. Select the one that BEST answers the question or completes the statement. *PRINT THE LETTER OF THE CORRECT ANSWER IN THE SPACE AT THE RIGHT.*

Questions 1-25.

DIRECTIONS: Select the word with the MOST appropriate meaning for the italicized word in each of Questions 1 through 25.

1. The directions were *explicit*.
   A. petulant   B. satiric   C. awkward
   D. unequivocal   E. foreign

2. The teacher explained *mutability*.
   A. change   B. harmony   C. annihilation
   D. ethics   E. candor

3. He was a *secular* man.
   A. holy   B. evil   C. worldly
   D. superior   E. small

4. They submitted a list of their *progeny*.
   A. experiments   B. books   C. holdings
   D. theories   E. offspring

5. She admired his *sententious* replies.
   A. simple   B. pithy   C. coherent
   D. lucid   E. inane

6. He believed in the ancient *dogma*.
   A. priest   B. prophet   C. seer
   D. doctrine   E. ruler

7. They studied a Grecian *archetype*.
   A. model   B. urn   C. epic   D. ode   E. play

8. The *insurrection* was described on the front page.
   A. surgery   B. pageant   C. ceremony
   D. game   E. revolt

9. He was known for his *procrastination*.
   A. justification   B. learning   C. delay
   D. ambition   E. background

10. The doctor analyzed the *toxic* ingredients. 10._____
    A. poisonous B. anemic C. trivial
    D. obscure E. distinct

11. It was a *portentous* occurrence. 11._____
    A. pleasant B. decisive C. ominous
    D. monetary E. hearty

12. His *espousal* of the plan was applauded. 12._____
    A. explanation B. rejection C. ridicule
    D. adoption E. revision

13. Her condition was *lachrymose*. 13._____
    A. improved B. tearful C. hopeful
    D. precocious E. tenuous

14. It was a *precarious* situation. 14._____
    A. uncomplicated B. peaceful C. precise
    D. uncertain E. precipitous

15. He was lost in a *reverie*. 15._____
    A. chancery B. dream C. forest
    D. cavern E. tarn

16. The hero was a young *gallant*. 16._____
    A. suitor B. fool C. gull
    D. lawyer E. executive

17. Their practices were *nefarious*. 17._____
    A. unprofitable B. ignorant C. multifarious
    D. wicked E. wishful

18. He insisted upon the *proviso*. 18._____
    A. stipulation B. pronunciation C. examination
    D. supply E. equipment

19. The spirit came from the *nether* regions. 19._____
    A. frozen B. lower C. lost
    D. bright E. mysterious

20. His actions were *malevolent*. 20._____
    A. unassuming B. silent C. evil
    D. peaceful E. constructive

21. He had a *florid* complexion. 21._____
    A. sanguine B. pallid C. fair
    D. sickly E. normal

22. The lawyer explained the legal *parlance*. 22.____
    A. action B. maneuver C. situation
    D. language E. procedure

23. They were present at the *interment*. 23.____
    A. concert B. trial C. embarkation
    D. burial E. performance

24. He made a *moot* point. 24.____
    A. definite B. sensible C. debatable
    D. strong E. correct

25. They carefully examined the *cryptic* message. 25.____
    A. occult B. legible C. valid
    D. familiar E. warning

Questions 26-40.

DIRECTIONS: Indicate the number of syllables in each of the following words.

26. vicissitude 26.____

27. blown 27.____

28. maintenance 28.____

29. symbolization 29.____

30. athletics 30.____

31. actually 31.____

32. friend 32.____

33. perseverance 33.____

34. physiology 34.____

35. pronunciation 35.____

36. vacuum 36.____

37. sophomore 37.____

38. opportunity 38.____

39. hungry 39.____

40. temperament 40.____

Questions 41-60.

DIRECTIONS: Indicate the one misspelled work in each of the following Questions 41 through 60 by indicating the letter of the misspelled word in the space at the right.

41. A. holiday B. noticeable C. fourty 41._____
    D. miniature E. yeast

42. A. grievance B. murmur C. occurance 42._____
    D. business E. captain

43. A. succeed B. vegatable C. pleasant 43._____
    D. picnicking E. shepherd

44. A. psychology B. plebian C. exercise 44._____
    D. fiery E. concise

45. A. ninety B. optimistic C. professor 45._____
    D. repitition E. siege

46. A. tarriff B. absence C. grammar 46._____
    D. license E. balloon

47. A. dissipation B. ecstasy C. prarie 47._____
    D. marriage E. consistent

48. A. supersede B. twelfth C. vacillate 48._____
    D. playright E. expense

49. A. fundamental B. government C. accomodate 49._____
    D. cafeteria E. surely

50. A. cemetary B. indispensable C. dormitory 50._____
    D. environment E. divine

51. A. irritible B. permissible C. irresistible 51._____
    D. rhythmical E. source

52. A. interprete B. opinion C. guard 52._____
    D. familiar E. possible

53. A. conscience B. existence C. loneliness 53._____
    D. leisure E. exhileration

54. A. villian B. weird C. seize 54._____
    D. tragedy E. crystal

55. A. develop B. bachelor C. dilemma 55._____
    D. operate E. synonym

28

56. A. university B. connoiseur C. aisle 56.____
    D. transferred E. division

57. A. zoology B. conscious C. aptitude 57.____
    D. restaurant E. sacriligious

58. A. tendency B. vital C. analyze 58.____
    D. consistant E. proceed

59. A. proceedure B. surround C. disastrous 59.____
    D. beginning E. arrival

60. A. encrease B. pursuing C. necessary 50.____
    D. tyranny E. strength

Questions 61-80.

DIRECTIONS: Indicate the part of speech for each italicized word in the following sentences by selecting the letter of the part of speech from the key above each set of questions.

   A. Noun
   B. Pronoun
   C. Verb
   D. Adjective
   E. Adverb

61. You are entirely *wrong*. 61.____

62. On *Sunday*, we will attend church. 62.____

63. *That* is the main problem. 63.____

64. He was invited to the party, *Saturday*. 64.____

65. I shall introduce a *technical* term. 65.____

66. It was a *novel* turn of events. 66.____

67. He wanted *that* gift for himself. 67.____

68. A few definitions will help *us* to understand. 68.____

69. He let them reach their own *conclusions*. 69.____

70. I must ask *you* to remain silent. 70.____

A. Preposition
B. Conjunction
C. Pronoun
D. Adverb
E. Adjective

71. *This* is a stupid answer.

72. He solved the mystery *without* the police.

73. She felt *secure* in his protection,

74. He believed in the *scientific* method.

75. Do not destroy their *traditional* beliefs.

76. They chartered the bus, *but* they did not go.

77. The young men are *quiet* with fear.

78. She talked *cheerfully* to the visitors.

79. The candidate was *certain* of victory.

80. I hope you will take *that* with you.

Questions 81-100.

DIRECTIONS: Indicate the use of each italicized word in the following sentences by choosing the letter of the CORRECT usage from the key above each set of questions.

A. Subject of Verb
B. Predicate Nominative or Subjective Complement
C. Predicate Adjective
D. Direct Object of Verb
E. Indirect Object of Verb

81. They made *him* president of the club.

82. There was nothing *odd* about the situation.

83. Give them *time* enough for thought.

84. He supervised the *work* himself.

85. Will you do *me* a favor?

86. The salad dressing tasted *good*.

87. In the crash, the *body* was thrown forward. 87.____

88. On a bench in the park was a single *man*. 88.____

89. There were two *men* who carried the trunk. 89.____

90. I am older than *you*. 90.____

      A. Object of Preposition
      B. Subject of Infinitive
      C. Direct Object of Verb
      D. Indirect Object of Verb
      E. Predicate Nominative or Subjective Complement

91. Let *them* suffer the consequences. 91.____

92. Offer *them* the key to the apartment. 92.____

93. He heard the *bell* ring. 93.____

94. Let *us* try another solution. 94.____

95. No one except *John* had volunteered. 95.____

96. Show *us* one example of your style. 96.____

97. Will you send *her* the flowers? 97.____

98. I want *you* to take her home. 98.____

99. He told his *father* that he would obey. 99.____

100. Do not write on the second *page*. 100.____

Questions 101-115.

DIRECTIONS: Indicate the kind of verbal italicized in the following sentences by choosing the appropriate letter from the key below.

      A. Gerund
      B. Participle
      C. Infinitive

101. The manuscript, *corrected* and typed, was on the desk. 101.____

102. He heard the bullet *ricochet*. 102.____

103. *Finding* the answer is a difficult task. 103.____

104. The animal, *hidden* from view, was trembling.   104.____

105. *Pretending* to be asleep, he listened attentively.   105.____

106. The professor, a *qualified* lecturer, entered the room.   106.____

107. They enjoyed *camping* at the lake.   107.____

108. Let them *come* to me.   108.____

109. He was annoyed by the *buzzing* sound.   109.____

110. It was a *stimulating* performance.   110.____

111. He had an accident while *returning* to the city.   111.____

112. *Encouraged* to study, the class opened the books.   112.____

113. He heard the gun *explode*.   113.____

114. They called him the *forgotten* man.   114.____

115. *Realizing* his mistake, he apologized.   115.____

Questions 116-130.

DIRECTIONS: Indicate the CORRECT punctuation for the following sentences by choosing the letter of the correct punctuation from the key below where brackets appear.

    A. Comma
    B. Semicolon
    C. Colon
    D. Dash
    E. No punctuation

116. He explained [ ] that he could not attend.   116.____

117. The executive [ ] prepared for the interview and entered the room.   117.____

118. She admitted [ ] that the suggestion was wrong.   118.____

119. He did not object [ ] to dealing with him.   119.____

120. The chairman disagreed [ ] the members did not.   120.____

121. You must report to duty on November 10 [ ] 2022.   121.____

122. The father [ ] and two sons went fishing.   122.____

123. Act on the following problems [ ] administration, supervision, and policy. 123.____

124. This is excellent [ ] it has insight. 124.____

125. "I will take the car [ ]" he said. 125.____

126. I will do it [ ] however, you must help me. 126.____

127. When the show ended [ ] he returned home. 127.____

128. Stop [ ] making all of that noise. 128.____

129. Be firm [ ] exercise your authority. 129.____

130. The first example is poor [ ] the second is good. 130.____

Questions 131-150.

DIRECTIONS: Place a *C* in the space at the right if the sentence is correctly punctuated and a *W* in the space at the right if the sentence is incorrectly punctuated.

131. Its later than you think. 131.____

132. While I was eating the toast burned. 132.____

133. The fire started at ten o'clock in the morning. 133.____

134. She asked, "Did you say, 'I will go?" 134.____

135. Richards handling of the question warranted praise. 135.____

136. July 4 is a holiday. 136.____

137. Oh perhaps you are right. 137.____

138. Will you answer the door, John? 138.____

139. While he was bathing the dog came in. 139.____

140. He was a calm gentle person. 140.____

141. He wore a new bow tie. 141.____

142. The shout "Block that kick" echoed upon the field. 142.____

143. Ladies and gentlemen take your seats. 143.____

144. However you must do your work. 144.____

145. My brothers are: John, Bill, and Charles.   145.____

146. While I was painting the neighbor opened the door.   146.____

147. One should fight for honor: not fame.   147.____

148. "Will you sing" he asked?   148.____

149. He played tennis, and then bowled.   149.____

150. On Monday April 5, we leave for Europe.   150.____

KEY (CORRECT ANSWERS)

1. D	31. 4	61. D	91. C	121. A
2. A	32. 1	62. A	92. D	122. E
3. C	33. 4	63. B	93. C	123. C
4. E	34. 5	64. A	94. C	124. D
5. B	35. 5	65. D	95. A	125. A
6. D	36. 2	66. D	96. C	126. B
7. A	37. 3	67. D	97. C	127. A
8. E	38. 5	68. B	98. C	128. E
9. C	39. 2	69. A	99. C	129. B
10. A	40. 3	70. B	100. A	130. B
11. C	41. C	71. C	101. B	131. W
12. D	42. C	72. A	102. B	132. W
13. B	43. B	73. D	103. A	133. C
14. D	44. B	74. E	104. B	134. W
15. B	45. D	75. E	105. A	135. W
16. A	46. A	76. B	106. B	136. C
17. D	47. C	77. E	107. A	137. W
18. A	48. D	78. D	108. C	138. C
19. B	49. C	79. E	109. B	139. W
20. C	50. A	80. C	110. B	140. W
21. A	51. A	81. D	111. A	141. C
22. D	52. A	82. C	112. B	142. W
23. D	53. E	83. D	113. C	143. W
24. C	54. A	84. D	114. B	144. W
25. A	55. C	85. E	115. A	145. W
26. 3	56. B	86. C	116. E	143. W
27. 1	57. E	87. A	117. E	147. W
28. 3	58. D	88. B	118. E	148. W
29. 5	59. A	89. A	119. E	149. W
30. 3	60. A	90. C	120. B	150. W

EXAMINATION SECTION
TEST 1

DIRECTIONS: Each question or incomplete statement is followed by several suggested answers or completions. Select the one that BEST answers the question or completes the statement. *PRINT THE LETTER OF THE CORRECT ANSWER IN THE SPACE AT THE RIGHT.*

Questions 1-22.

DIRECTIONS: Read through each group of words. Indicate in the space at the right the letter of the misspelled word.

1. A. miniature B. recession C. accommodate D. supress 1._____

2. A. mortgage B. illogical C. fasinate D. pronounce 2._____

3. A. calendar B. heros C. ecstasy D. librarian 3._____

4. A. initiative B. extraordinary C. villian D. exaggerate 4._____

5. A. absence B. sense C. dosn't D. height 5._____

6. A. curiosity B. ninety C. truely D. grammar 6._____

7. A. amateur B. definate C. meant D. changeable 7._____

8. A. excellent B. studioes C. achievement D. weird 8._____

9. A. goverment B. description C. sergeant D. desirable 9._____

10. A. proceed B. anxious C. neice D. precede 10._____

11. A. environment B. omitted C. apparant D. misconstrue 11._____

12. A. comparative B. hindrance C. benefited D. unanimous 12._____

37

13. A. embarrass   B. recommend   13._____
     C. desciple   D. argument

14. A. sophomore   B. suprintendent   14._____
     C. concievable   D. disastrous

15. A. agressive   B. questionnaire   15._____
     C. occurred   D. rhythm

16. A. peaceable   B. conscientious   16._____
     C. redicule   D. deterrent

17. A. mischievious   B. writing   17._____
     C. competition   D. athletics

18. A. auxiliary   B. synonymous   18._____
     C. maneuver   D. repitition

19. A. existence   B. optomistic   19._____
     C. acquitted   D. tragedy

20. A. hypocrisy   B. parrallel   20._____
     C. exhilaration   D. prevalent

21. A. convalesence   B. infallible   21._____
     C. destitute   D. grotesque

22. A. magnanimity   B. asassination   22._____
     C. incorrigible   D. pestilence

Questions 23-40.

DIRECTIONS: In Questions 23 through 40, one sentence fragment contains an error in punctuation or capitalization. Indicate the letter of the INCORRECT sentence fragment and place it in the space at the right.

23. A. Despite a year's work   23._____
     B. in a well-equipped laboratory
     C. my Uncle failed to complete his research
     D. now he will never graduate.

24. A. Gene, if you are going to sleep   24._____
     B. all afternoon I will enter
     C. that ladies' golf tournament
     D. sponsored by the Chamber of Commerce.

3 (#1)

25. A. Seeing the cat slink toward the barn,
    B. the farmer's wife jumped off the
    C. ladder picked up a broom, and began
    D. shouting at the top of her voice.

25.____

26. A. Extending over southeast Idaho and
    B. northwest Wyoming, the Tetons
    C. are noted for their height; however the
    D. highest peak is actually under 14,000 feet.

26.____

27. A. "Sarah, can you recall the name
    B. of the English queen
    C. who supposedly said, 'We are not
    D. amused?"

27.____

28. A. My aunt's graduation present to me
    B. cost, I imagine more than she could
    C. actually afford. It's a
    D. Swiss watch with numerous features.

28.____

29. A. On the left are examples of buildings
    B. from the Classical Period; two temples
    C. one of which was dedicated to Zeus; the
    D. Agora, a marketplace; and a large arch.

29.____

30. A. Tired of sonic booms, the people who
    B. live near Springfield's Municipal Airport
    C. formed an anti noise organization
    D. with the amusing name of Sound Off.

30.____

31. A. "Joe, Mrs. Sweeney said, "your family
    B. arrives Sunday. Since you'll be in
    C. the Labor Day parade, we could ask Mr.
    D. Krohn, who has a big car, to meet them."

31.____

32. A. The plumber emerged from the basement and
    B. said, "Mr. Cohen I found the trouble in
    C. your water heater. Could you move those
    D. Schwinn bikes out of my way?"

32.____

33. A. The President walked slowly to the
    B. podium, bowed to Edward Everett Hale
    C. the other speaker, and began his formal address:
    D. "Fourscore and seven years ago...."

33.____

34. A. Mr. Fontana, I hope, will arrive before
    B. the beginning of the ceremonies; however,
    C. if his plane is delayed, I have a substitute
    D. speaker who can be here at a moments' notice.

34.____

35. A. Gladys wedding dress, a satin creation,
    B. lay crumpled on the floor; her veil,
    C. torn and streaked, lay nearby. "Jilted!"
    D. shrieked Gladys. She was clearly annoyed.

35.____

36. A. Although it is poor grammar, the word
    B. hopefully has become television's newest
    C. pet expression; I hope (to use the correct
    D. form) that it will soon pass from favor.

36.____

37. A.   Plaza Apartment Hotel
    B.   103 Tower road
    C.   Hampstead, Iowa 52025
    D.   March 13, 2021

37.____

38. A. Circulation Department
    B. British History Illustrated
    C. 3000 Walnut Street
    D. Boulder Colorado 80302

38.____

39. A. Dear Sirs:
    B. Last spring I ordered a subscription to your
    C. magazine. I had read and enjoyed the May
    D. issue containing the article titled "kings."

39.____

40. A. I have not however, received a
    B. single issue. Will you check this?
    C. Sincerely,
    D. Maria Herrera

40.____

Questions 41-70.

DIRECTIONS: Questions 41 through 70 represent common grammatical concerns: subject-verb agreement, appropriate use of pronouns, and appropriate use of verbs. Read each sentence and indicate the letter of the grammatically CORRECT answer in the space at the right.

41. THE REIVERS, one of William Faulkner's last works, _____ made into a movie starring Steve McQueen.
    A. has been   B. have been   C. are being   D. were

41.____

42. He _____ on the ground, his eyes fastened on an ant slowly pushing a morsel of food toward the ant hill.
    A. layed   B. laid   C. had laid   D. lay

42.____

43. Nobody in the tri-cities _____ to admit that a flood could be disastrous.
    A. are willing   B. have been willing
    C. is willing   D. were willing

43.____

44. "_____," the senator asked, "have you convinced to run against the incumbent?"
    A. Who   B. Whom   C. Whomever   D. Womsoever

45. Of all the psychology courses that I took, Statistics 101 _____ the most demanding.
    A. was   B. are   C. is   D. were

46. Neither the conductor nor the orchestra members _____ the music to be applauded so enthusiastically.
    A. were expecting
    B. was expecting
    C. is expected
    D. has been expecting

47. The requirements for admission to the Lettermen's Club _____ posted outside the athletic director's office for months.
    A. was   B. was being   C. has been   D. have been

48. Please give me a list of the people _____ to compete in the kayak race.
    A. whom you think have planned
    B. who you think has planned
    C. who you think is planning
    D. who you think are planning

49. I saw Eloise and Abelard earlier today; _____ were riding around in a fancy 1956 MG.
    A. she and him   B. her and him   C. she and he   D. her and he

50. If you _____ the trunk in the attic, I'll unpack it later today.
    A. can sit
    B. are able to sit
    C. can set
    D. have sat

51. _____ all of the flour been used, or may I borrow three cups?
    A. Have   B. Has   C. Is   D. Could

52. In exasperation, the cycle shop's owner suggested that _____ there too long.
    A. us boys were
    B. we boys were
    C. us boys had been
    D. we boys had been

53. Idleness as well as money _____ the root of all evil.
    A. have been
    B. were to have been
    C. is
    D. are

54. Only the string players from the quartet—Gregory, Isaac, _____—remained after the concert to answer questions.
    A. him, and I
    B. he, and I
    C. him, and me
    D. he, and me

55. Of all the antiques that _____ for sale, Gertrude chose to buy a stupid glass thimble.
    A. was
    B. is
    C. would have
    D. were

56. The detective snapped, "Don't confuse me with theories about _____ you believe committed the crime!"
    A. who	B. whom	C. whomever	D. which

57. _____ when we first called, we might have avoided our present predicament.
    A. The plumber's coming
    B. If the plumber would have come
    C. If the plumber had come
    D. If the plumber was to have come

58. We thought the sun _____ in the north until we discovered that our compass was defective.
    A. had rose
    B. had risen
    C. had rised
    D. had raised

59. Each play of Shakespeare's _____ more than _____ share of memorable characters.
    A. contain its
    B. contains; its
    C. contains; it's
    D. contain; their

60. Our English teacher suggested to _____ seniors that either Tolstoy or Dickens _____ the outstanding novelist of the nineteenth century.
    A. we; was considered
    B. we; were considered
    C. us; was considered
    D. us; were considered

61. Sherlock Holmes, together with his great friend and companion Dr. Watson, _____ to aid the woman _____ had stumbled into the room.
    A. has agreed; who
    B. have agreed; whom
    C. has agreed; whom
    D. have agreed; who

62. Several of the deer _____ when they spotted my backpack _____ open in the meadow.
    A. was frightened; laying
    B. were frightened; lying
    C. were frightened; laying
    D. was frightened; lying

63. After the Scholarship Committee announces _____ selection, hysterics often _____.
    A. it's; occur
    B. its; occur
    C. their; occur
    D. their; occurs

64. I _____ the key on the table last night so you and _____ could find it.
    A. layed; her
    B. lay; she
    C. laid; she
    D. laid; her

65. Some of the antelope _____ wandered away from the meadow where the rancher _____ the block of salt.
    A. has; sat
    B. has; set
    C. have; had set
    D. has; sets

66. Macaroni and cheese _____ best to us (that is, to Andy and _____) when Mother adds extra cheddar cheese.
    A. tastes; I
    B. tastes; me
    C. taste; me
    D. taste; I

67. Frank said, "It must have been _____ called the phone company."
    A. she who
    B. she whom
    C. her who
    D. her whom

68. The herd _____ moving restlessly at every bolt of lightning; it was either Ted or _____ who saw the beginning of the stampede.
    A. was; me
    B. were; I
    C. was; I
    D. have been; me

69. The foreman _____ his lateness by saying that his alarm clock _____ until six minutes before eight.
    A. explains; had not rang
    B. explained; has not rung
    C. has explained; rung
    D. explained; hadn't rung

70. Of all the coaches, Ms. Cox is the only one who _____ that Sherry dives more gracefully than _____.
    A. is always saying; I
    B. is always saying; me
    C. are always saying; I
    D. were always saying; me

Questions 71-90.

DIRECTIONS: Choose the word in Questions 71 through 90 that is MOST opposite in meaning to the italicized word.

71. *fact*
    A. statistic
    B. statement
    C. incredible
    D. conjecture

72. *stiff*
    A. fastidious
    B. babble
    C. supple
    D. apprehensive

73. *blunt*
    A. concise
    B. tactful
    C. artistic
    D. humble

74. *foreign*
    A. pertinent
    B. comely
    C. strange
    D. scrupulous

75. *anger*
    A. infer
    B. pacify
    C. taint
    D. revile

76. *frank*
    A. earnest
    B. reticent
    C. post
    D. expensive

77. *secure*
   A. precarious   B. acquire   C. moderate   D. frenzied

77.____

78. *petty*
   A. harmonious   B. careful
   C. forthright   D. momentous

78.____

79. *concede*
   A. dispute   B. reciprocate
   C. subvert   D. propagate

79.____

80. *benefit*
   A. liquidation   B. bazaar
   C. detriment   D. profit

80.____

81. *capricious*
   A. preposterous   B. constant
   C. diabolical   D. careless

81.____

82. *boisterous*
   A. devious   B. valiant   C. girlish   D. taciturn

82.____

83. *harmony*
   A. congruence   B. discord   C. chagrin   D. melody

83.____

84. *laudable*
   A. auspicious   B. despicable
   C. acclaimed   D. doubtful

84.____

85. *adherent*
   A. partisan   B. stoic   C. renegade   D. recluse

85.____

86. *exuberant*
   A. frail   B. corpulent   C. austere   D. bigot

86.____

87. *spurn*
   A. accede   B. flail   C. efface   D. annihilate

87.____

88. *spontaneous*
   A. hapless   B. corrosive
   C. intentional   D. willful

88.____

89. *disparage*
   A. abolish   B. exude   C. incriminate   D. extol

89.____

90. *timorous*
   A. succinct   B. chaste   C. audacious   D. insouciant

90.____

KEY (CORRECT ANSWERS)

1. D	21. A	41. A	61. A	81. B
2. C	22. B	42. D	62.	82. D
3. B	23. C	43. C	63. B	83. B
4. C	24. B	44. B	64. C	84. B
5. C	25. C	45. A	65. C	85. C
6. C	26. C	46. A	66. B	86. C
7. B	27. D	47. D	67. A	87. A
8. B	28. B	48. A	68. C	88. C
9. A	29. B	49. C	69. D	89. D
10. C	30. C	50. C	70. A	90. C
11. C	31. A	51. B	71. D	
12. D	32. B	52. D	72. C	
13. C	33. B	53. C	73. B	
14. C	34. D	54. B	74. A	
15. A	35. A	55. D	75. B	
16. C	36. B	56. B	76. B	
17. A	37. B	57. C	77. A	
18. D	38. D	58. B	78. D	
19. B	39. D	59. B	79. A	
20. B	40. A	60. C	80. C	

SPELLING

EXAMINATION SECTION

TEST 1

DIRECTIONS: Each question or incomplete statement is followed by several suggested answers or completions. Select the one that BEST answers the question or completes the statement. *PRINT THE LETTER OF THE CORRECT ANSWER IN THE SPACE AT THE RIGHT.*

Questions 1-5.

DIRECTIONS: Questions 1 through 5 consist of four words. Indicate the letter of the word that is CORRECTLY spelled.

1. A. harassment B. harrasment 1.____
   C. harasment D. harrassment

2. A. maintainance B. maintenence 2.____
   C. maintainence D. maintenance

3. A. comparable B. comprable 3.____
   C. comparible D. commparable

4. A. suficient B. sufficiant 4.____
   C. sufficient D. suficiant

5. A. fairly   B. fairley   C. farely   D. fairlie   5.____

Questions 6-10.

DIRECTIONS: Questions 6 through 10 consist of four words. Indicate the letter of the word that is INCORRECTLY spelled.

6. A. pallor   B. ballid   C. ballet   D. pallid   6.____

7. A. urbane B. surburbane 7.____
   C. interurban D. urban

8. A. facial   B. physical   C. fiscle   D. muscle   8.____

9. A. interceed B. benefited 9.____
   C. analogous D. altogether

10. A. seizure B. irrelevant 10.____
    C. inordinate D. dissapproved

47

KEY (CORRECT ANSWERS)

1. A
2. D
3. A
4. C
5. A
6. B
7. B
8. C
9. A
10. D

TEST 2

DIRECTIONS: Each of Questions 1 through 15 consists of two words preceded by the letters A and B. In each question, one of the words may be spelled INCORRECTLY or both words may be spelled CORRECTLY. If one of the words in a question is spelled INCORRECTLY, print in the space at the right the capital letter preceding the INCORRECTLY spelled word. If both words are spelled CORRECTLY, print the letter C.

1. A. easely   B. readily   1.____
2. A. pursue   B. decend   2.____
3. A. measure   B. laboratory   3.____
4. A. exausted   B. traffic   4.____
5. A. discussion   B. unpleasant   5.____
6. A. campaign   B. murmer   6.____
7. A. guarantee   B. sanatary   7.____
8. A. communication B. safty   8.____
9. A. numerus   B. celebration   9.____
10. A. nourish   B. begining   10.____
11. A. courious   B. witness   11.____
12. A. undoubtedly   B. thoroughly   12.____
13. A. accessible   B. artifical   13.____
14. A. feild   B. arranged   14.____
15. A. admittence   B. hastily   15.____

KEY (CORRECT ANSWERS)

1.	A	6.	B	11.	A
2.	B	7.	B	12.	C
3.	C	8.	B	13.	B
4.	A	9.	A	14.	A
5.	C	10.	B	15.	A

TEST 3

DIRECTIONS: In each of the following sentences, one word is misspelled. Following each sentence is a list of four words taken from the sentence. Indicate the letter of the word which is MISSPELLED in the sentence. *PRINT THE LETTER OF THE CORRECT ANSWER IN THE SPACE AT THE RIGHT.*

1. The placing of any inflammable substance in any building, or the placing of any device or contrivance capable of producing fire, for the purpose of causing a fire is an attempt to burn.
    A. inflammable
    B. substance
    C. device
    D. contrivence

2. The word *break* also means obtaining an entrance into a building by any artifice used for that purpose, or by collussion with any person therein.
    A. obtaining
    B. entrance
    C. artifice
    D. colussion

3. Any person who with intent to provoke a breech of the peace causes a disturbance or is offensive to others may be deemed to have committed disorderly conduct.
    A. breech
    B. disturbance
    C. offensive
    D. committed

4. When the offender inflicts a grevious harm upon the person from whose possession, or in whose presence, property is taken, he is guilty of robbery.
    A. offender
    B. grevious
    C. possession
    D. presence

5. A person who wilfuly encourages or advises another person in attempting to take the latter's life is guilty of a felony.
    A. wilfuly
    B. encourages
    C. advises
    D. attempting

6. He maliciously demurred to an ajournment of the proceedings.
    A. maliciously
    B. demurred
    C. ajournment
    D. proceedings

7. His innocence at that time is irrelevant in view of his more recent villianous demeanor.
    A. innocence
    B. irrelevant
    C. villianous
    D. demeanor

8. The mischievous boys aggrevated the annoyance of their neighbor.
    A. mischievous
    B. aggrevated
    C. annoyance
    D. neighbor

2 (#3)

9. While his perseverence was commendable, his judgment was debatable. 9.____
   A. perseverence B. commendable
   C. judgment D. debatable

10. He was hoping the appeal would facilitate his aquittal. 10.____
    A. hoping B. appeal
    C. facilitate D. aquittal

11. It would be preferable for them to persue separate courses. 11.____
    A. preferable B. persue
    C. separate D. courses

12. The litigant was complimented on his persistance and achievement. 12.____
    A. litigant B. complimented
    C. persistance D. achievement

13. Ocassionally there are discrepancies in the descriptions of miscellaneous items. 13.____
    A. ocassionally B. discrepancies
    C. descriptions D. miscellaneous

14. The councilmanic seargent-at-arms enforced the prohibition. 14.____
    A. councilmanic B. seargeant-at-arms
    C. enforced D. prohibition

15. The teacher had an ingenious device for maintaining attendance. 15.____
    A. ingenious B. device
    C. maintaning D. attendance

16. A worrysome situation has developed as a result of the assessment that absenteeism is increasing despite our conscientious efforts. 16.____
    A. worrysome B. assessment
    C. absenteeism D. conscientious

17. I concurred with the credit manager that it was practicable to charge purchases on a biennial basis, and the company agreed to adhear to this policy. 17.____
    A. concurred B. practicable
    C. biennial D. adhear

18. The pastor was chagrined and embarassed by the irreverent conduct of one of his parishioners. 18.____
    A. chagrined B. embarassed
    C. irreverent D. parishioners

19. His inate seriousness was belied by his flippant demeanor. 19.____
    A. inate B. belied
    C. flippant D. demeanor

20. It was exceedingly regrettable that the excessive number of challenges in the court delayed the start of the trial.
    A. exceedingly
    B. regrettable
    C. excessive
    D. challanges

20.____

KEY (CORRECT ANSWERS)

1. D   11. B
2. D   12. C
3. A   13. A
4. B   14. B
5. A   15. C

6. C   16. A
7. C   17. D
8. B   18. B
9. A   19. A
10. D   20. D

TEST 4

Questions 1-11.

DIRECTIONS: Each question consists of three words in each question, one of the words may be spelled incorrectly or all three may be spelled correctly. For each question if one of the words is spelled INCORRECTLY, write the letter of the incorrect word in the space at the right. If all three words are spelled CORRECTLY, write the letter D in the space at the right.

SAMPLE I: (A) guide   (B) departmint   (C) stranger
SAMPLE II: (A) comply   (B) valuable   (C) window
In Sample I, departmint is incorrect. It should be spelled department.
Therefore, B is the answer.
In Sample II, all three words are spelled correctly. Therefore, D is the answer.

1. A. argument   B. reciept   C. complain   1.____
2. A. sufficient   B. postpone   C. visible   2.____
3. A. expirience   B. dissatisly   C. alternate   3.____
4. A. occurred   B. noticable   C. appendix   4.____
5. A. anxious   B. guarantee   C. calendar   5.____
6. A. sincerely   B. affectionately C. truly   6.____
7. A. excellant   B. verify   C. important   7.____
8. A. error   B. quality   C. enviroment   8.____
9. A. exercise   B. advance   C. pressure   9.____
10. A. citizen   B. expence   C. memory   10.____
11. A. flexable   B. focus   C. forward   11.____

Questions 12-15.

DIRECTIONS: Each of Questions 12 through 15 consists of a group of four words. Examine each group carefully; then in the space at the right, indicate
A. if only one word in the group is spelled correctly
B. if two words in the group are spelled correctly
C. if three words in the group are spelled correctly
D. if all four words in the group are spelled correctly

12. Wendsday, particular, similar, hunderd   12.____

2 (#4)

13. realize, judgment, opportunities, consistent13.____

14. equel, principle, assistense, committee14.____

15. simultaneous, privilege, advise, ocassionaly15.____

KEY (CORRECT ANSWERS)

1.	B	6.	D	11.	A
2.	D	7.	A	12.	B
3.	A	8.	C	13.	D
4.	B	9.	D	14.	A
5.	C	10.	B	15.	C

TEST 5

DIRECTIONS: Each of Questions 1 through 15 consists of two words preceded by the letters A and B. In each item, one of the words may be spelled INCORRECTLY or both words may be spelled CORRECTLY. If one of the words in a question is spelled INCORRECTLY, print in the space at the right the letter preceding the INCORRECTLY spelled word. If bot words are spelled CORRECTLY, print the letter C.

1.	A. justified	B. offering	1.____
2.	A. predjudice	B. license	2.____
3.	A. label	B. pamphlet	3.____
4.	A. bulletin	B. physical	4.____
5.	A. assure	B. exceed	5.____
6.	A. advantagous	B. evident	6.____
7.	A. benefit	B. occured	7.____
8.	A. acquire	B. graditude	8.____
9.	A. amenable	B. boundry	9.____
10.	A. deceive	B. voluntary	10.____
11.	A. imunity	B. conciliate	11.____
12.	A. acknoledge	B. presume	12.____
13.	A. substitute	B. prespiration	13.____
14.	A. reputable	B. announce	14.____
15.	A. luncheon	B. wretched	15.____

KEY (CORRECT ANSWERS)

1.	C	6.	A	11.	A
2.	A	7.	B	12.	A
3.	C	8.	B	13.	B
4.	C	9.	B	14.	A
5.	C	10.	C	15.	C

TEST 6

DIRECTIONS: Questions 1 through 15 contain lists of words, one of which is misspelled. Indicate the MISSPELLED word in each group. *PRINT THE LETTER OF THE CORRECT ANSWER IN THE SPACE AT THE RIGHT.*

1. A. felony   B. lacerate   1.____
    C. cancellation D. seperate

2. A. batallion   B. beneficial   2.____
    C. miscellaneous D. secretary

3. A. camouflage   B. changeable   3.____
    C. embarrass   D. inoculate

4. A. beneficial   B. disasterous   4.____
    C. incredible   D. miniature

5. A. auxilliary   B. hypocrisy   5.____
    C. phlegm   D. vengeance

6. A. aisle   B. cemetary   6.____
    C. courtesy   D. extraordinary

7. A. crystallize   B. innoculate   7.____
    C. eminent   D. symmetrical

8. A. judgment   B. maintainance   8.____
    C. bouillon   D. eery

9. A. isosceles   B. ukulele   9.____
    C. mayonaise   D. iridescent

10. A. remembrance   B. occurence   10.____
    C. correspondence D. countenance

11. A. corpuscles   B. mischievous   11.____
    C. batchelor   D. bulletin

12. A. terrace   B. banister   12.____
    C. concrete   D. masonery

13. A. balluster   B. gutter   13.____
    C. latch   D. bridging

14. A. personnell   B. navel   14.____
    C. therefor   D. emigrant

15. A. committee B. submiting
    C. amendment D. electorate

15.____

KEY (CORRECT ANSWERS)

1.	D	6.	B	11.	C
2.	A	7.	B	12.	D
3.	C	8.	B	13.	A
4.	B	9.	C	14.	A
5.	A	10.	B	15.	B

TEST 7

Questions 1-5.

DIRECTIONS: Questions 1 through 5 consist of groups of four words. Select answer
A if only one word is spelled correctly in a group
B if TWO words are spelled correctly in a group
C if THREE words are spelled correctly in a group
D if all FOUR words are spelled correctly in a group.

1. counterfeit, embarass, panicky, supercede   1._____

2. benefited, personnel, questionnaire, unparalelled   2._____

3. bankruptcy, describable, proceed, vacuum   3._____

4. handicapped, mispell, offerred, pilgrimmage   4._____

5. corduroy, interfere, privilege, separator   5._____

Questions 6-10.

DIRECTIONS: Questions 6 through 10 consist of four pairs of words each. Some of the words are spelled correctly; others are spelled incorrectly. For each question, indicate in the space at the right the letter preceding that pair of words in which BOTH words are spelled CORRECTLY.

6. A. hygienic, inviegle   B. omniscience, pittance   6._____
   C. plagarize, nullify   D. seargent, perilous

7. A. auxilary, existence   B. pronounciation, accordance 7._____
   C. ignominy, indegence   D. suable, baccalaureate

8. A. discreet, inaudible   B. hypocrisy, currupt   8._____
   C. liquidate, maintainance   D. transparancy, onerous

9. A. facility; stimulent   B. frugel, sanitary   9._____
   C. monetary, prefatory   D. punctileous, credentials

10. A. bankruptsy, perceptible B. disuade, resilient   10._____
    C. exhilerate, expectancy   D. panegyric, disparate

Questions 11-15.

DIRECTIONS: Each question or incomplete statement is followed by several suggested answers or completions. Select the one that BEST answers the question or completes the statement. PRINT THE LETTER OF THE CORRECT ANSWER IN THE SPACE AT THE RIGHT.

58

11. The silent *e* must be retained when the suffix –*able* is added to the word 11.____
    A. argue B. love C. move D. notice

12. The CORRECTLY spelled word in the choices below is 12.____
    A. kindergarden B. zylophone
    C. hemorrhage D. mayonaise

13. Of the following words, the one spelled CORRECTLY is 13.____
    A. begger B. cemetary
    C. embarassed D. coyote

14.
    A. dandilion B. wiry C. sieze D. rythmic 14.____

15. A. beligerent B. anihilation
    C. facetious D. adversery

KEY (CORRECT ANSWERS)

1.	B	6.	B	11.	D
2.	C	7.	D	12.	C
3.	D	8.	A	13.	D
4.	A	9.	C	14.	B
5.	D	10.	D	15.	C

TEST 8

DIRECTIONS: In each of the following sentences, one word is misspelled. Following each sentence is a list of four words taken from the sentence. Indicate the letter of the word which is MISSPELLED. *PRINT THE LETTER OF THE CORRECT ANSWER IN THE SPACE AT THE RIGHT.*

1. If the administrator attempts to withold information, there is a good likelihood that there will be serious repercussions.
   A. administrator
   B. withold
   C. likelihood
   D. repercussions

   1.____

2. He condescended to apologize, but we felt that a beligerent person should not occupy an influential position.
   A. condescended
   B. apologize
   C. beligerent
   D. influential

   2.____

3. Despite the sporadic delinquent payments of his indebtedness, Mr. Johnson has been an exemplery customer.
   A. sporadic
   B. delinquent
   C. indebtedness
   D. exemplery

   3.____

4. He was appreciative of the support he consistantly acquired, but he felt that he had waited an inordinate length of time for it.
   A. appreciative
   B. consistantly
   C. acquired
   D. inordinate

   4.____

5. Undeniably they benefited from the establishment of a receivership, but the question of statutary limitations remained unresolved.
   A. undeniably
   B. benefited
   C. receivership
   D. statutary

   5.____

6. Mr. Smith profered his hand as an indication that he considered it a viable contract, but Mr. Nelson alluded to the fact that his colleagues had not been consulted.
   A. profered
   B. viable
   C. alluded
   D. colleagues

   6.____

7. The treatments were beneficial according to the optomotrists, and the consensus was that minimal improvement could be expected.
   A. beneficial
   B. optomotrists
   C. consensus
   D. minimal

   7.____

8. Her frivolous manner was unbecoming because the air of solemnity at the cemetery was pervasive.
   A. frivalous
   B. solemnity
   C. cemetery
   D. pervasive

   8.____

60

9. The clandestine meetings were designed to make the two adversaries more amicable, but they served only to intensify their emnity.
   A. clandestine
   B. adversaries
   C. amicable
   D. emnity

9.____

10. Do you think that his innovative ideas and financial acumen will help stabalize the fluctuations of the stock market?
    A. innovative
    B. acumen
    C. stabalize
    D. fluctuations

10.____

11. In order to keep a perpetual inventory, you will have to keep an uninterrupted surveillance of all the miscellanious stock.
    A. perpetual
    B. uninterrupted
    C. surveillance
    D. miscellanious

11.____

12. She used the art of pursuasion on the children because she found that caustic remarks had no perceptible effect on their behavior.
    A. pursuasion
    B. caustic
    C. perceptible
    D. effect

12.____

13. His sacreligious outbursts offended his constituents, and he was summarily removed from office by the City Council.
    A. sacreligious
    B. constituents
    C. summarily
    D. Council

13.____

14. They exhorted the contestants to greater efforts, but the exhorbitant costs in terms of energy expended resulted in a feeling of lethargy.
    A. exhorted
    B. contestants
    C. exhorbitant
    D. lethargy

14.____

15. Since he was knowledgable about illicit drugs, he was served with a subpoena to appear for the prosecution.
    A. knowledgable
    B. illicit
    C. subpoena
    D. prosecution

15.____

16. In spite of his lucid statements, they denigrated his report and decided it should be succintly paraphrased.
    A. lucid
    B. denigrated
    C. succintly
    D. paraphrased

16.____

17. The discussion was not germane to the contraversy, but the indicted man's insistence on further talk was allowed.
    A. germane
    B. contraversy
    C. indicted
    D. insistence

17.____

18. The legislators were enervated by the distances they had traveled during the election year to fullfil their speaking engagements.
    A. legislators
    B. enervated
    C. traveled
    D. fullfil

18.____

19. The plaintiffs' attornies charge the defendant in the case with felonious assault.   19._____
    A. plaintiffs' B. attornies
    C. defendant   D. felonious

20. It is symptomatic of the times that we try to placate all, but a proposal for new forms of disciplinery action was promulgated by the staff.   20._____
    A. symptomatic B. placate
    C. disciplinery D. promulgated

KEY (CORRECT ANSWERS)

1.	B	11.	D
2.	C	12.	A
3.	D	13.	A
4.	B	14.	C
5.	D	15.	A
6.	A	16.	C
7.	B	17.	B
8.	A	18.	D
9.	D	19.	B
10.	C	20.	C

TEST 9

DIRECTIONS: Each of Questions 1 through 15 consists of a single word which is spelled either correctly or incorrectly. If the word is spelled CORRECTLY, you are to print the letter C (Correct) in the space at the right. If the word is spelled INCORRECTL, you are to print the letter W (Wrong).

1. pospone   1.____
2. diffrent   2.____
3. height   3.____
4. carefully   4.____
5. ability   5.____
6. temper   6.____
7. deslike   7.____
8. seldem   8.____
9. alcohol   9.____
10. expense   10.____
11. vegatable   11.____
12. dispensary   12.____
13. specemin   13.____
14. allowance   14.____
15. exersise   15.____

KEY (CORRECT ANSWERS)

1.	W	6.	C	11.	W
2.	W	7.	W	12.	C
3.	C	8.	W	13.	W
4.	C	9.	C	14.	C
5.	C	10.	C	15.	W

TEST 10

DIRECTIONS: Each of Questions 1 through 10 consists of four words, one of which may be spelled incorrectly or all four words may be spelled correctly. If one of the words in a question is spelled incorrectly, print in the space at the right the capital letter preceding the word which is spelled INCORRECTLY. If all four words are spelled CORRECTLY, print the letter E.

1. A. dismissal   B. collateral   1._____
   C. leisure   D. proffession

2. A. subsidary   B. outrageous   2._____
   C. liaison   D. assessed

3. A. already   B. changeable   3._____
   C. mischevous   D. cylinder

4. A. supersede   B. deceit   4._____
   C. dissension   D. imminent

5. A. arguing   B. contagious   5._____
   C. comparitive   D. accessible

6. A. indelible   B. existance   6._____
   C. presumptuous D. mileage

7. A. extention   B. aggregate   7._____
   C. sustenance   D. gratuitous

8. A. interrogate   B. exaggeration   8._____
   C. vacillate   D. moreover

9. A. parallel   B. derogatory   9._____
   C. admissible   D. appellate

10. A. safety   B. cumalative   10._____
    C. disappear   D. usable

KEY (CORRECT ANSWERS)

1. D   6. B
2. A   7. A
3. C   8. E
4. E   9. C
5. C   10. B

TEST 11

DIRECTIONS: Each of questions 1 through 10 consists of four words, one of which may be spelled incorrectly or all four words may be spelled correctly. If one of the words in a question is spelled INCORRECTLY, print in the space at the right the capital letter preceding the word which is spelled incorrectly. If all four words are spelled CORRECTLY, print the letter E.

1. A. vehicular   B. gesticulate   1.____
   C. manageable   D. fullfil

2. A. inovation   B. onerous   2.____
   C. chastise   D. irresistible

3. A. familiarize   B. dissolution   3.____
   C. oscillate   D. superflous

4. A. census   B. defender   4.____
   C. adherence   D. inconceivable

5. A. voluminous   B. liberalize   5.____
   C. bankrupcy   D. conversion

6. A. justifiable   B. executor   6.____
   C. perpatrate   D. dispelled

7. A. boycott   B. abeyence   7.____
   C. enterprise   D. circular

8. A. spontaineous   B. dubious   8.____
   C. analyze   D. premonition

9. A. intelligible   B. apparently   9.____
   C. genuine   D. crucial

10. A. plentiful   B. ascertain   10.____
    C. carreer   D. preliminary

KEY (CORRECT ANSWERS)

1.	D	6.	C
2.	A	7.	B
3.	D	8.	A
4.	E	9.	E
5.	C	10.	C

TEST 12

DIRECTIONS: Each of questions 1 through 25 consists of four words, one of which may be spelled incorrectly or all four words may be spelled correctly. If one of the words in a question is spelled INCORRECTLY, print in the space at the right the capital letter preceding the word which is spelled incorrectly. If all four words are spelled CORRECTLY, print the letter E.

1. A. temporary B. existance 1.____
   C. complimentary D. altogether

2. A. privilege B. changeable 2.____
   C. jeopardize D. commitment

3. A. grievous B. alloted 3.____
   C. outrageous D. mortgage

4. A. tempermental B. accommodating 4.____
   C. bookkeeping D. panicky

5. A. auxiliary B. indispensable 5.____
   C. ecstasy D. fiery

6. A. dissappear B. buoyant 6.____
   C. imminent D. parallel

7. A. loosly B. medicine 7.____
   C. schedule D. defendant

8. A. endeavor B. persuade 8.____
   C. retroactive D. desparate

9. A. usage B. servicable 9.____
   C. disadvantageous D. remittance

10. A. beneficary B. receipt 10.____
    C. excitable D. implement

11. A. accompanying B. intangible 11.____
    C. offerred D. movable

12. A. controlling B. seize 12.____
    C. repetitious D. miscellaneous

13. A. installation B. accommodation 13.____
    C. consistant D. illuminate

14. A. incidentaly B. privilege 14.____
    C. apparent D. chargeable

2 (#12)

15. A. prevalent B. serial   15.____
    C. briefly   D. disatisfied

16. A. reciprocal   B. concurrence   16.____
    C. persistence D. withold

17. A. deferred   B. suing   17.____
    C. fulfilled D. pursuant

18. A. questionable   B. omission   18.____
    C. acknowledgment D. insistent

19. A. guarantee B. committment   19.____
    C. mitigate   D. publicly

20. A. prerogative   B. apprise   20.____
    C. extrordinary   D. continual

21. A. arrogant   B. handicapped   21.____
    C. judicious D. perennial

22. A. permissable   B. deceive   22.____
    C. innumerable   D. retrieve

23. A. notable   B. allegiance   23.____
    C. reimburse D. illegal

24. A. wholly   B. disbursement   24.____
    C. hindrance D. conciliatory

25. A. guidance   B. condemn   25.____
    C. publically D. coercion

67

KEY (CORRECT ANSWERS)

1.	B		11.	C
2.	E		12.	E
3.	B		13.	C
4.	A		14.	A
5.	E		15.	D
6.	A		16.	D
7.	A		17.	E
8.	D		18.	A
9.	B		19.	B
10.	A		20.	C

21. E
22. A
23. E
24. E
25. C

EXAMINATION SECTION
TEST 1

DIRECTIONS: In each of the following groups, one of the four sentences contains an error in grammar, usage, diction, or punctuation. Indicate the INCORRECT sentence. *PRINT THE LETTER OF THE CORRECT ANSWER IN THE SPACE AT THE RIGHT.*

1. A. He acted as if he had never heard the story.
    B. The lecturer spoke so long his audience became restless.
    C. The author of "The Yearling" has written another book about Florida.
    D. It looks now like he will not be promoted after all.

    1.____

2. A. Swing music is different from the popular music of ten years ago.
    B. Mary bought the hat at once lest she change her mind.
    C. No one having received permission to call a meeting, the plan was dropped.
    D. Being that you are here, we can proceed with the discussion.

    2.____

3. A. After a long and bitter discussion, the meeting was adjoined at 6 o' clock.
    B. He owns property in an adjoining county.
    C. When you joined the club, you were a sophomore.
    D. No one should plan a long journey for pleasure in these days.

    3.____

4. A. My brother is so much taller than I that hardly any one believes we are twins.
    B. The account he gave of the accident was different in many particulars.
    C. Your sister is so kind to you that I don't see how you can love your brother more than her.
    D. You have given more thought and time to the solving of this problem than anybody else has.

    4.____

5. A. They told us how they had suffered.
    B. It is interesting (a) to the student, (b) to the parent, and (c) to the teacher.
    C. There were blue, green and red banners.
    D. "Will you help", he asked?

    5.____

6. A. Who do you suggest should be appointed chairman of our committee?
    B. Whom do you think they met on their way to the concert last night?
    C. Who do you believe would choose such men as their representatives?
    D. Whom do you think will visit us next spring to see the cherry blossoms?

    6.____

7. A. He will try and do as you request.
    B. This was a matter between him and me.
    C. They agreed to distribute the candy among all the children.
    D. Jones won by Smith's missing a chance.

    7.____

8. A. There are only a few shovelfuls of coal left.
    B. The batter tried to gain time by blowing his nose between every ball.
    C. A novel or five short stories were to be read.
    D. This group of stories is concerned with family problems.

    8.____

9. A. Dinner being over, the table may now be cleared.
    B. He is wiser, but not so old as his brother.
    C. There is nothing so enervating as too much rest.
    D. I was too late for the train, so I returned home and, after arriving there, noticed the ominous clouds in the west.

10. A. Her very manner makes one think of a cleanly person.
    B. His motives were as contemptible as his actions.
    C. His meager contribution is more preferable than her refusal to participate at all.
    D. An umpire must be a disinterested judge.

11. A. The remainder of the day was spent at home.
    B. He asked for the loan of a clean handkerchief.
    C. Neither painting nor fighting feed men.
    D. He emigrated from Germany in 1939.

12. A. Although he is a lawyer for ten years he has never appeared in a court.
    B. The drivers object to paying their proportion of the increase.
    C. He would have been the first man to acknowledge the contradiction.
    D. She would have liked to wear her new gown at the ball.

13. A. I suggest he do as he is told.
    B. Clubs with membership between 100 to 500 are not listed in this catalogue.
    C. I ask that the prisoner be given his liberty.
    D. He could not help wondering whether he would be the next victim.

14. A. Her tears had no effect on him whatsoever.
    B. The facts were different than what we had feared.
    C. He was driving somebody else's car.
    D. Immigration into the United States has been reduced.

15. A. Looking at the problem calmly, a solution seems not only possible but probable.
    B. Were he to appear, I'd throw the lie into his face.
    C. I don't object to Carter's going; I do object to his representing us.
    D. After he had lain in one position for an hour, he felt cramped and stiff.

16. A. If we except Bert, no one prepared the lesson thoroughly.
    B. "Jack is the winner," he announced, "Bill is in second place, and Stan is in third."
    C. The teacher appointed two of us, Anne and me, to distribute the papers.
    D. He had only to speak to gain our support.

17. A. The family are not agreed on next summer's vacation plans.
    B. Yours and theirs are right next to ours.
    C. In the fight for women's suffrage one judge's decision had little effect, for the most part, upon the ladies' determination.
    D. This time Mr. Andrews spoke like he really meant it.

18. A. The doctor prescribed at least a three weeks' rest for me.
    B. Neither Fred nor the twins are coming.
    C. I find those kind of gloves impractical for me.
    D. Most English teachers penalize the use of <u>O's</u> and <u>etc.'s</u> in compositions.

19. A. Give the money to whoever needs it most.
    B. We are in New York City for the past ten years.
    C. Everyone being willing, we decided to try a moonlight hike up the Tuckerman Ravine Trail.
    D. Madeline looks beautiful in purple.

19.____

20. A. If Brutus had refused Antony a chance to speak, history might have been changed.
    B. We had always wanted to visit Zion National Park, White Sands National Monument, and Death Valley.
    C. We cannot, however, scarcely believe Cora's wild tale of a burglar.
    D. Who do you think will win the Rose Bowl game?

20.____

21. A. There lay the puppy squealing piteously.
    B. Natives of certain African tribes are, on the average, taller than we.
    C. For landscape planting why not choose one of the native shrubs; for example, winterberry, viburnum, or blueberry?
    D. I don't doubt but what you are right, but I reject your reasoning.

21.____

22. A. I hope that Paul's mother will leave him go to the party.
    B. This Sunday on the parkway there were fewer tie-ups and less congestion than on the previous Sunday.
    C. Teresa would have liked to take the trip, but she couldn't afford it.
    D. It seems to be she who made the blunder.

22.____

23. A. We wanted a tree that was beautiful all year round; therefore we planted a dogwood.
    B. I wanted the victor to be him, not her.
    C. Mt. Kinley in Alaska is higher than any mountain in North America.
    D. The men's and boys' departments are next to each other.

23.____

24. A. All that is left standing in the bombed area is a few brick walls.
    B. I found, when I reached the theatre, that I left home without the tickets.
    C. Every available officer, including fifteen privates, was sent on the mission.
    D. It is I who am most concerned over the implications of the new bill.

24.____

25. A. Our school has more students than any other school in the borough.
    B. I don't know but that he is correct.
    C. I think we can count on John being present.
    D. Tom has two brothers-in-law.

25.____

26. A. She has had more advantages than he.
    B. The doctor is not in at present, but he'll return at three o'clock.
    C. This country must either set up flood controls or be prepared to lose billions of dollars annually.
    D. The pupils were told by the teacher to bring their project home from school with them.

26.____

27. A. He was doubtless aware that his supporters were deserting him.
    B. The lazy pupil, of course, will tend to write the minimum amount of words acceptable.
    C. It was his practice to feed whoever appeared at his door.
    D. He did not resent the intrusion so much as he despised the intruder.

27.____

28. A. It's a problem that we've been unable to solve satisfactorily.
    B. If anybody objects to our plan, let's tell them to try to make a better one.
    C. When the thirsty horse had drunk its fill, it trotted briskly down the road.
    D. I left my pen in this room but seem unable to find it.

    28.___

29. A. They preferred the site at Hurley Street and Second Avenue because of its proximity to the proposed bus terminal at Twenty-fourth Street.
    B. The farther south you drive in Blackwell County, the more you understand the reason for Conniston's moving north.
    C. "Inasmuch as Baker is a resident here for twenty years," declared Carter, "we should give serious consideration to his suggestions."
    D. His approach to the committee was certainly not conducive to a cordial reception of his proposals, which were, at best, of doubtful validity.

    29.___

30. A. In his teaching, he always kept the children's interests and needs in mind.
    B. He prefers this kind of book to any other.
    C. Although he was fond of the theatre, he would never go to see a play, at the Sheffield Theatre because he didn't like its owner.
    D. If he were to resign now, people would say he was unwilling to face the issue.

    30.___

31. A. On the last day of the school term, Mr. Jansen will take Miss Brill's enrolling room; Mrs. Jackson, Mr. Fein's; and Miss Knowland, mine.
    B. Did the Student Council raise any objection to John's running for President of the General Organization?
    C. The spokesman said that on February 15 the school dietitian called each of the cafeteria employees individually into her office and told them to resign from the union.
    D. Dan would like to have seen the Orange Bowl game on television.

    31.___

32. A. Being that I am older than you, I am probably stronger.
    B. He was afraid of being late for the party if he stayed to discuss the plans any longer.
    C. Being widely known as a man of sound opinions, he felt that his reputation was at stake.
    D. His being called by the principal caused him to weep and tremble.

    32.___

33. A. Everybody who has paid the full purchase price should call for his set of books now.
    B. Only a person of great determination and stamina could have persisted in that endeavor to the point of success.
    C. There is no explanation for the strange phenomenon, it just occurs regularly early every morning.
    D. Had he not been so averse to criticism, he could have had the benefit of Desmond's opinion.

    33.___

34. A. Hearing the bells and the whistles, the New Year was greeted noisily by everybody at the party.
    B. Besides her own family of four boys, my grandmother reared two adopted children.
    C. A preposition is a relational word; an adjective is an attributive word.
    D. If I were a good speller, I should get better marks in English.

    34.___

35.   A. My teacher won't leave me come into the classroom when I am late.
      B. I'll lend you the book, provided you prepare a report on it for our next meeting.
      C. He is not the kind of person upon whom one can depend.
      D. The proposal that we should all go together was accepted enthusiastically.

36.   A. Had you heard the argument, you would be ready to excuse his anger.
      B. If you will hold the pen like I do, it will not give you any trouble.
      C. Should you see my sister, please ask her to come home at once.
      D. Let's start early so that we'll be in time for the beginning of the play.

37.   A. In recent years the metals in many articles have been substituted by plastics.
      B. They are not in Boston now, but I think they're going to that city next week.
      C. Having heard all the testimony in the case, the jury was charged by the judge.
      D. Either two bolts or one metal strap is required for the job.

38.   A. I shall reward whoever completed the job first.
      B. These data have been prepared by me, and you are welcome to make use of them.
      C. This is one of the issues in the salary question that is still to be reviewed.
      D. I want the responsibilities to be divided equally among the several members.

39.   A. "Do you wish to reconsider any of your answers?" he asked.
      B. Due to lack of attendance, the traveling circus was forced to suspend operations.
      C. I have no objection to their using the tennis court this afternoon.
      D. There was, in the mail, an inquiry by a young couple for a house with two or three bedrooms.

40.   A. Had you not lain there during the drill, you might have been reported for breaking the rules.
      B. Yes, the apple tastes sweet.
      C. Is he not the man whom you saw forcing his way into the meeting?
      D. Everyone but Jerry and I agreed to the compromise proposal on the salary question.

41.   A. He always tried his best; he almost always achieved success.
      B. "Now, when we need him most," she declared, "he has declined to continue as a member of the committee."
      C. The papers lay undisturbed in the attic for more than fifty years.
      D. No sooner had he received his inheritance when he bought a new car.

42.   A. The children asked, "When shall we start our program?"
      B. They feared that the child might be lost.
      C. We have less books in chemistry than in physics.
      D. If you do not pay attention to lights, you may be hit by an automobile.

43.   A. They're not sure that your suggestion is suitable for their purpose.
      B. Suddenly collecting his wits, he began to talk rapidly about the events leading up to the accident.
      C. Dickens wrote "David Copperfield"; Thackeray, "Vanity Fair."
      D. Many students graduate high school in less than four years.

44. A. We had scarcely reached our door than the rain began to come down in torrents. 44.___
    B. The reason I am discouraged is that I have failed twice in my attempt to be elected.
    C. Is this the man who you thought had an interesting story to tell?
    D. Once inside the barn, the horse was no longer frightened.

45. A. None of the boys was willing to have the game post-poned. 45.___
    B. My grandmother used to say, "A stitch in time saves nine."
    C. This kind of apples ripens earlier than any other in our section of the country.
    D. They planned to meet my friend's brother and I at the bus terminal.

KEY (CORRECT ANSWERS)

1. D	11. C	21. D	31. C	41. D
2. D	12. A	22. A	32. A	42. C
3. D	13. B	23. C	33. C	43. D
4. B	14. B	24. B	34. A	44. A
5. D	15. A	25. C	35. A	45. D
6. D	16. B	26. D	36. B	
7. A	17. D	27. B	37. A	
8. B	18. C	28. B	38. A	
9. D	19. B	29. C	39. B	
10. C	20. C	30. A	40. D	

TEST 2

DIRECTIONS: In each of the following groups, one of the four sentences contains an error in grammar, usage, diction, or punctuation. Indicate the INCORRECT sentence. *PRINT THE LETTER OF THE CORRECT ANSWER IN THE SPACE AT THE RIGHT.*

1. A. If you'll lend me some thread, I'll make you a dress.   1.____
   B. He dresses just like he did in the West.
   C. She walks slowly and cautiously, just as I do when I'm very tired.
   D. I don't know whether I should go or stay.

2. A. Give me a few minutes to think, I shall have the answer.   2.____
   B. We went to Albany, a large city in New York State, on a business trip.
   C. We hope to hear from you as soon as you reach Topeka.
   D. We traveled all day at top speed, but failed to reach home in time for dinner.

3. A. I haven't seen him for more than two years.   3.____
   B. I have been absent due to the illness of my son.
   C. Who's going to know you're here, if none of us calls your name?
   D. By the time the treaty is signed, we shall have lost our rights to the property.

4. A. I wish I were going away, too.   4.____
   B. We, she and I, have made many trips to the West.
   C. The clay can easily be shaped by one who has the necessary skill.
   D. He is reported to be killed in an airplane accident.

5. A. He let on that he was sick whenever there was work to be done.   5.____
   B. The prize was divided among the members of the crew.
   C. These data are submitted for your approval.
   D. He climbed off the platform and ran away.

6. A. Although you speak clearly and to the point, you have not convinced me.   6.____
   B. Shall we go anywhere after lunch today?
   C. The flowers smell sweet after an April shower.
   D. After discussing the matter with my mother and I, my father reluctantly agreed to postpone the trip.

7. A. The storm was severe, but it did not harm the ship.   7.____
   B. Did you see the boy whom, we all think, is the leader of the group?
   C. He was assisted by his friend who lives in a nearby apartment.
   D. They went into the house to read the account of the trial.

8. A. He couldn't hardly see what he had written on the paper.   8.____
   B. Mary confidently expected to see Albert at the theatre.
   C. I fully intended to go to church Easter Sunday.
   D. We had not yet heard from John when the news of the accident reached us.

9. A. Now, at last, you are coming to the point.   9.____
   B. The mistress was at home, even though she did not come to the door.
   C. They are alike in this particular, e.g., they are both over twenty years of age.
   D. Standing in the doorway, he could hear the typewriter clicking.

75

10. A. He told us to follow him and we did not do so.
    B. The ocean liner that docked in the harbor yesterday is called the Queen Elizabeth.
    C. How could he have grown so much during the last year!
    D. I'm living here two years, but I don't know my neighbors.

10.___

11. A. The return trip was equally as delightful as the trip to the coast.
    B. Mary and Sue saw each other often after their graduation.
    C. I like him very much, despite his many faults.
    D. I will go to see him Thursday next.

11.___

12. A. And that, my friends, was the way I nearly lost my job.
    B. But I was not really lazy; the heat was most enervating.
    C. Never again! Curiosity can kill more than cats.
    D. "Why do you continue to suffer in silence", she asked?

12.___

13. A. We saw a penny rolling around the corner.
    B. "John and Henry," he insisted, "were in their room."
    C. Everybody came in and took his seat.
    D. Taking the watch apart, it seemed to be a very complicated mechanism.

13.___

14. A. You looked good in that dress.
    B. I bought a red and green dress to wear at your sister's party.
    C. May I leave early to-day for a change?
    D. There is a sale of men's and ladies' suits in this store.

14.___

15. A. He stayed inside the yard all morning.
    B. The coal was put in under the stairs.
    C. These kind of apples are not grown in New York or in New Jersey.
    D. It does look like rain, but all signs fail in dry weather.

15.___

16. A. The party who called before lunch refused to leave his name.
    B. For the sake of argument, let us assume that the moon is inhabited.
    C. I should like to spend the summer somewhere in Canada.
    D. This boy is careful and not likely to make many mistakes.

16.___

17. A. My father did not like fishing, hiking, or swimming; in fact, he refused to play golf.
    B. Chicago was very different than what I had imagined.
    C. If you cannot effect a change in his attitude, we'll lose his support entirely.
    D. He found the climate in Arizona very healthful.

17.___

18. A. He was improved some in spelling and in oral reading.
    B. This rule, which is still in effect, was adopted three years ago.
    C. The principal will recommend whoever has the best record.
    D. We'll lend you our truck, provided you take good care of it.

18.___

19. A. The boy blew up his balloon until it burst.
    B. Most every week, the farmer brings us fresh eggs from the country.
    C. Neither you nor I am in a position to complain about the arrangements.
    D. I can't recall his asking us to pay him a visit.

19.___

20. A. Yesterday, he said, "Hello."
    B. Between you and I, these are the facts.
    C. I have seen my mother.
    D. We have not heard from John.

21. A. This sure is a hard problem.
    B. He got off the horse.
    C. Only Charles was there.
    D. I was there yesterday, I assure you.

22. A. He and I do not agree.
    B. If I were you, I would go.
    C. We knew that it was not her.
    D. DYNASTS, by Thomas Hardy, is a novel.

23. A. Who did he see?
    B. If he should fall, we should all be lost.
    C. I intended to go.
    D. He is reported to have been killed.

24. A. Only Charles will come.
    B. They are alike in this particular.
    C. I should like to give you tickets, but I haven't any.
    D. Shall we go any place today with this data?

25. A. If I was young, I would dance.
    B. She gave them to us girls.
    C. She helped John and me.
    D. I know whom he saw.

26. A. He asked us to watch him.
    B. I believe him to be rich.
    C. She knew the guide to be me.
    D. She used three cupsful of flour in the cake.

27. A. We knew it was she.
    B. I approve of his giving her the ring.
    C. This series of books are excellent.
    D. Everyone has studied his lesson.

28. A. The material was oak and pine.
    B. He don't know his own strength.
    C. The instructor, as well as the class, was alarmed.
    D. The committee disagree on this point.

29. A. I do not know whether I can tell you.
    B. Three days ago I saw him.
    C. I cannot encourage you any.
    D. What is one among many?

30. A. Don't blame me for it.
    B. Loan me five dollars.
    C. I have met but four.
    D. May I leave early tonight?

31. A. She rides like I do.
    B. Can he run a hundred yards in ten seconds?
    C. These data are correct.
    D. He was sick with rheumatism.

32. A. James and John saw each other often.
    B. The return trip was equally delightful.
    C. I could hardly do it.
    D. She couldn't hardly see.

33. A. I have no hope of seeing him before winter.
    B. He stayed inside the yard.
    C. I didn't say nothing.
    D. It rolled under the desk.

34. A. I approved of him accepting the position.
    B. Three times four is twelve.
    C. Each man carries a gun.
    D. The tidings were brought to her.

35. A. Ethics is a difficult course.
    B. Everyone knows what to do.
    C. You and I are going to the concert.
    D. The factory's manager was very young.

36. A. He was extremely kind to me yesterday.
    B. I talked to him in regard to the subscription.
    C. They were so good to me.
    D. The teacher spoke clear and emphatic.

37. A. He was very much amused at her.
    B. I intended to have gone.
    C. He went away, far into the desert.
    D. I shall not go without his agreeing.

38. A. It must be here somewhere.
    B. The reason is that there is no bread.
    C. Of all other cities, New York is the largest.
    D. The pickles were excellent.

39. A. This is a new kind of rose.
    B. Which is the oldest, John or James?
    C. It looks like rain.
    D. I bought this from the dealer.

40. A. Because of the intransigence of one member of the committee, no agreement could be reached.
    B. The enemy's guns tried in vain to reduce the ramifications on the opposite shore.
    C. The farmer was advised to let the land lie fallow.
    D. It was an unsuitable diet for a man who followed a sedentary occupation.

41. A. He frequently hurt people's feelings with his terse remarks.
    B. The perspicacity revealed by his comments won the approval of his superiors.
    C. He was aggravated by a severe cold.
    D. An ewe and a ram were bought at the same time for the purpose of mating.

42. A. An aroused public opinion militated against a fair trial for the defendant in that county.
    B. The market was surfeited with new cars.
    C. Since basketball was limited to intramural games, no money was needed for trips.
    D. The three prime ministers of the Benelux countries signed, in a matter of minutes, a bilateral treaty which had taken months to prepare.

43. A. Marauding bands terrorized the area.
    B. In the face of the bad news his levity was frowned upon.
    C. Refusing to answer was interpreted as tantamount to guilt.
    D. The consultant in Macy's considered the combination of colors indecorous.

44. A. He was so credulous as to be a detriment to the firm.
    B. The white marble columns rested on pediments of pink marble.
    C. The proponents of the scheme were ready to reap the benefits.
    D. He was praised for having accomplished a creditable piece of work in the face of great difficulties.

45. A. His penchant for gambling was soon to lead to disaster.
    B. The impresario stopped in the middle of her aria to upbraid the new manager.
    C. She departed, leaving a trail of disturbing innuendoes in her wake.
    D. The most troublesome of the impediments was considered first.

46. A. The old countess was waiting to ask the artist what he really meant by a piquant face.
    B. The doctor's prognosis proved to be right.
    C. The Marseillaise has been described as the impassioned cry of an aroused people.
    D. When the lectures on logistics began, philosophy took on a new meaning for him.

47. A. The unhealthy climate made the campaign a costly one.
    B. Man is said to be a naturally gregarious animal.
    C. The winner of the lottery was soon luxuriating in his new wealth.
    D. The jury reached no decision because of one adamant member.

48. A. Rip Van Winkle's wife was known as a termagant.
    B. Use of the word was interpreted as an error on the part of the author's amnuensis.

C. General Washington could hardly believe Arnold's duplicity.
D. The guns thundered the salutary greeting customarily given to the head of a state.

49. A. She tried in vain to find a euphemistic phrase with which to express her contempt.
    B. The Javanese peccadillo was kept in an ornate silver cage.
    C. The prisoner received word of his fate impassively.
    D. His turgid style of writing pleased no one but himself.

50. A. The new boats were immediately assigned to internecine duties.
    B. He spoke from copious notes.
    C. The chemists were amazed at the tensile strength of the new fiber.
    D. The owner and lessee were both in court.

KEY (CORRECT ANSWERS)

1. B	11. D	21. A	31. A	41. C
2. B	12. D	22. C	32. D	42. D
3. B	13. D	23. A	33. C	43. D
4. D	14. A	24. D	34. A	44. B
5. A	15. C	25. A	35. D	45. B
6. D	16. A	26. D	36. D	46. D
7. B	17. B	27. C	37. B	47. A
8. A	18. A	28. B	38. C	48. D
9. C	19. B	29. C	39. B	49. B
10. D	20. B	30. B	40. B	50. A

ENGLISH EXPRESSION
EXAMINATION SECTION
TEST 1

DIRECTIONS: Each question or incomplete statement is followed by several suggested answers or completions. Select the one that BEST answers the question or completes the statement. *PRINT THE LETTER OF THE CORRECT ANSWER IN THE SPACE AT THE RIGHT.*

Questions 1-9.

DIRECTIONS: The following sentences contain problems in grammar, usage diction (choice of words), and idiom. Some sentences are correct. No sentence contains more than one error. You will find that the error, if there is one, is underlined and lettered. Assume that all other elements of the sentence are correct and cannot be changed. In choosing answers, follow the requirements of standard written English. If there is an error, select the *one underlined* part that must be changed in order to make the sentence correct. If there is no error, mark E.

1. <u>In planning</u> your future, <u>one must be</u> as honest with yourself as possible, make careful 1.____
     A   B
   decisions about the best course <u>to follow to achieve</u> a particular purpose, and, above all,
             C
   have the courage <u>to stand by those</u> decisions. <u>No error</u>
         D   E

2. <u>Even though</u> history does not actually repeat itself, knowledge <u>of</u> history <u>can give</u> 2.____
    A   B   C
   current problems a familiar, <u>less</u> formidable look. <u>No error</u>
            D   E

3. The Curies <u>had almost exhausted</u> their resources, and <u>for a time it seemed</u> 3.____
        A   B
   unlikely that <u>they ever</u> would find the <u>solvent to their financial problems</u>. <u>No error</u>
       C   D   E

4. <u>If the rumors are</u> correct, Deane <u>will not be convicted</u>, for each of the officers 4.____
    A   B
   on the court realizes that Colson and Holdman may be <u>the real culprit and</u> that
                       C
   <u>their</u> testimony is not completely trustworthy. <u>No error</u>
    D   E

5. The citizens of Washington, <u>like Los Angeles</u>, prefer to commute by automobile,   5.____
                                    A

even though motor vehicles contribute <u>nearly as many</u> contaminants to the air
                                                        B

<u>as do all other</u> sources <u>combined</u>. <u>No error</u>
       C   D   E

6. <u>By the time Robert Vasco completes</u> his testimony, every major executive of our   6.____
                      A

company but Ray Ashurst <u>and I</u> <u>will have been</u> <u>accused of</u> complicity in the stock
                                B   C   D

swindle. <u>No error</u>
           E

7. <u>Within six months</u> the store was operating <u>profitably and efficient</u>; shelves   7.____
        A   B

<u>were well stocked</u>, goods were selling rapidly, and the cash register
     C

<u>was ringing constantly</u>. <u>No error</u>
        D   E

8. Shakespeare's comedies have an advantage <u>over Shaw</u> <u>in that Shakespeare's</u> were   8.____
                                          A   B

<u>written primarily</u> to entertain and <u>not to</u> argue for a cause. <u>No error</u>
     C   D   E

9. Any true insomniac <u>is well aware of</u> the futility of <u>such measures as</u> drinking   9.____
                       A   B

hot milk, <u>regular hours, deep breathing</u>, counting sheep, and <u>concentrating on</u>
                      C   D

black velvet. <u>No error</u>
               E

Questions 10-15.

DIRECTIONS: In each of the following sentences, some part of the sentence or the entire sentence is underlined. Beneath each sentence you will find five ways of phrasing the underlined part. The first of these repeats the original; the other four are different. If you think the original is better than any of the alternatives, choose answer A; otherwise choose one of the others. In choosing answers, follow the requirements of standard written English; that is, pay attention to grammar, choice of words, sentence construction, and punctuation. Choose the answer that produces the most effective sentence—clear and exact, without awkwardness or ambiguity. Do not make a choice that changes the meaning of the original sentence.

10. The tribe of warriors believed that boys and girls should be <u>reared separate, and, as soon as he was weaned, the boys were taken from their mothers.</u>   10.____

    A. reared separate, and, as soon as he was weaned, the boys were taken from their mothers

3 (#1)

- B. reared separate, and, as soon as he was weaned, a boy was taken from his mother
- C. reared separate, and, as soon as he was weaned, the boys were taken from their mothers
- D. reared separately, and, as soon as a boy was weaned, they were taken from their mothers
- E. reared separately, and, as soon as a boy was weaned, he was taken from his mother

11. <u>Despite Vesta being only the third largest, it is by far the brightest of the known asteroids.</u>
    - A. Despite Vesta being only the third largest, it is by far the brightest of the known asteroids.
    - B. Vesta, though only the third largest asteroid, is by far the brightest of the known ones.
    - C. Being only the third largest, yet Vesta is by far the brightest of the known asteroids.
    - D. Vesta, though only the third largest of the known asteroids, is by far the brightest.
    - E. Vesta is only the third largest of the asteroids, it being, however, the brightest one.

11._____

12. As a result of the discovery of the Dead Sea Scrolls, our understanding of the roots of Christianity <u>has had to be revised considerably.</u>
    - A. has had to be revised considerably
    - B. have had to be revised considerably
    - C. has had to undergo revision to a considerable degree
    - D. have had to be subjected to considerable revision
    - E. has had to be revised in a considerable way

12._____

13. Because <u>it is imminently suitable to</u> dry climates, adobe has been a traditional building material throughout the southwestern states.
    - A. it is imminently suitable to
    - B. it is eminently suitable for
    - C. It is eminently suitable when in
    - D. of its eminent suitability with
    - E. of being imminently suitable in

13._____

14. Martell is more concerned with demonstrating that racial prejudice exists <u>than preventing it from doing harm, which explains</u> why his work is not always highly regarded.
    - A. Martell is more concerned with demonstrating that racial prejudice exists than preventing it from doing harm, which explains
    - B. Martell is more concerned with demonstrating that racial prejudice exists than with preventing it from doing harm, and this explains
    - C. Martell is more concerned with demonstrating that racial prejudice exists than with preventing it from doing harm, an explanation of
    - D. Martell's greater concern for demonstrating that racial prejudice exists than preventing it from doing harm—this explains
    - E. Martell's greater concern for demonstrating that racial prejudice exists than for preventing it from doing harm explains

14._____

15. Throughout this history of the American West there runs a steady commentary on the deception and mistreatment of the Indians.   15.____
    A. Throughout this history of the American West there runs a steady commentary on the deception and mistreatment of the Indians.
    B. There is a steady commentary provided on the deception and mistreatment of the Indians and it runs throughout this history of the American West.
    C. The deception and mistreatment of the Indians provide a steady comment that runs throughout this history of the American West.
    D. Comment on the deception and mistreatment of the Indians is steadily provided and runs throughout this history of the American West.
    E. Running throughout this history of the American West is a steady commentary that is provided on the deception and mistreatment of the Indians.

Questions 16-20.

DIRECTIONS: In each of the following questions you are given a complete sentence to be rephrased according to the directions which follow it. You should rephrase the sentence mentally to save time, although you may make notes in your test book if you wish. Below each sentence and its directions are listed words or phrases that may occur in your revised sentence. When you have thought out a good sentence, look in the choices A through E for the word or entire phrase that is included in your revised sentence, and print the letter of the correct answer in the space at the right. The word or phrase you choose should be the most accurate and most nearly complete of all the choices given, and should be part of a sentence that meets the requirements of standard written English. Of course, a number of different sentences can be obtained if the sentence is revised according to directions, and not all of these possibilities can be included in only five choices. If you should find that you have thought of a sentence that contains none of the words or phrases listed in the choices, you should attempt to rephrase the sentence again so that it includes a word or phrase that is listed. Although the directions may at times require you to change the relationship between parts of the sentence or to make slight changes in meaning in other ways, make only those changes that the directions require; that is, keep the meaning the same, or as nearly the same as the directions permit. If you think that more than one good sentence can be made according to the directions, select the sentence that is most exact, effective, and natural in phrasing and construction.

EXAMPLES

I. Sentence: Coming to the city as a young man, he found a job as a newspaper reporter.
   Directions: Substitute He came for Coming.
   A. and so he found   B. and found
   C. and there he had found   D. and then finding
   E. and had found

Your rephrased sentence will probably read: "He came to the city as a young man and found a job as a newspaper reporter." This sentence contains the correct answer: <u>B. and found</u>. A sentence which used one of the alternate phrases would <u>change the</u> meaning or <u>intention</u> of the original sentence, would be a <u>poorly written sentence</u>, or would be <u>less effective</u> than another possible revision.

II. <u>Sentence</u>: Owing to her wealth, Sarah had many suitors.
<u>Directions</u>: Begin with <u>Many men courted</u>.
   A. so   B. while   C. although   D. because   E. and

Your rephrased sentence will probably read: "Many men courted Sarah because she was wealthy." This new sentence contains only choice D, which is the correct answer. None of the other choices will fit into an effective, correct sentence that retains the original meaning.

16. The archaeologists could only mark out the burial site, for then winter came.
   Begin with <u>Winter came before</u>.
     A. could do nothing more   B. could not do anything
     C. could only do   D. could do something
     E. could do anything more

17. The white reader often receives some insight into the reasons why black men are angry from descriptions by a black writer of the injustice they encounter in a white society.
   Begin with <u>A black writer often gives</u>.
     A. when describing   B. by describing
     C. he has described   D. in the descriptions
     E. because of describing

18. The agreement between the university officials and the dissident students provides for student representation on every university committee and on the board of trustees.
   Substitute <u>provides that</u> for <u>provides for</u>.
     A. be   B. are   C. would have
     D. would be   E. is to be

19. English Romanticism had its roots in German idealist philosophy, first described in England by Samuel Coleridge.
   Begin with <u>Samuel Coleridge was the first in</u>.
     A. in which English   B. and from it English
     C. where English   D. the source of English
     E. the birth of English

20. Four months have passed since his dismissal, during which time Alan has looked for work daily.
   Begin with <u>Each day</u>.
     A. will have passed   B. that have passed   C. that passed
     D. were to pass   E. <u>had passed</u>

KEY (CORRECT ANSWERS)

1.	B	11.	D
2.	E	12.	A
3.	D	13.	B
4.	C	14.	E
5.	A	15.	A
6.	B	16.	E
7.	B	17.	B
8.	A	18.	A
9.	C	19.	D
10.	E	20.	B

ENGLISH EXPRESSION
CHOICE OF EXPRESSION
COMMENTARY

One special form of the English Expression multiple-choice question in current use requires the candidate to select from among five (5) versions of a particular part of a sentence (or of an entire sentence), the one version that expresses the idea of the sentence most clearly, effectively, and accurately. Thus, the candidate is required not only to recognize errors, but also to choose the best way of phrasing a particular part of the sentence.

This is a test of choice of expression, which assays the candidate's ability to express himself correctly and effectively, including his sensitivity to the subtleties and nuances of the language.

SAMPLE QUESTIONS

DIRECTIONS: In each of the following sentences, some part of the sentence or the entire sentence is underlined. The underlined part presents a problem in the appropriate use of language. Beneath each sentence you will find five ways of writing the underlined part. The first of these indicates no change (that is, it repeats the original), but the other four are all different. If you think the original sentence is better than any of the suggested changes, you should choose answer A; otherwise you should mark one of the other choices. Select the BEST answer and print the letter in the space at the right.

This is a test of correctness and effectiveness of expression. In choosing answers, follow the requirements of standard written English; that is, pay attention to acceptable usage in grammar, diction (choice of words), sentence construction, and punctuation. Choose the answer that produces the most effective sentence—clear and exact, without awkwardness or ambiguity. Do not make a choice that changes the meaning of the original sentence.

SAMPLE QUESTION 1

Although these states now trade actively with the West, and although they are willing to exchange technological information, their arts and thoughts and social structure <u>remains substantially similar to what it has always been</u>.

    A. remains substantially similar to what it has always been
    B. remain substantially unchanged
    C. remains substantially unchanged
    D. remain substantially similar to what they have always been
    E. remain substantially without being changed

The purpose of questions of this type is to determine the candidate's ability to select the clearest and most effective means of expressing what the statement attempts to say. In this example, the phrasing in the statement, which is repeated in A, presents a problem of agreement between a subject and its verb (<u>their arts and thought and social structure</u> and <u>remains</u>), a problem of agreement between a pronoun and its antecedent (<u>their arts and thought and social structure</u> and <u>it</u>), an a problem of precise and concise phrasing (<u>remains</u>

substantially similar to what it has always been for remains substantially unchanged). Each of the four remaining choices in some way corrects one or more of the faults in the sentence, but only one deals with all three problems satisfactorily. Although C presents a more careful and concise wording of the phrasing of the statement and, in the process, eliminates the problem of agreement between pronoun and antecedent, it fails to correct the problem of agreement between the subject and its verb. In D, the subject agrees with its verb and the pronoun agrees with its antecedent, but the phrasing is not so accurate as it should be. The same difficulty persists in E. Only in B are all the problems presented corrected satisfactory. The question is not difficult.

SAMPLE QUESTION 2

Her latest novel is the largest in scope, the most accomplished in technique, and it is more significant in theme than anything she has written.
  A. it is more significant in theme than anything
  B. It is most significant in theme of anything
  C. more significant in theme than anything
  D. the most significant in theme than anything
  E. the most significant in theme of anything

This question is of greater difficulty than the preceding one. The problem posed in the sentence and repeated in A is essentially one of parallelism; Does the underlined portion of the sentence follow the pattern established by the first two elements of the series (the largest...the most accomplished)? It does not, for it introduces a pronoun and verb (it is) that the second term of the series indicates should be omitted and a degree of comparison (more significant) that is not in keeping with the superlatives used earlier in the sentence. B uses the superlative degree of significant but retains the unnecessary it is; C removes the it is, but retains the faulty comparative form of the adjective. D corrects both errors in parallelism, but introduces an error in idiom (the most...than). Only E corrects all the problems without introducing another fault.

SAMPLE QUESTION 3

Desiring to insure the continuity of their knowledge, magical lore is transmitted by the chiefs to their descendants.
  A. magical lore is transmitted by the chiefs
  B. transmission of magical lore is made by the chiefs
  C. the chiefs' magical lore is transmitted
  D. the chiefs transmit magical lore
  E. the chiefs make transmission of magical lore
The CORRECT answer is D.

SAMPLE QUESTION 4

As Malcolm walks quickly and confident into the purser's office, the rest of the crew wondered whether he would be charged with the theft.
  A. As Malcolm walks quickly and confident
  B. As Malcolm was walking quick and confident
  C. As Malcom walked quickly and confident

D. As Malcolm walked quickly and confidently
E. As Malcolm walks quickly and confidently
The CORRECT answer is D.

SAMPLE QUESTION 5

The chairman, <u>granted the power to assign any duties to whoever he</u> wished, was still unable to prevent bickering.
A. granted the power to assign any duties to whoever he wished
B. granting the power to assign any duties to whoever he wished
C. being granted the power to assign any duties to whoever he wished
D. having been granted the power to assign any duties to whosoever he wished
E. granted the power to assign any duties to whomever he wished
The CORRECT answer is E.

SAMPLE QUESTION 6

Certainly, well-seasoned products are more expensive, <u>but those kinds prove chaper</u> in the end.
A. but those kinds prove cheaper
B. but these kinds prove cheaper
C. but that kind proves cheaper
D. but those kind prove cheaper
E. but this kind proves cheaper
The CORRECT answer is A.

SAMPLE QUESTION 7

"We shall not," he shouted, "whatever the <u>difficulties." "lose faith in the success of our plan!!</u>"
A. difficulties," "lose faith in the success of our plan!"
B. difficulties, "lose faith in the success of our plan"!
C. "difficulties, lose faith in the success of our plan!"
D. difficulties, lose faith in the success of our plan"!
E. difficulties, lose faith in the success of our plan!"

SAMPLE QUESTION 8

<u>Climb up the tree</u>, the lush foliage obscured the chattering monkeys.
A. Climbing up the tree
B. Having climbed up the tree
C. Clambering up the tree
D. After we had climbed up the tree
E. As we climbed up the tree
The CORRECT answer is E.

EXAMINATION SECTION
TEST 1

DIRECTIONS: See DIRECTIONS for Sample Questions on Page 1. *PRINT THE LETTER OF THE CORRECT ANSWER IN THE SPACE AT THE RIGHT.*

1. At the opening of the story, Charles Gilbert <u>has just come</u> to make his home with his two unmarried aunts.
   A. No change
   B. hadn't hardly come
   C. has just came
   D. had just come
   E. has hardly came

2. The sisters, who are no longer young, <u>are use to living</u> quiet lives.
   A. No change
   B. are used to live
   C. are use'd to living
   D. are used to living
   E. are use to live

3. They <u>willingly except</u> the child.
   A. No change
   B. willingly eccepted
   C. willingly accepted
   D. willingly acepted
   E. willingly accept

4. As the months pass, Charles' presence <u>affects many changes</u> in their household.
   A. No change
   B. affect many changes
   C. effects many changes
   D. effect many changes
   E. affected many changes

5. These changes <u>is not all together</u> to their liking.
   A. No change
   B. is not altogether
   C. are not all together
   D. are not altogether
   E. is not alltogether

6. In fact, they have some difficulty in adapting <u>theirselves</u> to these changes
   A. No change
   B. in adopting theirselves
   C. in adopting themselves
   D. in adapting theirselves
   E. in adapting themselves

7. That is the man <u>whom I believe</u> was the driver of the car.
   A. No change
   B. who I believed
   C. whom I believed
   D. who to believe
   E. who I believe

8. John's climb to fame was more rapid <u>than his brother's</u>.
   A. No change
   B. than his brother
   C. than that of his brother's
   D. than for his brother
   E. than the brother

9. We knew that he had formerly swam on an Olympic team.
    A. No change
    B. has formerly swum
    C. did formerly swum
    D. had formerly swum
    E. has formerly swam

10. Not one of us loyal supporters ever get a pass to a game.
    A. No change
    B. ever did got a pass
    C. ever has get a pass
    D. ever had get a pass
    E. ever gets a pass

11. He was complemented on having done a fine job.
    A. No change
    B. was compliminted
    C. was compleminted
    D. was complimented
    E. did get complimented

12. This play is different from the one we had seen last night.
    A. No change
    B. have seen
    C. had saw
    D. have saw
    E. saw

13. A row of trees was planted in front of the house.
    A. No change
    B. was to be planted
    C. were planted
    D. were to be planted
    E. are planted

14. The house looked its age in spite of our attempts to beautify it.
    A. No change
    B. looks its age
    C. looked its' age
    D. looked it's age
    E. looked it age

15. I do not know what to council in this case.
    A. No change
    B. where to council
    C. when to councel
    D. what to counsel
    E. what to counsil

16. She is more capable than any other girl in the office.
    A. No change
    B. than any girl
    C. than any other girls
    D. than other girl
    E. than other girls

17. At the picnic the young children behaved very good.
    A. No change
    B. behave very good
    C. behaved better
    D. behave very well
    E. behaved very well

18. I resolved to go irregardless of the consequences.
    A. No change
    B. to depart irregardless of
    C. to go regarding of
    D. to go regardingly of
    E. to go regardless of

19. The new movie has a number of actors which have been famous on Broadway.   19.____
    A. No change
    B. which had been famous
    C. who had been famous
    D. that are famous
    E. who have been famous

20. I am certain that these books are not our's.   20.____
    A. No change
    B. have not been ours'
    C. have not been our's
    D. are not ours
    E. are not ours'

21. Each of your papers is filed for future reference.   21.____
    A. No change
    B. Each of your papers are filed
    C. Each of your papers have been filed
    D. Each of your papers are to be filed
    E. Each of your paper is filed

22. I wish that he would take his work more serious.   22.____
    A. No change
    B. he took his work more serious
    C. he will take his work more serious
    D. he shall take his work more seriously
    E. he would take his work more seriously

23. After the treasurer report had been read, the chairman called for the reports of the committees.   23.____
    A. No change
    B. After the treasure's report had been read
    C. After the treasurers' report had been read
    D. After the treasurerer's report had been read
    E. After the treasurer's report had been read

24. Last night the stranger lead us down the mountain.   24.____
    A. No change
    B. leaded us down the mountain
    C. let us down the mountain
    D. led us down the mountain
    E. had led us down the mountain

25. It would not be safe for either you or I to travel in Viet Nam.   25.____
    A. No change
    B. for either you or me
    C. for either I or you
    D. for either of you or I
    E. for either of I or you

KEY (CORRECT ANSWERS)

1.	A		11.	D
2.	D		12.	E
3.	E		13.	A
4.	C		14.	A
5.	D		15.	D
6.	E		16.	A
7.	E		17.	E
8.	A		18.	E
9.	D		19.	E
10.	E		20.	D

21. A
22. E
23. E
24. D
25. B

TEST 2

DIRECTIONS: See DIRECTIONS for Sample Questions on Page 1. *PRINT THE LETTER OF THE CORRECT ANSWER IN THE SPACE AT THE RIGHT.*

1. Both the body and the mind <u>needs exercise</u>.
   A. No change
   B. have needs of exercise
   C. is needful of exercise
   D. needed exercise
   E. need exercise

   1.____

2. <u>It's paw injured</u>, the animal limped down the road.
   A. No change
   B. It's paw injured
   C. Its paw injured
   D. Its' paw injured
   E. Its paw injure

   2.____

3. The butter <u>tastes rancidly</u>.
   A. No change
   B. tastes rancid
   C. tasted rancidly
   D. taste rancidly
   E. taste rancid

   3.____

4. <u>Who do you think</u> has sent me a letter?
   A. No change
   B. Whom do you think
   C. Whome do you think
   D. Who did you think
   E. Whom can you think

   4.____

5. If more nations <u>would have fought</u> against tyranny, the course of history would have been different.
   A. No change
   B. would fight
   C. could have fought
   D. fought
   E. had fought

   5.____

6. Radio and television programs, along with other media of communication, <u>helps us to appreciate the arts and to keep informed</u>.
   A. No change
   B. helps us to appreciate the arts and to be informed
   C. helps us to be appreciative of the arts and to keep informed
   D. helps us to be appreciative of the arts and to be informed
   E. help us to appreciate the arts and to keep informed

   6.____

7. Music, <u>for example most always</u> has listening and viewing audiences numbering in the hundreds of thousands.
   A. No change
   B. for example, most always
   C. for example, almost always
   D. for example nearly always
   E. for example, near always

   7.____

8. When operas are performed on radio or television, <u>they effect the listener</u>.
   A. No change
   B. they inflict the listener
   C. these effect the listeners
   D. they affects the listeners
   E. they affect the listener

   8.____

9. After hearing then the listener wants to buy recordings of the music.   9.____
   A. No change
   B. After hearing them, the listener wants
   C. After hearing them, the listener want
   D. By hearing them the listener wants
   E. By hearing them, the listener wants

10. To we Americans the daily news program has become important.   10.____
    A. No change   B. To we the Americans
    C. To us Americans   D. To us the Americans
    E. To we and us Americans

11. This has resulted from it's coverage of a days' events.   11.____
    A. No change
    B. from its coverage of a days' events
    C. from it's coverage of a day's events
    D. from its' coverage of a day's events
    E. from its coverage of a day's events

12. In schools, teachers advice their students to listen to or to view certain programs.   12.____
    A. No change
    B. teachers advise there students
    C. teachers advise their students
    D. the teacher advises their students
    E. teachers advise his students

13. In these ways we are preceding toward the goal of an educated and an   13.____
    informed public.
    A. No change
    B. we are preeceding toward the goal
    C. we are proceeding toward the goal
    D. we are preceding toward the goal
    E. we are proceeding toward the goal

14. The cost of living is raising again.   14.____
    A. No change   B. are raising again
    C. is rising again   D. are rising again
    E. is risen again

15. We did not realize that the boys' father had forbidden them to keep there   15.____
    puppy.
    A. No change
    B. had forbade them to keep there puppy
    C. had forbade them to keep their puppy
    D. has forbidden them to keep their puppy
    E. had forbidden them to keep their puppy

16. Her willingness to help others' was her outstanding characteristic.   16.____
    A. No change
    B. Her willingness to help other's,
    C. Her willingness to help others's
    D. Her willingness to help others
    E. Her willingness to help each other

17. Because he did not have an invitation, the girls objected to him going.   17.____
    A. No change
    B. the girls object to him going
    C. the girls objected to him's going
    D. the girls objected to his going
    E. the girls object to his going

18. Weekly dances have become a popular accepted feature of the summer   18.____
    schedule.
    A. No change
    B. have become a popular accepted feature
    C. have become a popular excepted feature
    D. have become a popularly excepted feature
    E. have become a popularly accepted feature

19. I couldn't hardly believe that he would desert our party.   19.____
    A. No change   B. would hardly believe
    C. didn't hardly believe   D. should hardly believe
    E. could hardly believe

20. I found the place in the book more readily than she.   20.____
    A. No change   B. more readily than her
    C. more ready than she   D. more quickly than her
    E. more ready than her

21. A good example of American outdoor activities are sports.   21.____
    A. No change   B. is sports
    C. are sport   D. are sports events
    E. are to be found in sports

22. My point of view is much different from your's.   22.____
    A. No change   B. much different from your's
    C. much different than yours   D. much different from yours
    E. much different than yours'

23. The cook was suppose to use two spoonfuls of dressing for each serving.   23.____
    A. No change
    B. was supposed to use two spoonsful
    C. was suppose to use two spoonsful
    D. was supposed to use two spoonsfuls
    E. was supposed to use two spoonfuls

4 (#2)

24. If anyone has any doubt about the values of the tour, refer him to me.   24.____
    A. No change
    B. refer him to I
    C. refer me to he
    D. refer them to me
    E. refer he to I

25. We expect that the affects of the trip will be neneficial.   25.____
    A. No change
    B. the effects of the trip will be beneficial
    C. the effects of the trip should be beneficial
    D. the affects of the trip would be beneficial
    E. the effects of the trip will be benificial

KEY (CORRECT ANSWERS)

1.	E		11.	E
2.	C		12.	C
3.	B		13.	E
4.	A		14.	C
5.	E		15.	E
6.	E		16.	D
7.	C		17.	D
8.	E		18.	E
9.	B		19.	E
10.	C		20.	A

21.	B
22.	D
23.	E
24.	A
25.	B

TEST 3

DIRECTIONS: See DIRECTIONS for Sample Questions on Page 1. *PRINT THE LETTER OF THE CORRECT ANSWER IN THE SPACE AT THE RIGHT.*

1. That, my friend is not the proper attitude.
   A. No change
   B. That my friend
   C. That my fried,
   D. That—my friend
   E. That, my friend,

   1.____

2. The girl refused to admit that the note was her's.
   A. No change
   B. that the note were her's
   C. that the note was hers'
   D. that the note was hers
   E. that the note might be hers

   2.____

3. There were fewer candidates that we had been lead to expect
   A. No change
   B. was fewer candidates than we had been lead
   C. were fewer candidates than we had been lead
   D. was fewer candidates than we had been led
   E. were fewer candidates than we had been led

   3.____

4. When I first saw the car, its steering wheel was broke.
   A. No change
   B. its' steering wheel was broken
   C. it's steering wheel had been broken
   D. its steering wheel were broken
   E. its steering wheel was broken

   4.____

5. I find that the essential spirit for we beginners is missing.
   A. No change
   B. we who begin are missing
   C. us beginners are missing
   D. us beginners is missing
   E. we beginners are missing

   5.____

6. I believe that you had ought to study harder.
   A. No change
   B. you should have ought
   C. you had better
   D. you ought to have
   E. you ought

   6.____

7. This is Tom, whom I am sure, will be glad to help you.
   A. No change
   B. Tom whom, I am sure,
   C. Tom, whom I am sure
   D. Tom who I am sure,
   E. Tom, who, I am sure,

   7.____

8. His father or his mother has read to him every night since he was very small.
   A. No change
   B. did read to him
   C. have been reading to him
   D. had read to him
   E. have read to him

   8.____

99

9. He become an authority
   A. No change
   B. becomed an authority
   C. become the authority
   D. became an authority
   E. becamed an authority

10. I know of no other reason in the club who is more kind-hearted than her.
    A. No change
    B. who are more kind-hearted than they
    C. who are more kind-hearted than them
    D. whom are more kind-hearted than she
    E. who is more kind-hearted than she

11. After Bill had ran the mile, he was breathless.
    A. No change
    B. had runned the mile
    C. has ran the mile
    D. had ranned the mile
    E. had run the mile

12. Wilson has scarcely no equal as a pitcher.
    A. No change
    B. has scarcely an equal
    C. has hardly no equal
    D. had scarcely no equal
    E. has scarcely any equals

13. It was the worse storm that the inhabitants of the island could remember.
    A. No change
    B. were the worse storm
    C. was the worst storm
    D. was the worsest storm
    E. was the most worse storm

14. If only we had began before it was too late.
    A. No change
    B. we had began
    C. we would have begun
    D. we had begun
    E. we had beginned

15. Lets evaluate our year's work.
    A. No change
    B. Let us' evaluate
    C. Lets' evaluate
    D. Lets' us evaluate
    E. Let's evaluate

16. This is an organization with which I wouldn't want to be associated with.
    A. No change
    B. with whom I wouldn't want to be associated with
    C. that I wouldn't want to be associated
    D. with which I would want not to be associated with
    E. with which I wouldn't want to be associated

17. The enemy fled in many directions, leaving there weapons on the field.
    A. No change
    B. leaving its weapons
    C. letting their weapons
    D. leaving alone there weapons
    E. leaving their weapons

18. I hoped that John could effect a compromise between the approved forces.
    A. No change
    B. could accept a compromise between
    C. could except a compromise between
    D. would have effected a compromise among
    E. could effect a compromise among

19. I was surprised to learn that he has not always spoke English fluently.
    A. No change
    B. that he had not always spoke English
    C. that he did not always speak English
    D. that he has not always spoken English
    E. that he could not always speak English

20. The lawyer promised to notify my father and I of his plans for a new trial.
    A. No change
    B. to notify I and my father
    C. to notify me and our father
    D. to notify my father and me
    E. to notify mine father and me

21. The most important feature of the series of tennis lessons were the large amount of strokes taught.
    A. No change
    B. were the large number
    C. was the large amount
    D. was the largeness of the amount
    E. was the large number

22. That the prize proved to be beyond her reach did not surprise him.
    A. No change
    B. has not surprised him
    C. had not ought to have surprised him
    D. should not surprise him
    E. would not have surprised him

23. I am not all together in agreement with the author's point of view.
    A. No change
    B. all together of agreement
    C. all together for agreement
    D. altogether with agreement
    E. altogether in agreement

24. Windstorms have recently established a record which meteorologists hope will not be equal for many years to come.
    A. No change
    B. will be equal
    C. will not be equalized
    D. will be equaled
    E. will not be equaled

25. A large number of Shakespeare's soliloquies must be considered <u>as representing thought</u>, not speech.   25.____
    A. No change
    B. as representative of speech, not thought
    C. as represented by thought, not speech
    D. as indicating thought, not speech
    E. as representative of thought, more than speech

KEY (CORRECT ANSWERS)

1. E
2. D
3. E
4. E
5. D

6. E
7. E
8. A
9. D
10. E

11. E
12. B
13. C
14. D
15. E

16. E
17. E
18. A
19. D
20. D

21. E
22. A
23. E
24. E
25. A

TEST 4

DIRECTIONS: See DIRECTIONS for Sample Questions on Page 1. *PRINT THE LETTER OF THE CORRECT ANSWER IN THE SPACE AT THE RIGHT.*

1. A sight to inspire fear <u>are wild animals on the lose</u>.
   A. No change
   B. are wild animals on the loose
   C. is wild animals on the loose
   D. is wild animals on the lose
   E. are wild animals loose

   1._____

2. For many years, the settlers <u>had been seeking to workship as they please</u>.
   A. No change
   B. had seeked to workship as they pleased
   C. sought to workship as they please
   D. sought to have worshiped as they pleased
   E. had been seeking to worship as they pleased

   2._____

3. The girls stated that the dresses were <u>their's</u>.
   A. No change   B. there's   C. theirs
   D. theirs'   E. there own

   3._____

4. <u>Please fellows</u> don't drop the ball.
   A. No change
   B. Please, fellows
   C. Please fellows;
   D. Please, fellows,
   E. Please! fellows

   4._____

5. Your sweater <u>has laid</u> on the floor for a week.
   A. No change
   B. has been laying
   C. has been lying
   D. laid
   E. has been lain

   5._____

6. I wonder whether <u>you're sure that scheme of yours'</u> will work.
   A. No change
   B. your sure that scheme of your's
   C. you're sure that scheme of yours
   D. your sure that scheme of yours
   E. you're sure that your scheme's

   6._____

7. Please let <u>her and me</u> do it.
   A. No change   B. she and I
   C. she and me   D. her and I
   E. her and him

   7._____

8. I expected him to be angry <u>and to scold</u> her.
   A. No change
   B. and that he would scold
   C. and that he might scold
   D. and that he should scold
   E. , scolding

   8._____

9. Knowing little about algebra, it was difficult to solve the equation. 9.____
   A. No change
   B. the equation was difficult to solve
   C. the solution to the equation was difficult to find
   D. I found it difficult to solve the equation
   E. it being difficult to solve the equation

10. He worked more diligent now that he had become vice president of the company. 10.____
    A. No change
    B. works more diligent
    C. works more diligently
    D. began to work more diligent
    E. worked more diligently

11. Flinging himself at the barricade he pounded on it furiously. 11.____
    A. No change
    B. Flinging himself at the barricade: he
    C. Flinging himself at the barricade—he
    D. Flinging himself at the barricade; he
    E. Flinging himself at the barricade, he

12. When he begun to give us advise, we stopped listening. 12.____
    A. No change
    B. began to give us advise
    C. begun to give us advice
    D. began to give us advice
    E. begin to give us advice

13. John was only one of the boys whom as you know was not eligible. 13.____
    A. No change
    B. who as you know were
    C. whom as you know were
    D. who as you know was
    E. who as you know is

14. Why was Jane and he permitted to go? 14.____
    A. No change
    B. was Jane and him
    C. were Jane and he
    D. were Jane and him
    E. weren't Jane and he

15. Take courage Tom: we all make mistakes. 15.____
    A. No change
    B. Take courage Tom—we
    C. Take courage, Tom; we
    D. Take courage, Tom we
    E. Take courage! Tom: we

16. Henderson, the president of the class and who is also captain of the team, will lead the rally. 16.____
    A. No change
    B. since he is captain of the team
    C. captain of the team
    D. also being captain of the team
    E. who be also captain of the team

17. Our car has always run good on that kind of gasoline. 17.____
    A. No change
    B. run well
    C. ran good
    D. ran well
    E. done good

18. There was a serious difference of opinion among her and I.
    A. No change
    B. among she and I
    C. between her and I
    D. between her and me
    E. among her and me

19. "This is most unusual," said Helen, "the mailman has never been this late before."
    A. No change
    B. Helen, "The
    C. Helen—"The
    D. Helen; "The
    E. Helen." The

20. The three main characters in the story are Johnny Hobart a teenager, his mother a widow, and the local druggist.
    A. No change
    B. teenager; his mother, a widow; and
    C. teenager; his mother a widow; and
    D. teenager, his mother, a widow and
    E. teenager, his mother, a widow; and

21. How much has food costs raised during the past year?
    A. No change
    B. have food costs rose
    C. have food costs risen
    D. has food costs risen
    E. have food costs been raised

22. "Will you come too" she pleaded?
    A. No change
    B. too,?"she pleaded
    C. too?" she pleaded
    D. too," she pleaded?
    E. too, she pleaded?"

23. If he would have drank more milk, his health would have been better.
    A. No change
    B. would drink
    C. had drank
    D. had he drunk
    E. had drunk

24. Jack had no sooner laid down and fallen asleep when the alarm sounded.
    A. No change
    B. no sooner lain down and fallen asleep than
    C. no sooner lay down and fell asleep when
    D. no sooner laid down and fell asleep than
    E. no sooner lain down than he fell asleep when

25. Jackson is one of the few Sophomores, who has ever made the varsity team.
    A. No change
    B. one of the few Sophomores, who have
    C. one of the few sophomores, who has
    D. one of the few sophomores who have
    E. one of the few sophomores who has

KEY (CORRECT ANSWERS)

1.	C		11.	E
2.	E		12.	D
3.	C		13.	B
4.	D		14.	C
5.	C		15.	C
6.	C		16.	C
7.	A		17.	B
8.	A		18.	D
9.	D		19.	E
10.	E		20.	B

21. C
22. C
23. E
24. B
25. D

TEST 5

DIRECTIONS: See DIRECTIONS for Sample Questions on Page 1. *PRINT THE LETTER OF THE CORRECT ANSWER IN THE SPACE AT THE RIGHT.*

1. The lieutenant had ridden almost a kilometer when the scattering shells <u>begin landing</u> uncomfortably close.
    A. No change
    B. beginning to land
    C. began to land
    D. having begun to land
    E. begin to land

    1.____

2. <u>Having studied eight weeks</u>, he now feels sufficiently prepared for the examination.
    A. No change
    B. For eight weeks he studies so
    C. Due to eight weeks of study
    D. After eight weeks of studying
    E. Since he's been spending the last eight weeks in study

    2.____

3. <u>Coming from the Greek, and the word "democracy" means government by the people</u>.
    A. No change
    B. "Democracy," the word which comes from the Greek, means government by the people.
    C. Meaning government by the people, the word "democracy" comes from the Greek.
    D. Its meaning being government by the people in Greek, the word is "democracy."
    E. The word "democracy" comes from the Greek and means government by the people.

    3.____

4. Moslem universities were one of the chief agencies <u>in the development</u> and spreading Arabic civilization.
    A. No change
    B. in the development of
    C. to develop
    D. in developing
    E. for the developing of

    4.____

5. The water of Bering Strait <u>were closing</u> to navigation by ice early in the fall.
    A. No change
    B. has closed
    C. have closed
    D. had been closed
    E. closed

    5.____

6. The man, <u>since he grew up</u> on the block, felt sentimental when returning to it.
    A. No change
    B. having grown up
    C. growing up
    D. since he had grown up
    E. whose growth had been

    6.____

7. Jack and Jill watched the canoe to take their parents out of sight round the bend of the creek.
   A. No change
   B. The canoe, taking their parents out of sight, rounds the bend as Jack and Jill watch.
   C. Jack and Jill watched the canoe round the bend of the creek, taking their parents out of sight,
   D. The canoe rounded the bend of the creek as it took their parents out of sight, Jack and Jill watching.
   E. Jack and Jill watching, the canoe is rounding the bend of the creek to take their parents out of sight.

7.____

8. Chaucer's best-known work is THE CANTERBURY TALES, a collection of stories which he tells with a group of pilgrims as they travel to the town of Canterbury.
   A. No change
   B. which he tells through
   C. who tell
   D. told by
   E. told through

8.____

9. The Estates-General, the old feudal assembly of France, had not met for one hundred and seventy-five years when it convened in 1789.
   A. No change
   B. has not met
   C. has not been meeting
   D. had no meeting
   E. has no meeting

9.____

10. Just forty years ago, there had been fewer than one hundred symphony orchestras in the United States.
    A. No change
    B. there had
    C. there were
    D. there was
    E. there existed

10.____

11. Mrs. Smith complained that her son's temper tantrums aggravated her and caused her to have a headache.
    A. No change
    B. gave her aggravation
    C. were aggravating to her
    D. aggravated her condition
    E. instigated

11.____

12. A girl like I would never be seen in a place like that.
    A. No change   B. as I   C. as me
    D. like I am   E. like me

12.____

13. Between you and me, my opinion is that this room is certainly nicer than the first one we saw.
    A. No change
    B. between you and I
    C. among you and me
    D. betwixt you and I
    E. between we

13.____

3 (#5)

14. It is important to know for <u>what kind of a person you are working</u>.
    A. No change
    B. what kind of a person for whom you are working
    C. what kind of person you are working
    D. what kind of person you are working for
    E. what kind of a person you are working for

14.____

15. I had <u>all ready</u> finished the book before you came in.
    A. No change
    B. already
    C. previously
    D. allready
    E. all

15.____

16. <u>Ask not for who the bell tolls, it tolls for thee</u>.
    A. No change
    B. Ask not for whom the bell tolls, it tolls for thee.
    C. Ask not whom the bell tolls for; it tolls for thee.
    D. Ask not for whom the bell tolls; it tolls for thee.
    E. As not who the bell tolls for: It tolls for thee.

16.____

17. It is a far better thing I do, than <u>ever I did</u> before.
    A. No change
    B. never I did
    C. I have ever did
    D. I have ever been done
    E. ever have I done

17.____

18. <u>Ending a sentence with a preposition is something up with which I will not put</u>.
    A. No change
    B. Ending a sentence with a preposition is something with which I will not put up.
    C. To end a sentence with a preposition is that which I will not put up with.
    D. Ending a sentence with a preposition is something of which I will not put up.
    E. Something I will not put up with is ending a sentence with a preposition.

18.____

19. Everyone <u>took off their hats and stand up</u> to sing the national anthem.
    A. No change
    B. took off their hats and stood up
    C. take off their hats and stand up
    D. took off his hat and stood up
    E. have taken off their hats and standing up

19.____

20. <u>She promised me that if she had the opportunity she would have came irregardless of the weather</u>.
    A. No change
    B. She promised me that if she had the opportunity she would have come regardless of the weather.
    C. She assured me that had she had the opportunity he would have come regardless of the weather.
    D. She assured me that if she would have had the opportunity she would have come regardless of the weather.

20.____

E. She promised me that if she had had the opportunity she would have came irregardless of the weather.

21. The man decided it would be advisable to marry a girl <u>somewhat younger than him</u>.
    A. No change
    B. somehow younger than him
    C. some younger than him
    D. somewhat younger from him
    E. somewhat younger than he

22. Sitting near the campfire, the old man told <u>John and I about many exciting adventures he had had</u>.
    A. No change
    B. John and me about many exciting adventures he had,
    C. John and I about much exciting adventure which he'd had
    D. John and me about many exciting adventures he had had
    E. John and me about many exciting adventures he has had.

23. <u>If you had stood at home and done your homework</u>, you would not have failed the course.
    A. No change
    B. If you had stood at home and done you're homework,
    C. If you had staid at home and done your homework,
    D. Had you stayed at home and done your homework,
    E. Had you stood at home and done your homework,

24. The children didn't, as a rule, <u>do anything beyond</u> what they were told to do.
    A. No change
    B. do hardly anything beyond
    C. do anything except
    D. do hardly anything except for
    E. do nothing beyond

25. <u>Either the girls or him is</u> right.
    A. No change
    B Either the girls or he is
    C. Either the girls or him are
    D. Either the girls or he are
    E. Either the girls nor he is

KEY (CORRECT ANSWERS)

1. C
2. A
3. E
4. D
5. D

6. B
7. C
8. D
9. A
10. C

11. D
12. E
13. A
14. C
15. B

16. D
17. E
18. E
19. D
20. C

21. E
22. D
23. D
24. A
25. B

WORD MEANING
COMMENTARY

DESCRIPTION OF THE TEST

On many examinations, you will have questions about the meaning of words, or vocabulary.

In this type of question you have to state what a word or phrase means. (A phrase is a group of words.) This word or phrase is in CAPITAL letters in a sentence. You are also given for each question five other words or groups of words — lettered A, B, C, D, and E — as possible answers. One of thes words or groups of words means the same as the word or group of words in CAPITAL letters. Only one is right. You are to pick out the one that is right and select the letter of your answer.

HINTS FOR ANSWERING WORD-MEANING QUESTIONS

Read each question carefully.

Choose the best answer of the five choices even though it is not the word you might use yourself.

Answer first those that you know. Then do the others.

If you know that some of the suggested answers are not right, pay no more attention to them.

Be sure that you have selected an answer for every question, even if you have to guess.

SAMPLE QUESTIONS

DIRECTIONS: For the following questions, select the word or group of words lettered A, B, C, D, or E that means MOST NEARLY the same as the word in capital letters. Indicate the letter of the CORRECT answer for each question.

SAMPLE QUESTIONS 1 AND 2

1. The letter was SHORT. SHORT means *MOST NEARLY*

   A. tall   B. wide   C. brief   D. heavy   E. dark

   EXPLANATION
   SHORT is a word you have used to describe something that is small, or not long, or little, etc. Therefore you would not have to spend much time figuring out the right answer. You would choose C. brief.

2. The young man is VIGOROUS. VIGOROUS means *MOST NEARLY*

   A. serious   B. reliable   C. courageous
   D. strong   E. talented

   EXPLANATION
   VIGOROUS is a word that you have probably used yourself or read somewhere. It carries with it the idea of being active, full of pep, etc. Which one of the five choices comes closest to meaning that? Certainly not A. serious, B. reliable, or E. talented; C. courageous — maybe, D. strong — maybe. But between courageous or strong, you would have to agree that strong is the better choice. Therefore, you would choose D.

WORD MEANING
EXAMINATION SECTION
TEST 1

DIRECTIONS: For the following questions, select the word or group of words lettered A, B, C, D, or E that means MOST NEARLY the same as the word in capital letters. *PRINT THE LETTER OF THE CORRECT ANSWER IN THE SPACE AT THE RIGHT.*

1. The lane was NARROW and led to a mountain lake. 1.____
   - A. attractive
   - B. not wide
   - C. overgrown
   - D. rough
   - E. without trees

2. Blow the horn as you APPROACH the gate. 2.____
   - A. discover
   - B. leave
   - C. draw near
   - D. pass through
   - E. unlock

3. It was part of our BARGAIN that you should wash dishes. 3.____
   - A. agreement   B. debt   C. goal   D. plan   E. wish

4. I shall remember that little valley FOREVER. 4.____
   - A. often   B. yet   C. always   D. next   E. no more

5. The boy was EAGER to go on the trip. 5.____
   - A. able   B. afraid   C. anxious   D. likely   E. willing

6. The children were having a DISPUTE over the boy. 6.____
   - A. conversation
   - B. crying spell
   - C. disagreement
   - D. performance
   - E. tantrum

7. The man was punished for his BRUTAL act. 7.____
   - A. bloody
   - B. cruel
   - C. deadly
   - D. defenseless
   - E. ugly

8. We LAUNCHED our new business with great hope for the future. 8.____
   - A. concluded   B. started   C. pursued   D. steered   E. watched

9. The two streets INTERSECT at the edge of town. 9.____
   - A. run parallel
   - B. change names
   - C. end
   - D. become thoroughfares
   - E. cross

10. She suffered from an UNCOMMON disease. 10.____
    - A. ordinary   B. painful   C. contagious   D. rare   E. new

11. The antique chair was very FRAGILE.

    A. delicate   B. worn   C. beautiful   D. well-made   E. useless

12. They picked EDIBLE mushrooms.

    A. poisonous   B. well-formed   C. unusual   D. large   E. eatable

13. He found the reception at the airport very GRATIFYING.

    A. surprising   B. deafening   C. pleasant
    D. disagreeable   E. impolite

14. DEFECTIVE brakes caused the mishap.

    A. old-fashioned   B. uneven   C. squeaking
    D. unused   E. faulty

15. After a little EXERTION the box was moved.

    A. argument   B. delay   C. coaxing   D. effort   E. planning

KEY (CORRECT ANSWERS)

1. B
2. C
3. A
4. C
5. C

6. C
7. B
8. B
9. E
10. D

11. A
12. E
13. C
14. E
15. D

TEST 2

DIRECTIONS: For the following questions, select the word or group of words lettered A, B, C, D, or E that means MOST NEARLY the same as the word in capital letters. *PRINT THE LETTER OF THE CORRECT ANSWER IN THE SPACE AT THE RIGHT.*

1. The RAPIDITY of the attack surprised us. 1.____
   - A. power
   - B. effectiveness
   - C. possibility
   - D. strangeness
   - E. swiftness

2. She enjoyed CONVERSING with her friends. 2.____
   - A. meeting   B. laughing   C. talking   D. dining   E. traveling

3. There was a small VENT near the end of the tube. 3.____
   - A. cap   B. screw   C. opening   D. joint   E. pump

4. With great CAUTION we opened the barn door. 4.____
   - A. care   B. fear   C. distrust   D. danger   E. difficulty

5. The old man's coat was THREADBARE. 5.____
   - A. spotted   B. tight   C. new   D. ill-made   E. shabby

6. I was sorry that I could not decide OTHERWISE. 6.____
   - A. immediately
   - B. differently
   - C. favorably
   - D. positively
   - E. eagerly

7. The GIGANTIC switchboard controlled all the lights in the theatre. 7.____
   - A. complicated
   - B. up-to-date
   - C. automatic
   - D. huge
   - E. stationary

8. The balls were made of SYNTHETIC rubber. 8.____
   - A. artificial   B. hard   C. cheap   D. imported   E. crude

9. He was MERELY a servant in the house. 9.____
   - A. occasionally
   - B. in no way
   - C. unhappily
   - D. formerly
   - E. no more than

10. The prisoner CONFERRED with his lawyer. 10.____
    - A. argued
    - B. interfered
    - C. dined
    - D. sympathized
    - E. consulted

11. The soldier's GALLANTRY went unnoticed. 11.____
    - A. strength
    - B. fright
    - C. disobedience
    - D. injury
    - E. bravery

117

12. The music was chosen for its SOOTHING effect. 12.____
    A. tuneful   B. calming   C. magic   D. exciting   E. solemn

13. The owners were advised to REINFORCE the wall. 13.____
    A. rebuild   B. lengthen   C. lower   D. strengthen   E. repaint

14. They performed their duties with UTMOST ease. 14.____
    A. noticeable   B. some   C. surprising   D. greatest   E. increasing

15. We picnicked near a CASCADE. 15.____
    A. pond   B. camp   C. waterfall   D. trail   E. slope

KEY (CORRECT ANSWERS)

1. E
2. C
3. C
4. A
5. E
6. B
7. D
8. A
9. E
10. E
11. E
12. B
13. D
14. D
15. C

TEST 3

DIRECTIONS: For the following questions, select the word or group of words lettered A, B, C, D, or E that means MOST NEARLY the same as the word in capital letters. *PRINT THE LETTER OF THE CORRECT ANSWER IN THE SPACE AT THE RIGHT.*

1. The chairman was anxious to ADJOURN the meeting. 1.____
   A. conduct   B. attend   C. start   D. address   E. close

2. The gown was made of a GLOSSY fabric. 2.____
   A. shiny   B. embroidered   C. many-colored
   D. transparent   E. expensive

3. An ocean voyage in a small boat can be very HAZARDOUS. 3.____
   A. thrilling   B. slow   C. dangerous   D. rough   E. tiresome

4. The weatherman predicted VARIABLE winds. 4.____
   A. drying   B. strong   C. cool   D. light   E. changeable

5. Not long after the play began, the children began to FIDGET. 5.____
   A. clap   B. move restlessly
   C. cry   D. laugh aloud
   E. shriek

6. That person has a habit of MEDDLING. 6.____
   A. stumbling   B. interfering   C. play jokes
   D. cheating   E. being late

7. Young children are frequently INQUISITIVE. 7.____
   A. curious   B. saucy   C. restless   D. shy   E. tearful

8. The FALSITY of the report was apparent at first glance. 8.____
   A. uselessness   B. untidiness   C. incompleteness
   D. incorrectness   E. disagreeableness

9. Orders were given to LIBERATE the prisoners by noon. 9.____
   A. question   B. transfer   C. free   D. sentence   E. fingerprint

10. She is HABITUALLY late for her dental appointments. 10.____
    A. usually   B. seldom   C. extremely   D. slightly   E. never

11. The soldiers were given SPACIOUS living quarters. 11.____
    A. pleasant   B. well-aired   C. crowded
    D. well-furnished   E. roomy

119

12. The witnesses gave STRAIGHTFORWARD answers. 12.___

    A. hasty   B. frank   C. conflicting   D. helpful   E. serious

13. His income EXCEEDS that of his brother. 13.___

    A. is less regular than   B. is greater than
    C. is the same as   D. is less than
    E. is spent sooner than

14. He SHUNNED all of his neighbors. 14.___

    A. disapproved   B. welcomed   C. quarreled with
    D. avoided   E. insulted

15. Many of the natives are ILLITERATE. 15.___

    A. unable to read   B. unclean   C. unable to vote
    D. unmanageable   E. sickly

KEY (CORRECT ANSWERS)

1. E
2. A
3. C
4. E
5. B
6. B
7. A
8. D
9. C
10. A
11. E
12. B
13. B
14. D
15. A

TEST 4

DIRECTIONS: For the following questions, select the word or group of words lettered A, B, C, D, or E that means MOST NEARLY the same as the word in capital letters. *PRINT THE LETTER OF THE CORRECT ANSWER IN THE SPACE AT THE RIGHT.*

1. We have always found this medicine to be RELIABLE.

    A. dependable B. easy to use C. pleasant-tasting
    D. bitter E. fast-acting

2. The cloth was left to BLEACH in the sun.

    A. dry B. soak C. whiten D. shrink E. rot

3. The work is ORDINARILY done on time.

    A. seldom B. without fail C. necessarily
    D. hardly ever E. usually

4. Jim is a very DISCOURTEOUS boy.

    A. impolite B. daring C. untruthful D. uneasy E. cautious

5. Paris is noted for its BOULEVARDS.

    A. crooked streets B. parks C. art galleries
    D. churches E. broad avenues

6. The group formed the SEMICIRCLE quickly.

    A. half-circle B. double circle C. complete circle
    D. uneven E. very small circle

7. The machine that he designed was PORTABLE.

    A. business-like B. practical C. of foreign manufacture
    D. easily transported E. difficult to use

8. The food supply DWINDLED during the winter.

    A. spoiled B. became less C. froze
    D. was wasted E. was rationed

9. The vase was one of the PERMANENT exhibits at the museum.

    A. historical B. lasting C. popular
    D. artistic E. well-planned

10. We could not understand why he left so ABRUPTLY.

    A. suddenly B. soon C. absent-mindedly
    D. mysteriously E. noisily

KEY (CORRECT ANSWERS)

1. A
2. C
3. E
4. A
5. E

6. A
7. D
8. B
9. B
10. A

WORD MEANING
EXAMINATION SECTION
TEST 1

DIRECTIONS: Each question or incomplete statement is followed by several suggested answers or completions. Select the one that BEST answers the question or completes the statement. *PRINT THE LETTER OF THE CORRECT ANSWER IN THE SPACE AT THE RIGHT.*

1. He implied that he would work overtime if necessary.
   In this sentence, the word *implied* means

   A. denied
   B. explained
   C. guaranteed
   D. hinted

   1.____

2. The bag of the vacuum cleaner was inflated.
   In this sentence, the word *inflated* means

   A. blown up with air
   B. filled with dirt
   C. loose
   D. torn

   2.____

3. Burning material during certain hours is prohibited.
   In this sentence, the word *prohibited* means

   A. allowed   B. forbidden   C. legal   D. required

   3.____

4. He was rejected when he applied for the job. In this sentence, the word *rejected* means

   A. discouraged
   B. put to work
   C. tested
   D. turned down

   4.____

5. The foreman was able to substantiate his need for extra supplies.
   In this sentence, the word *substantiate* means

   A. estimate   B. meet   C. prove   D. reduce

   5.____

6. The new instructions supersede the old ones.
   In this sentence, the word *supersede* means

   A. explain   B. improve   C. include   D. replace

   6.____

7. Shake the broom free of surplus water and hang it up to dry.
   In this sentence, the word *surplus* means

   A. dirty   B. extra   C. rinse   D. soapy

   7.____

8. When a crack is filled, the asphalt must be tamped.
   In this sentence, the word *tamped* means

   A. cured
   B. heated
   C. packed down
   D. wet down

   8.____

9. The apartment was left vacant.
   In this sentence, the word *vacant* means

   A. clean   B. empty   C. furnished   D. locked

   9.____

10. The caretaker spent the whole day doing various repairs.
    In this sentence, the word *various* means

    A. different   B. necessary   C. small   D. special

11. He came back to assist his partner.
    In this sentence, the word *assist* means

    A. call   B. help   C. stop   D. question

12. A person who is biased cannot be a good foreman.
    In this sentence, the word *biased* means

    A. easy-going   B. prejudiced
    C. strict   D. uneducated

13. The lecture for the new employees was brief.
    In this sentence, the word *brief* means

    A. educational   B. free
    C. interesting   D. short

14. He was asked to clarify the order.
    In this sentence, the word *clarify* means

    A. follow out   B. make clear
    C. take back   D. write out

15. The employee was commended by his foreman.
    In this sentence, the word *commended* means

    A. assigned   B. blamed   C. picked   D. praised

16. Before the winter, the lawnmower engine was dismantled.
    In this sentence, the word *dismantled* means

    A. oiled   B. repaired
    C. stored away   D. taken apart

17. They excavated a big hole on the project lawn.
    In this sentence, the word *excavated* means

    A. cleaned out   B. discovered
    C. dug out   D. filled in

18. The new man was told to sweep the exterior area.
    In this sentence, the word *exterior* means

    A. asphalt   B. nearby   C. outside   D. whole

19. The officer refuted the statement of the driver.
    As used in this sentence, the word *refuted* means MOST NEARLY

    A. disproved   B. elaborated upon
    C. related   D. supported

20. The mechanism of the parking meter is not intricate.
    As used in this sentence, the word *intricate* means MOST NEARLY

    A. cheap
    B. complicated
    C. foolproof
    D. strong

21. The weight of each box fluctuates.
    As used in this sentence, the word *fluctuates* means MOST NEARLY

    A. always changes
    B. decreases
    C. increases gradually
    D. is similar

22. The person chosen to investigate the new procedure should be impartial.
    As used in this sentence, the word *impartial* means MOST NEARLY

    A. experienced
    B. fair
    C. forward looking
    D. important

23. Carelessness in the safekeeping of keys will not be tolerated.
    As used in this sentence, the word *tolerated* means MOST NEARLY

    A. forgotten
    B. permitted
    C. punished lightly
    D. understood

24. The traffic was easily diverted.
    As used in this sentence, the word *diverted* means MOST NEARLY

    A. controlled
    B. speeded up
    C. stopped
    D. turned aside

25. A transcript of the report was prepared in the office.
    As used in this sentence, the word *transcript* means MOST NEARLY

    A. brief
    B. copy
    C. record
    D. translation

26. The change was authorized by the supervisor.
    As used in this sentence, the word *authorized* means MOST NEARLY

    A. completed   B. corrected   C. ordered   D. permitted

27. The supervisor read the excerpt of the collector's report.
    According to this sentence, the supervisor read _____ the report.

    A. a passage from
    B. a summary of
    C. the original of
    D. the whole of

28. During the probation period, the worker proved to be inept.
    The word *inept* means MOST NEARLY

    A. incompetent
    B. insubordinate
    C. satisfactory
    D. uncooperative

29. The putative father was not living with the family.
    The word *putative* means MOST NEARLY

    A. reputed
    B. unemployed
    C. concerned
    D. indifferent

30. The adopted child researched various documents of vital statistics in an effort to discover the names of his natural parents.
    The words *vital statistics* mean MOST NEARLY statistics relating to

    A. human life B. hospitals
    C. important facts D. health and welfare

31. Despite many requests for them, there was a scant supply of new blotters.
    The word *scant* means MOST NEARLY

    A. adequate B. abundant
    C. insufficient D. expensive

32. Did they replenish the supply of forms in the cabinet?
    The word *replenish* means MOST NEARLY

    A. straighten up B. refill
    C. sort out D. use

33. Employees may become bored if they are assigned diverse duties.
    The word *diverse* means MOST NEARLY

    A. interesting B. different
    C. challenging D. enjoyable

Questions 34-37.

DIRECTIONS: Each of Questions 34 through 37 consists of a capitalized word followed by four suggested meanings of the word. Select the word or phrase which means MOST NEARLY the same as the capitalized word.

34. PROFICIENCY

    A. vocation B. competency
    C. repugnancy D. prominence

35. BIBLIOGRAPHY

    A. description B. stenography
    C. photograph D. compilation of books

36. FIDELITY

    A. belief B. treachery
    C. strength D. loyalty

37. ACCELERATE

    A. adjust B. press C. quicken D. strip

38. One of the machinists in your shop enjoys the reputation of being a great equivocator.
    This means MOST NEARLY that he

    A. takes pride and is happy in his work
    B. generally hedges and often gives misleading answers
    C. is a strong union man with great interest in his fellow workers' welfare
    D. is good at resolving disputes

39. When a person has the reputation of persistently making foolish or silly remarks, it may be said that he is   39.____

    A. inane
    B. meticulous
    C. a procrastinator
    D. a prevaricator

40. When two mechanics, called A and B, make measurements of the same workpiece and find significant discrepancies in their measurements, it is MOST NEARLY correct to state that   40.____

    A. mechanic B made an erroneous reading
    B. mechanic A was careless in making his measurements
    C. both mechanics made their measurements correctly
    D. there was considerable difference in the two sets of measurements

41. A foreman who *expedites* a job,   41.____

    A. abolishes it
    B. makes it bigger
    C. slows it down
    D. speeds it up

42. If a man is working at a *uniform* speed, it means he is working at a speed which is   42.____

    A. changing   B. fast   C. slow   D. steady

43. To say that a caretaker is *obstinate* means that he is   43.____

    A. cooperative
    B. patient
    C. stubborn
    D. willing

44. To say that a caretaker is *negligent* means that he is   44.____

    A. careless   B. neat   C. nervous   D. late

45. To say that something is *absurd* means that it is   45.____

    A. definite
    B. not clear
    C. ridiculous
    D. unfair

46. To say that a foreman is *impartial* means that he is   46.____

    A. fair   B. improving   C. in a hurry   D. watchful

47. A man who is *lenient* is one who is   47.____

    A. careless
    B. harsh
    C. inexperienced
    D. mild

48. A man who is *punctual* is one who is   48.____

    A. able   B. polite   C. prompt   D. sincere

49. If you think one of your men is too *awkward* to do a job, it means you think he is too   49.____

    A. clumsy   B. lazy   C. old   D. weak

50. A person who is *seldom* late, is late   50.____

    A. always   B. never   C. often   D. rarely

KEY (CORRECT ANSWERS)

1. D	11. B	21. A	31. C	41. D
2. A	12. B	22. B	32. B	42. D
3. B	13. D	23. B	33. B	43. C
4. D	14. B	24. D	34. B	44. A
5. C	15. D	25. B	35. D	45. C
6. D	16. D	26. D	36. D	46. A
7. B	17. C	27. A	37. C	47. D
8. C	18. C	28. A	38. B	48. C
9. B	19. A	29. A	39. B	49. A
10. A	20. B	30. A	40. D	50. D

TEST 2

DIRECTIONS: Each question or incomplete statement is followed by several suggested answers or completions. Select the one that BEST answers the question or completes the statement. *PRINT THE LETTER OF THE CORRECT ANSWER IN THE SPACE AT THE RIGHT.*

1. The Department of Health can certify that conditions in a housing accommodation are detrimental to life or health.
   As used in the above sentence, the word *detrimental* means MOST NEARLY

   A. injurious   B. serious
   C. satisfactory   D. necessary

2. The Administrator shall have the power to revoke any adjustment in rents granted either the landlord or the tenant.
   As used in the above sentence, the word *revoke* means MOST NEARLY

   A. increase   B. decrease   C. rescind   D. restore

Questions 3-5.

DIRECTIONS: Each of Questions 3 through 5 consists of a capitalized word followed by four suggested meanings of the word. Select the word which means MOST NEARLY the same as the capitalized word.

3. DOGMATISM

   A. dramatism   B. positiveness
   C. doubtful   D. tentativeness

4. ELECTRODE

   A. officer   B. electrolyte
   C. terminal   D. positive

5. EMIT

   A. return   B. enter   C. omit   D. discharge

6. The word *inflammable* means MOST NEARLY

   A. burnable   B. acid   C. poisonous   D. explosive

7. The word *disinfect* means MOST NEARLY

   A. deodorize   B. sterilize   C. bleach   D. dissolve

8. He wanted to ascertain the facts before arriving at a conclusion.
   The word *ascertain* means MOST NEARLY

   A. disprove   B. determine   C. convert   D. provide

9. Did the supervisor assent to her request for annual leave?
   The word *assent* means MOST NEARLY

   A. allude   B. protest   C. agree   D. refer

129

10. The new worker was fearful that the others would rebuff her.
    The word *rebuff* means MOST NEARLY

    A. ignore   B. forget   C. copy   D. snub

11. The supervisor of that office does not condone lateness.
    The word *condone* means MOST NEARLY

    A. mind   B. excuse   C. punish   D. remember

12. Each employee was instructed to be as concise as possible when preparing a report.
    The word *concise* means MOST NEARLY

    A. exact   B. sincere   C. flexible   D. brief

13. The shovelers should not distribute the asphalt faster than it can be properly handled by the rakers.
    As used above, *distribute* means MOST NEARLY

    A. dump   B. pick-up   C. spread   D. heat

14. Any defective places should be cut out.
    As used above, *defective* means MOST NEARLY

    A. low   B. hard   C. soft   D. faulty

15. *Sphere of authority* is called

    A. constituency   B. dictatorial
    C. jurisdiction   D. vassal

16. Rollers are made in several sizes.
    As used above, *several* means MOST NEARLY

    A. large   B. heavy   C. standard   D. different

17. Sometimes a roller is run over an old surface to detect weak spots.
    As used above, *detect* means MOST NEARLY

    A. compact   B. remove   C. find   D. strengthen

18. Reconstruction of the old base is sometimes required as a preliminary operation.
    As used above, *preliminary* means MOST NEARLY

    A. first   B. necessary   C. important   D. local

19. If a man makes an *absurd* remark, he makes one which is MOST NEARLY

    A. misleading   B. ridiculous
    C. unfair   D. wicked

20. A worker who is *adept* at his job is one who is MOST NEARLY

    A. cooperative   B. developed
    C. diligent   D. skilled

21. If a man states a condition is *general,* he means it is MOST NEARLY

    A. artificial   B. prevalent
    C. timely   D. transient

Questions 22-50.

DIRECTIONS: Each of Questions 22 through 50 consists of a sentence in which a word is italicized. Of the four words following each sentence, select the word whose meaning is MOST NEARLY the same as the meaning of the italicized word.

22. The agent's first *assignment* was to patrol on Hicks Avenue.
    A. test   B. sign   C. job   D. deadline

23. Agents get many *inquiries* from the public.
    A. complaints
    B. suggestions
    C. compliments
    D. questions

24. The names of all fifty states were written in *abbreviated* form.
    A. shortened
    B. corrected
    C. eliminated
    D. illegible

25. The meter was examined and found to be *defective*.
    A. small   B. operating   C. destroyed   D. faulty

26. Agent Roger's reports are *legible*, but Agent Baldwin's are not.
    A. similar   B. readable   C. incorrect   D. late

27. The time allowed, as shown by the meter, had *expired*.
    A. started   B. broken   C. ended   D. violated

28. The busy *commercial* area is quiet in the evenings.
    A. deserted   B. growing   C. business   D. local

29. The district office *authorized* the giving of summonses to illegally parked trucks.
    A. suggested
    B. approved
    C. prohibited
    D. recorded

30. Department property must be used *exclusively* for official business.
    A. occasionally
    B. frequently
    C. only
    D. properly

31. The District Commander *banned* driving in the area.
    A. detoured
    B. permitted
    C. encouraged
    D. prohibited

32. Two copies of the summons are *retained* by the Enforcement Agent.
    A. kept
    B. distributed
    C. submitted
    D. signed

33. The Agent *detected* a parking violation.
    A. cancelled
    B. discovered
    C. investigated
    D. reported

34. *Pedestrians* may be given summonses for violating traffic regulations.

   A. Bicycle riders   B. Horsemen
   C. Motorcyclists   D. Walkers

35. Parked cars are not allowed to *obstruct* traffic.

   A. direct   B. lead   C. block   D. speed

36. It was *obvious* to the Agent that the traffic light was broken.

   A. uncertain   B. surprising
   C. possible   D. clear

37. The signs stated that parking in the area was *restricted* to vehicles of foreign diplomats.

   A. allowed   B. increased   C. desired   D. limited

38. Each violation carries an *appropriate* fine.

   A. suitable   B. extra   C. light   D. heavy

39. Strict enforcement of parking regulations helps to *alleviate* traffic congestion.

   A. extend   B. build   C. relieve   D. increase

40. The Bureau has a rule which states that an Agent shall speak and act *courteously* in any relationship with the public.

   A. respectfully   B. timidly
   C. strangely   D. intelligently

41. City traffic regulations prohibit parking at *jammed* meters.

   A. stuck   B. timed   C. open   D. installed

42. A *significant* error was made by the collector.

   A. doubtful   B. foolish   C. important   D. strange

43. It is better to *disperse* a crowd.

   A. hold back   B. quiet   C. scatter   D. talk to

44. Business groups wish to *expand* the program.

   A. advertise   B. defeat   C. enlarge   D. expose

45. The procedure was *altered* to assist the storekeepers.

   A. abolished   B. changed
   C. improved   D. made simpler

46. The collector was instructed to *survey* the damage to the parking meter.

   A. examine   B. give the reason for
   C. repair   D. report

47. It is *imperative* that a collector's report be turned in after each collection.

   A. desired   B. recommended
   C. requested D. urgent

48. The collector was not able to *extricate* the key.

    A. find
    B. free
    C. have a copy made of
    D. turn

49. Parking meters have *alleviated* one of our major traffic problems.

    A. created
    B. lightened
    C. removed
    D. solved

50. Formerly drivers with learners' permits could drive only on *designated* streets.

    A. dead-end
    B. not busy
    C. one way
    D. specified

KEY (CORRECT ANSWERS)

1. A	11. B	21. B	31. D	41. A
2. C	12. D	22. C	32. A	42. C
3. B	13. C	23. D	33. B	43. C
4. C	14. D	24. A	34. D	44. C
5. D	15. C	25. D	35. C	45. B
6. A	16. D	26. B	36. D	46. A
7. B	17. C	27. C	37. D	47. D
8. B	18. A	28. C	38. A	48. B
9. C	19. B	29. B	39. C	49. B
10. D	20. D	30. C	40. A	50. D

TEST 3

DIRECTIONS: Each question or incomplete statement is followed by several suggested answers or completions. Select the one that BEST answers the question or completes the statement. *PRINT THE LETTER OF THE CORRECT ANSWER IN THE SPACE AT THE RIGHT.*

1. Sprinkler systems in buildings can retard the spread of fires.
   As used in this sentence, the word *retard* means MOST NEARLY

   A. quench   B. slow   C. reveal   D. aggravate

2. Although there was widespread criticism, the director refused to curtail the program.
   As used in this sentence, the word *curtail* means MOST NEARLY

   A. change   B. discuss   C. shorten   D. expand

3. Argon is an inert gas.
   As used in this sentence, the word *inert* means MOST NEARLY

   A. unstable   B. uncommon   C. volatile   D. inactive

4. The firemen turned their hoses on the shed and the main building simultaneously.
   As used in this sentence, the word *simultaneously* means MOST NEARLY

   A. in turn   B. without hesitation
   C. with great haste   D. at the same time

5. The officer was rebuked for his failure to act promptly. As used in this sentence, the word *rebuked* means MOST NEARLY

   A. demoted   B. reprimanded
   C. discharged   D. reassigned

6. Parkways in the city may be used to facilitate responses to fire alarms.
   As used in this sentence, the word *facilitate* means MOST NEARLY

   A. reduce   B. alter   C. complete   D. ease

7. Fire extinguishers are most effective when the fire is incipient.
   As used in this sentence, the word *incipient* means MOST NEARLY

   A. accessible   B. beginning
   C. red hot   D. confined

8. It is important to convey to new members the fundamentals of the procedure.
   As used in this sentence, the words *convey to* means MOST NEARLY

   A. prove for   B. confirm for
   C. suggest to   D. impart to

9. The explosion was a graphic illustration of the effects of neglect and carelessness.
   As used in this sentence, the word *graphic* means MOST NEARLY

   A. terrible   B. typical   C. unique   D. vivid

10. The worker was assiduous in all things relating to his duties.
    As used in this sentence, the word *assiduous* means MOST NEARLY

    A. aggressive   B. careless   C. persistent   D. cautious

11. A worker must be adept to be successful at his work.
    As used in this sentence, the word *adept* means MOST NEARLY

    A. ambitious   B. strong   C. agile   D. skillful

12. The extinguisher must be inverted before it will operate. As used in this sentence, the word *inverted* means MOST NEARLY

    A. turned over   B. completely filled
    C. lightly shaken   D. unhooked

13. Assume that the bridge operator may at times be assigned to the task of coordinating the bridge crew for the various routine jobs.
    As used in this sentence, the word *coordinating* means MOST NEARLY

    A. ordering   B. testing
    C. scheduling   D. instructing

14. The worker made an insignificant error.
    As used in this sentence, the word *insignificant* means MOST NEARLY

    A. latent   B. serious
    C. accidental   D. minor

15. An Assistant Supervisor should be attentive.
    As used in this sentence, the word *attentive* means MOST NEARLY

    A. watchful   B. prompt   C. negligent   D. willing

16. The Assistant Supervisor reported a cavity in the roadway.
    As used in this sentence, the word *cavity* means MOST NEARLY

    A. lump   B. wreck   C. hollow   D. oil-slick

17. Anyone working in traffic must be cautious.
    As used in this sentence, the word *cautious* means MOST NEARLY

    A. brave   B. careful   C. expert   D. fast

Questions 18-20.

DIRECTIONS: Each of Questions 18 through 20 consists of a capitalized word followed by four suggested meanings of the word. Select the word or phrase which means MOST NEARLY the same as the capitalized word.

18. OSMOSIS

    A. combining   B. diffusion
    C. ossification   D. incantation

19. COLLOIDAL

    A. mucinous   B. powdered   C. hairy   D. beautiful

20. PRETEXT

    A. ritual
    B. fictitious reason
    C. sermon
    D. truthful motive

21. *Easily broken or snapped* defines the word

    A. brittle   B. pliable   C. cohesive   D. volatile

22. *At right angles to a given line or surface* defines the word

    A. horizontal
    B. oblique
    C. perpendicular
    D. adjacent

23. *Tools with cutting edges for enlarging or shaping holes* are

    A. screwdrivers
    B. pliers
    C. reamers
    D. nippers

24. *An instrument used for measuring very small distances* is called a

    A. gage
    B. compass
    C. slide ruler
    D. micrometer

25. When the phrase *acrid smoke* is used, it refers to smoke that is

    A. irritating
    B. dense
    C. black
    D. very hot

26. The officer gave explicit directions on how the work was to be done.
    As used in this sentence, the word *explicit* means MOST NEARLY

    A. implied   B. clear   C. vague   D. brief

27. After the fire had been extinguished, the debris was taken outside and soaked.
    As used in this sentence, the word *debris* means MOST NEARLY

    A. wood   B. rubbish   C. couch   D. paper

28. The trapped man blanched when he saw the life net below him.
    As used in this sentence, the word *blanched* means MOST NEARLY

    A. turned pale
    B. sprang forward
    C. flushed
    D. fainted

29. The worker and his supervisor discussed the problem candidly.
    As used in this sentence, the word *candidly* means MOST NEARLY

    A. angrily
    B. frankly
    C. tolerantly
    D. understandingly

30. The truck came careening down the street.
    As used in this sentence, the word *careening* means MOST NEARLY

    A. with sirens screaming
    B. at a slow speed
    C. swaying from side to side
    D. out of control

31. The population of the province is fairly homogeneous.
    As used in this sentence, the word *homogeneous* means MOST NEARLY

    A. devoted to agricultural pursuits
    B. conservative in outlook
    C. essentially alike
    D. sophisticated

32. The reports of injuries during the past month are being tabulated.
    As used in this sentence, the word *tabulated* means MOST NEARLY

    A. analyzed
    B. placed in a file
    C. put in the form of a table
    D. verified

33. The terms offered were tantamount to surrender.
    As used in this sentence, the word *tantamount* means MOST NEARLY

    A. equivalent   B. opposite
    C. preferable   D. preliminary

34. The man's injuries were superficial.
    As used in this sentence, the word *superficial* means MOST NEARLY

    A. on the surface   B. not fatal
    C. free from infection D. not painful

35. This experience warped his outlook on life.
    As used in this sentence, the word *warped* means MOST NEARLY

    A. changed   B. improved
    C. strengthened   D. twisted

36. Hotel guests usually are transients.
    As used in this sentence, the word *transients* means MOST NEARLY

    A. persons of considerable wealth
    B. staying for a short time
    C. visitors from other areas
    D. untrustworthy persons

37. The pupil's work specimen was considered unsatisfactory because of his failure to observe established tolerances. As used in this sentence, the word *tolerances* means MOST NEARLY

    A. safety precautions
    B. regard for the rights of others
    C. allowable variations in dimensions
    D. amount of waste produced in an operation

38. Punishment was severe because the act was considered willful.
    As used in this sentence, the word *willful* means MOST NEARLY

    A. brutal   B. criminal
    C. harmful   D. intentional

39. The malfunctioning of the system was traced to a defective thermostat.
    As used in this sentence, the word *thermostat* means MOST NEARLY a device that reacts to changes in

    A. amperage
    B. water pressure
    C. temperature
    D. atmospheric pressure

40. His garden contained a profusion of flowers, shrubs, and bushes.
    As used in this sentence, the word *profusion* means MOST NEARLY

    A. abundance
    B. display
    C. representation
    D. scarcity

41. The inspector would not approve the work because it was out of plumb.
    As used in this sentence, the words *out of plumb* means MOST NEARLY not

    A. properly seasoned
    B. of the required strength
    C. vertical
    D. fireproof

42. The judge admonished the witness for his answer.
    As used in this sentence, the word *admonished* means MOST NEARLY

    A. complimented
    B. punished
    C. questioned
    D. warned

43. A millimeter is a measure of length.
    The length represented by *one millimeter* is

    A. one-thousandth of a meter
    B. one thousand meters
    C. one-millionth of a meter
    D. one million meters

44. It is not possible to misconstrue his letter.
    As used in this sentence, the word *misconstrue* means MOST NEARLY

    A. decipher
    B. forget
    C. ignore
    D. misinterpret

45. The wire connecting the two terminals must be kept taut.
    As used in this sentence, the word *taut* means MOST NEARLY without

    A. defects
    B. slack
    C. electrical charge
    D. pressure

46. Reaching the summit appeared beyond the capacity of the hikers.
    As used in this sentence, the word *summit* means MOST NEARLY

    A. canyon   B. peak   C. plateau   D. ravine

47. The plot was thwarted by the quick action of the police. As used in this sentence, the word *thwarted* means MOST NEARLY

    A. blocked
    B. discovered
    C. punished
    D. solved

48. An abrasive was required by the machinist to complete his task.
    As used in this sentence, the word *abrasive* means a substance used for

    A. coating
    B. lubricating
    C. measuring
    D. polishing

49. The facades of the building were dirty and grimy.
    As used in this sentence, the word *facades* means MOST NEARLY

    A. cellars
    B. fronts
    C. residents
    D. surroundings

50. Several firemen were injured by the detonation.
    As used in this sentence, the word *detonation* means MOST NEARLY

    A. accident   B. collapse   C. collision   D. explosion

KEY (CORRECT ANSWERS)

1. B	11. D	21. A	31. C	41. C
2. C	12. A	22. C	32. C	42. D
3. D	13. C	23. C	33. A	43. A
4. D	14. D	24. D	34. A	44. D
5. B	15. A	25. A	35. D	45. B
6. D	16. C	26. B	36. B	46. B
7. B	17. B	27. B	37. C	47. A
8. D	18. B	28. A	38. D	48. D
9. D	19. A	29. B	39. C	49. B
10. C	20. B	30. C	40. A	50. D

WORD MEANING

EXAMINATION SECTION
TEST 1

DIRECTIONS: Each question or incomplete statement is followed by several suggested answers or completions. Select the one that BEST answers the question or completes the statement. *PRINT THE LETTER OF THE CORRECT ANSWER IN THE SPACE AT HE IGHT.*

1. He received a large reward.
   In this sentence, the word *reward* means

   A. capture   B. recompense   C. key   D. praise

   1.____

2. The aide was asked to transmit a message. In this sentence, the word *transmit* means

   A. change   B. send   C. take   D. type

   2.____

3. The pest control aide requested the tenant to call the Health Department.
   In this sentence, the word *requested* means the pest control aide

   A. asked   B. helped   C. informed   D. warned

   3.____

4. The driver had to return the department's truck. In this sentence, the word *return* means

   A. borrow   B. fix   C. give back   D. load up

   4.____

5. The aide discussed the purpose of the visit. In this sentence, the word *purpose* means

   A. date   B. hour   C. need   D. reason

   5.____

6. The tenant suspected the aide who knocked at her door. In this sentence, the word *suspected* means

   A. answered   B. called   C. distrusted   D. welcomed

   6.____

7. The aide was positive that the child hit her. In this sentence, the word *positive* means

   A. annoyed   B. certain   C. sorry   D. surprised

   7.____

8. The tenant declined to call the Health Department. In this sentence, the word *declined* means

   A. agreed   B. decided   C. refused   D. wanted

   8.____

9. The porter cleaned the vacant room.
   In this sentence, the word *vacant* means NEARLY the same as

   A. empty   B. large   C. main   D. crowded

   9.____

10. The supervisor gave a brief report to his men.
    In this sentence, the word *brief* means NEARLY the same as

    A. long   B. safety   C. complete   D. short

    10.____

141

11. The supervisor told him to connect the two pieces.
    In this sentence, the word *connect* means NEARLY the same as

    A. join B. paint C. return D. weigh

12. Standing on the top of a ladder is risky.
    In this sentence, the word *risky* means NEARLY the same as

    A. dangerous B. sensible C. safe D. foolish

13. He raised the cover of the machine.
    In this sentence, the word *raised* means NEARLY the same as

    A. broke B. lifted C. lost D. found

14. The form used for reporting the finished work was revised. In this sentence, the word *revised* means NEARLY the same as

    A. printed B. ordered C. dropped D. changed

15. He did his work rapidly.
    In this sentence, the word *rapidly* means NEARLY the same a

    A. carefully B. quickly C. slowly D. quietly

16. The worker was occasionally late.
    In this sentence, the word *occasionally* means NEARLY the same as

    A. sometimes B. often C. never D. always

17. He selected the best tool for the job.
    In this sentence, the word *selected* means NEARLY the same as

    A. bought B. picked C. lost D. broke

18. He needed assistance to lift the package.
    In this sentence, the word *assistance* means NEARLY the same as

    A. strength B. time C. help D. instructions

19. The tools were issued by the supervisor.
    In this sentence, the word *issued* means NEARLY the same as

    A. collected B. cleaned up C. given out D. examined

20. A permit for a tap for unmetered water will be issued only on prepayment of all charges for water to be used. In this sentence, the word *prepayment* means

    A. promise of payment   B. payment in advance
    C. payment as water is used D. monthly payment

21. Upon application, the department will endeavor to locate a service pipe by means of an electrical indicator.
    In this sentence, the word *endeavor* means

    A. try   B. help   C. assist   D. explore

22. It shall be unlawful for any person to operate certain equipment without previous permission from the department. In this sentence, the word *previous* means

    A. written   B. oral   C. prior   D. provisional

23. All persons must comply with the rules and regulations. In this sentence, the word *comply* means

    A. agree   B. coincide
    C. work carefully   D. act in accord

24. No unauthorized person shall tamper with a water supply valve.
    In this sentence, the words *tamper with* means

    A. open   B. operate   C. alter   D. shut

25. The use of water is permitted subject to such conditions as the department may consider reasonable.
    In this sentence, the word *reasonable* means

    A. necessary   B. inexpensive   C. fair   D. desirable

26. An owner must engage a licensed plumber. In this sentence, the word *engage* means

    A. hire   B. pay   C. contact   D. inform

27. The charges for a machine part are usually for the furnishing, delivering, and installing of the part. In this sentence, the word *furnishing* means

    A. preparing   B. manufacturing   C. finishing   D. supplying

28. The investigator attempted to ascertain the facts.
    As used in this sentence, the word *ascertain* means MOST NEARLY to

    A. disprove   B. find out   C. go beyond   D. explain

29. The speaker commenced the lecture with an anecdote.
    As used in this sentence, the word *commenced* means MOST NEARLY

    A. concluded   B. illustrated   C. enlivened   D. started

30. The use of a hydrant may be authorized for construction purposes.
    As used in this sentence, the word *authorized* means

    A. possible   B. permitted   C. intended   D. stopped

31. Conservation of the water supply is a major goal of the department.
    As used in this sentence, the word *conservation* means MOST NEARLY

    A. estimating
    B. increasing
    C. preserving
    D. purifying

32. Consumers should inspect their faucets frequently to guard against leaks.
    As used in this sentence, the word *consumers* means MOST NEARLY

    A. citizens
    B. owners
    C. producers
    D. users

33. The wire was connected to the adjacent terminal.
    As used in this sentence, the word *adjacent* means MOST NEARLY

    A. out of order
    B. metallic
    C. nearby
    D. negative

34. Some of the equipment supplied to the inspector was defective.
    As used in this sentence, the word *defective* means MOSTNEARLY

    A. expensive
    B. faulty
    C. old
    D. unnecessary

35. The inspector was told to use discretion in dealing with the public.
    As used in this sentence, the word *discretion* means MOST NEARLY

    A. courtesy
    B. firmness
    C. judgment
    D. persuasion

36. It is unlawful to demolish any building without first obtaining a permit.
    As used in this sentence, the word *demolish* means MOST NEARLY

    A. build
    B. make alterations in
    C. occupy
    D. tear down

37. The clerk rendered an account of the cash received.
    As used in this sentence, the word *rendered* means MOST NEARLY

    A. concealed
    B. corrected
    C. forged
    D. gave

38. The permit was revoked by the department.
    As used in this sentence, the word *revoked* means MOST NEARLY

    A. approved
    B. cancelled
    C. renewed
    D. reviewed

39. The incident received much attention in the newspapers. As used in this sentence, the word *incident* means MOST NEARLY

    A. campaign
    B. crime
    C. event
    D. merger

40. The modification of the procedure was approved by the supervisor.
    As used in this sentence, the word *modification* means MOST NEARLY

    A. change
    B. interpretation
    C. repeal
    D. termination

41. The workers combined the contents of the two boxes. The word *combined* means

    A. sifted through
    B. put together
    C. tore apart
    D. forgot about

42. Don't touch the lever on the left side. The word *lever* means

    A. button
    B. rope
    C. handle
    D. gun

43. All litter should be taken away. The word *litter* means

    A. paint
    B. bowls
    C. rubbish
    D. evidence

44. The inspection of the street was complete. The word *inspection* means

    A. cleaning
    B. examination
    C. repair
    D. painting

45. The route must be followed exactly.
    The word *route* means

    A. foreman
    B. truck
    C. way
    D. recipe

46. Don't injure your back.
    The word *injure* means

    A. bend
    B. use
    C. hurt
    D. exercise

47. John repaired the machine.
    The word *repaired* means

    A. fixed
    B. broke
    C. ran
    D. oiled

48. Put the lid on the box.
    The word *lid* means

    A. cover
    B. ribbon
    C. rope
    D. wrapping

49. The rear of the truck should be washed.
    The word *rear* means

    A. hood
    B. front
    C. back
    D. roof

50. Coworkers must assist each other while at work. The word *assist* means

    A. help
    B. outdo
    C. like
    D. hurt

KEY (CORRECT ANSWERS)

1. B	11. A	21. A	31. C	41. B
2. B	12. A	22. C	32. D	42. C
3. A	13. B	23. D	33. C	43. C
4. C	14. D	24. C	34. B	44. B
5. D	15. B	25. C	35. C	45. C
6. C	16. A	26. A	36. D	46. C
7. B	17. B	27. D	37. D	47. A
8. C	18. C	28. B	38. B	48. A
9. A	19. C	29. D	39. C	49. C
10. D	20. B	30. B	40. A	50. A

TEST 2

DIRECTIONS: Each question or incomplete statement is followed by several suggested answers or completions. Select the one that BEST answers the question or completes the statement. *PRINT THE LETTER OF THE CORRECT ANSWER IN THE SPACE AT THE RIGHT.*

1. It is possible to construct a leak-proof home.
   The OPPOSITE of *construct* is

   A. build B. erect C. plant D. wreck

   1.____

2. The driver had to repair the flat tire.
   The OPPOSITE of the word *repair* is

   A. destroy B. fix C. mend D. patch

   2.____

3. The student tried to shout the answer.
   The OPPOSITE of the word *shout* is

   A. scream B. shriek C. whisper D. yell

   3.____

4. Daily visits are the best.
   The OPPOSITE of the word *visits* is

   A. absences B. exercises C. lessons D. trials

   4.____

5. It is important to arrive early in the morning.
   The OPPOSITE of the word *arrive* is

   A. climb B. descend C. enter D. leave

   5.____

6. Mike is a group leader.
   The OPPOSITE of the word *leader* is

   A. boss B. chief C. follower D. overseer

   6.____

7. The exterior of the house needs painting.
   The OPPOSITE of the word *exterior* is

   A. inside B. outdoors C. outside D. surface

   7.____

8. He conceded the victory.
   The OPPOSITE of the word *conceded* is

   A. admitted B. denied C. granted D. reported

   8.____

9. He watched the team begin.
   The OPPOSITE of the word *begin* is

   A. end B. fail C. gather D. win

   9.____

10. Your handwriting is illegible.
    The OPPOSITE of the word *illegible* is

    A. clear B. confused C. jumbled D. unclear

    10.____

11. The one of the following words that has the OPPOSITE meaning of *partition* is

    A. division   B. connection   C. barrier   D. compartment

12. The one of the following words that has the OPPOSITE meaning of *obvious* is

    A. concealed   B. known   C. clear   D. apparent

13. The one of the following words that has the OPPOSITE meaning of *assist* is

    A. hinder   B. offer   C. demand   D. aid

14. The one of the following words that has the OPPOSITE meaning of *obsolete* is

    A. neglected   B. traditional   C. rare   D. new

15. The one of the following words that has the OPPOSITE meaning of *stagnant* is

    A. murky   B. active   C. calm   D. dirty

16. The number of applicants exceeded the anticipated figure. As used in this sentence, the word *anticipated* means MOST NEARLY

    A. expected   B. required   C. revised   D. necessary

17. The clerk was told to collate the pages of the report. As used in this sentence, the word *collate* means MOST NEARLY

    A. destroy   B. edit   C. correct   D. assemble

18. Mr. Wells is not authorized to release the information. As used in this sentence, the word *authorized* means MOST NEARLY

    A. inclined   B. pleased   C. permitted   D. trained

19. The secretary chose an appropriate office for the meeting. As used in this sentence, the word *appropriate* means MOST NEARLY

    A. empty   B. decorated   C. nearby   D. suitable

20. The employee performs a complex set of tasks each day. As used in this sentence, the word *complex* means MOST NEARLY

    A. difficult   B. important   C. pleasant   D. large

21. In talking with a homeowner, an inspector should always be polite. As used in this sentence, the word *polite* means

    A. cold   B. courteous   C. aggressive   D. modest

22. In talking with a client, a worker should not discuss trivial matters. As used in this sentence, the word *trivial* means

    A. related   B. essential   C. significant   D. unimportant

23. The one of the following words that is SIMILAR in meaning to *revise* is   23.____

    A. edit   B. confuse   C. complicate   D. dismiss

24. The one of the following words that is SIMILAR in meaning to *abandon* is   24.____

    A. quit   B. use   C. remain   D. discourage

25. The one of the following words that is SIMILAR in meaning to *adjacent* is   25.____

    A. far   B. detached   C. bordering   D. distant

26. The one of the following words that is SIMILAR in meaning to *coarse* is   26.____

    A. fine   B. smooth   C. rough   D. slick

27. The one of the following words that is SIMILAR in meaning to *orifice* is   27.____

    A. chamber   B. enclosure   C. opening   D. device

28. The aide arrived on time.
    In this sentence, the word *arrived* means   28.____

    A. awoke   B. came   C. left   D. delayed

29. The salesman had to deliver books to each person he visited.
    In this sentence, the word *deliver* means   29.____

    A. give   B. lend   C. mail   D. sell

30. When estimating materials for interior plaster, consideration must be given to the number   30.____
    of coats.
    As used in this sentence, the word *estimating* means

    A. calculating approximately   B. purchasing
    C. mixing together   D. finishing

31. As used in the sentence in Question 30 above, the word *consideration* means   31.____

    A. extra weight   B. careful thought
    C. firmness   D. additions

32. When computing quantities of plaster for the scratch coat, no allowance may be made for   32.____
    the space occupied by the metal lath.
    As used in this sentence, the word *computing* means

    A. figuring   B. preparing   C. slaking   D. packing

33. As used in the sentence in Question 32 above, the word *allowance* means   33.____

    A. deduction   B. addition   C. leeway   D. closing

34. The supervisor made a ridiculous statement.   34.____
    As used in this sentence, the word *ridiculous* means MOST NEARLY

    A. incorrect   B. evil   C. unfriendly   D. foolish

35. That worker is engaged in a hazardous job.
    As used in this sentence, the word *hazardous* means MOST NEARLY

    A. inconvenient   B. dangerous   C. difficult   D. demanding

36. Breaks in water distribution mains are front page news for the very reason that they occur infrequently.
    As used in this sentence, the word *infrequently* means MOST NEARLY

    A. at regular intervals   B. often
    C. rarely   D. unexpectedly

37. Several kinds of self-caulking substitutes for lead have been developed.
    As used in this sentence, the word *substitutes* means MOST NEARLY

    A. additives   B. replacements   C. hardeners   D. softeners

38. Cast iron is essentially an alloy of iron and carbon. As used in this sentence, the word *essentially* means MOST NEARLY

    A. never   B. basically   C. barely   D. sometimes

39. When water moves through pipe, friction is developed between the water and the inside surface of the pipe. As used in this sentence, the word *friction* means MOST NEARLY

    A. resistance   B. heat   C. slippage   D. pressure

40. A person who is confident he can complete a task is said to be

    A. courageous   B. sure   C. bright   D. successful

41. If a child sleeping peacefully is awakened by a sudden cry, he is likely to be

    A. ill   B. uncomfortable   C. startled   D. hungry

42. He could not get his truck on the highway. A *highway* is a type of

    A. lot   B. road   C. scale   D. sidewalk

43. The large vehicle was being repaired.
    Which of the following is a *vehicle*?

    A. Truck   B. Building   C. Boiler   D. Table

44. The fence needs to be painted.
    The one of the following which is MOST like a *fence* is a

    A. door   B. crane   C. wall   D. building

45. Furniture is not taken with the regular garbage collection.
    Which of the following is *furniture*?

    A. Sofas and chairs   B. Cars and trucks
    C. Brooms and mops   D. Bags and boxes

46. The group was assigned to do special work. Which of the following is a *group*? 46.____

    A. Truck   B. Boat   C. Team   D. Foreman

47. Sanitation men often use tools in their work. 47.____
    The one of the following which is MOST often considered a *tool* is a

    A. tire   B. shovel   C. glove   D. basket

48. The man claimed that he could not lift the box. The word *lift* means MOST NEARLY 48.____

    A. bury   B. pick up   C. refill   D. clean

49. Place all the boxes below the second shelf. The word *below* means 49.____

    A. under   B. into   C. beside   D. over

50. This street should be clean when the sanitation men finish. 50.____
    The word *clean* means free of

    A. obstacles   B. pedestrians   C. traffic   D. dirt

KEY (CORRECT ANSWERS)

1. D	11. B	21. B	31. B	41. C
2. A	12. A	22. D	32. A	42. B
3. C	13. A	23. A	33. A	43. A
4. A	14. D	24. A	34. D	44. C
5. D	15. B	25. C	35. B	45. A
6. C	16. A	26. C	36. C	46. C
7. A	17. D	27. C	37. B	47. B
8. B	18. C	28. B	38. B	48. B
9. A	19. D	29. A	39. A	49. A
10. A	20. A	30. A	40. B	50. D

TEST 3

DIRECTIONS: Each question or incomplete statement is followed by several suggested answers or completions. Select the one that BEST answers the question or completes the statement. *PRINT THE LETTER OF THE CORRECT ANSWER IN THE SPACE AT THE RIGHT.*

Questions 1-6.

DIRECTIONS: In the paragraph below, some of the underlined words have been purposely changed and spoil the meaning that the rest of the paragraph is meant to give. Read the paragraph carefully. Then, answer Questions 1 through 6.

    The motor vehicle supervisor who is <u>responsible</u> for training drivers in the operation of <u>special</u> equipment cannot expect a man to carry out all of his duties <u>poorly</u> <u>immediately</u> after receiving instruction. The employee may be overwhelmed by all of the details he must master, <u>happy</u> because he is <u>associated</u> with new fellow workers, or fearful that he may not <u>succeed</u> on the job. It is the supervisor's <u>job</u> to make the <u>operator</u> feel at ease and <u>discourage</u> his self-confidence. The supervisor must also vary the speed of the <u>driving</u> according to the operator's <u>capacity</u> to <u>absorb</u> the instruction without undue pressure or confusion. All learners <u>progress</u> through <u>several</u> stages of <u>development</u> <u>unless</u> they become expert in their duties. As the operator's skills <u>increase,</u> he will require <u>more</u> instruction but the supervisor should be available to correct <u>mistakes</u> promptly to prevent wrong <u>habits</u> being formed.

1. Of the following words underlined in the above paragraph, the one that does NOT give the real meaning that the rest of the paragraph is meant to give is

   A. responsible   B. special   C. happy   D. immediately

2. Of the following words underlined in the above paragraph, the one that does NOT give the real meaning that the rest of the paragraph is meant to give is

   A. overwhelmed   B. happy   C. associated   D. succeed

3. Of the following words underlined in the above paragraph, the one that does NOT give the real meaning that the rest of the paragraph is meant to give is

   A. job   B. operator   C. discourage   D. self-confidence

4. Of the following words underlined in the above paragraph, the one that does NOT give the real meaning that the rest of the paragraph is meant to give is

   A. driving   B. capacity   C. absorb   D. pressure

5. Of the following words underlined in the above paragraph, the one that does NOT give the real meaning that the rest of the paragraph is meant to give is

   A. progress   B. several   C. development   D. unless

6. Of the following words underlined in the above paragraph, the one that does NOT give the real meaning that the rest of the paragraph is meant to give is

   A. increase   B. more   C. mistakes   D. habits

Questions 7-13.

DIRECTIONS: Each of Questions 7 through 13 consists of a capitalized word followed by four suggested meanings of the word. Select the word or phrase which means MOST NEARLY the same as the capitalized word.

7. ACCELERATE

   A. adjust B. press C. quicken D. strip

8. ALIGN

   A. bring into line B. carry out
   C. happen by chance D. join together

9. CONTRACTION

   A. agreement B. denial
   C. presentation D. shrinkage

10. INTERVAL

    A. ending B. mixing together of
    C. space of time D. weaken

11. LUBRICATE

    A. bend back B. make slippery
    C. rub out D. soften

12. OBSOLETE

    A. broken-down B. hard to find
    C. high-priced D. out of date

13. RETARD

    A. delay B. flatten C. rest D. tally

14. Any major components of a fire communication system should be meticulously maintained.
    In the preceding sentence, the word *meticulously* means MOST NEARLY

    A. indifferently B. perfunctorily
    C. painstakingly D. languidly

Questions 15-17.

DIRECTIONS: Questions 15 through 17 are to be answered in accordance with the following statement.

In order to facilitate prompt assembly of designated members, the officer in charge, Bureau of Fire Communications, shall maintain accurate current data on all such matters.

15. The word *facilitate,* as used in the above statement, means MOST NEARLY

    A. authorize   B. expedite   C. command   D. hinder

16. The word *designated,* as used in the above statement, means MOST NEARLY

    A. required   B. versatile   C. skillful   D. selected

17. The word *data,* as used in the above statement, means MOST NEARLY

    A. calculations   B. information   C. forecasts   D. surveillance

Questions 18-19.

DIRECTIONS: Questions 18 and 19 are to be answered in accordance with the following statement.

In the event of severe disruption of circuits....members of this squad may be.... detailed to Bureau of Fire Communications for duration of such emergency.

18. The word *disruption,* as used in the above sentence, means MOST NEARLY

    A. overloading   B. breakdown   C. disuse   D. concurrence

19. The word *detailed,* as used in the above statement, means MOST NEARLY

    A. assigned   B. reported   C. demoted   D. promoted

20. The officer in command, after verification that the alarm was false, shall transmit by radio the signal 9-2 followed by box number.
    The word *verification,* as used in the above sentence, means MOST NEARLY

    A. confirmation   B. consideration   C. notification   D. confutation

Questions 21-23.

DIRECTIONS: Questions 21 through 23 are to be answered on the basis of the following statement.

The manual of Fire Communications was planned to serve the Fire Department as guide and reference in effective use of its vast, versatile communications network.... Complete understanding of its phases and precepts, together with prompt compliance with all requirements and actions set in motion by its coded signals and radio transmissions, are essential.

21. The word *versatile,* as used in the above statement, means MOST NEARLY

    A. steady   B. many-sided   C. constant   D. wavering

22. The word *precepts,* as used in the above statement, means MOST NEARLY

    A. forerunners   B. paragraphs   C. rules   D. sections

23. The word *compliance,* as used in the above statement, means MOST NEARLY   23._____

    A. variance   B. dissension   C. divergence   D. conformance

24. A person who is influenced in making a decision by preconceived opinions is said to be   24._____

    A. subjective   B. obstinate   C. hateful   D. ignorant

25. No time was set for the conference.   25._____
    The word below that BEST describes this fact is

    A. indefinite   B. decisive   C. ignored   D. powerful

26. The truck could not go under the bridge because the bridge was too low.   26._____
    The reason the truck could not go under the bridge was that the bridge was not _____ enough.

    A. high   B. long   C. strong   D. wide

Questions 27-29.

DIRECTIONS: Questions 27 through 29 are to be answered on the basis of the following statement.

In structures exceeding 150 ft. in height, adequate means shall be provided for taking care of the expansion and contraction of all vertical lines of pipe. In addition, adequate means shall be provided to properly support all vertical lines of pipe.

27. The word *adequate,* as used above, means MOST NEARLY   27._____

    A. liquid devices
    B. properly designed and sufficient
    C. strong and thick walled
    D. in very great numbers

28. The word *expansion,* as used above, means MOST NEARLY a(n)   28._____

    A. bulbous swelling
    B. transverse projection
    C. large increase in diameter
    D. an increase in length

29. The word *contraction,* as used above, means MOST NEARLY   29._____

    A. contract to install the vertical line
    B. reduction in length
    C. to group all vertical lines together
    D. to decrease the equivalent length

30. A common mistake is to assume that the strength of equipment is the most important factor.   30._____
    As used in the above sentence, the word *assume* means MOST NEARLY

    A. determine   B. take for granted
    C. figure   D. make sure

KEY (CORRECT ANSWERS)

1.	C	11.	B	21.	B
2.	B	12.	D	22.	C
3.	C	13.	A	23.	D
4.	A	14.	C	24.	A
5.	D	15.	B	25.	A
6.	B	16.	D	26.	A
7.	C	17.	B	27.	B
8.	A	18.	B	28.	D
9.	D	19.	A	29.	B
10.	C	20.	A	30.	B

VERBAL ANALOGIES

EXAMINATION SECTION
TEST 1

DIRECTIONS: In Questions 1 to 10, the first two *italicized* words have a relationship to each other. Determine that relationship, and then match the third *italicized* word with the one of the lettered choices with which it has the same relationship as the words of the first pair have to each other. PRINT THE LETTER OF THE CORRECT ANSWER IN THE SPACE AT THE RIGHT.

In order to help you understand the procedure, a sample question is given:

SAMPLE: *dog* is to *bark* as *cat* is to
    A. animal   B. small   C. meow
    D. pet   E. snarl

The relationship between *dog* and *bark* is that the sound which a dog normally emits is a bark. In the same way, the sound which a cat emits is a meow. Thus, C is the CORRECT answer.

1. *Fine* is to *speeding* as *jail* is to
   - A. bars
   - B. prisoner
   - C. warden
   - D. confinement
   - E. steal

2. *Orchid* is to *rose* as *gold* is to
   - A. watch
   - B. copper
   - C. mine
   - D. coin
   - E. mint

3. *Pistol* is to *machine gun* as *button* is to
   - A. coat
   - B. bullet
   - C. zipper
   - D. tailor
   - E. needle and thread

4. *Spontaneous* is to *unrehearsed* as *planned* is to
   - A. completed
   - B. organized
   - C. restricted
   - D. understood
   - E. informal

5. *Friendly* is to *hostile* as *loyalty* is to
   - A. fealty
   - B. evil
   - C. devotion
   - D. warlike
   - E. treachery

6. *Fear* is to *flight* as *bravery* is to
   - A. courage
   - B. danger
   - C. resistance
   - D. injury
   - E. unyielding

7. *Economical* is to *stingy* as *sufficient* is to
   - A. abundant
   - B. adequate
   - C. expensive
   - D. needy
   - E. greedy

8. *Astronomer* is to *observation* as *senator* is to   8.___

   A. caucus   B. election   C. convention
   D. legislation   E. patronage

9. *Hunger* is to *food* as *exhaustion* is to   9.___

   A. labor   B. play   C. illness
   D. debility   E. rest

10. *Entertainment* is to *boredom* as *efficiency* is to   10.___

    A. ignorance   B. government   C. waste
    D. expert   E. time and motion studies

KEY (CORRECT ANSWERS)

1. E   6. C
2. B   7. A
3. C   8. D
4. B   9. E
5. E   10. C

TEST 2

DIRECTIONS: In Questions 1 to 10, the first two *italicized* words have a relationship to each other. Determine that relationship, and then match the third *italicized* word with the one of the lettered choices with which it has the same relationship as the words of the first pair have to each other. *PRINT THE LETTER OF THE CORRECT ANSWER IN THE SPACE AT THE RIGHT.*

1. *Diamond* is to *glass* as *platinum* is to 1.____
   - A. jewelry
   - B. metal
   - C. aluminum
   - D. mine
   - E. white

2. *Water* is to *aqueduct* as *electricity* is to 2.____
   - A. meter
   - B. battery
   - C. fuse
   - D. wire
   - E. solenoid

3. *Oratory* is to *filibuster* as *reign* is to 3.____
   - A. tyrant
   - B. terror
   - C. government
   - D. bluster
   - E. confusion

4. *Gravity* is to *gaiety* as *taunt* is to 4.____
   - A. ridicule
   - B. console
   - C. avoid
   - D. amuse
   - E. condone

5. *Electron* is to *atom* as *earth* is to 5.____
   - A. sun
   - B. solar system
   - C. moon
   - D. planet
   - E. center

6. *Flattery* is to *adulation* as *cruelty* is to 6.____
   - A. pain
   - B. barbarity
   - C. censorious
   - D. compassion
   - E. duality

7. *Rowboat* is to *oar* as *automobile* is to 7.____
   - A. land
   - B. engine
   - C. driver
   - D. passenger
   - E. piston

8. *Friction* is to *oil* as *war* is to 8.____
   - A. conference
   - B. peace
   - C. munitions
   - D. satellite
   - E. retaliation

9. *Disease* is to *infection* as *reaction* is to 9.____
   - A. control
   - B. injury
   - C. relapse
   - D. stipulation
   - E. sensation

10. *Persecution* is to *martyr* as *swindle* is to 10.____
    - A. embezzler
    - B. refuge
    - C. confidence man
    - D. bank
    - E. dupe

KEY (CORRECT ANSWERS)

1. C
2. D
3. E
4. B
5. B

6. B
7. B
8. A
9. E
10. E

TEST 3

DIRECTIONS: In Questions 1 to 10, the first two *italicized* words have a relationship to each other. Determine that relationship, and then match the third *italicized* word with the one of the lettered choices with which it has the same relationship as the words of the first pair have to each other. *PRINT THE LETTER OF THE CORRECT ANSWER IN THE SPACE AT THE RIGHT.*

1. *Woman* is to *man* as *Mary* is to 1._____
   A. woman   B. child   C. female   D. John   E. male

2. *Land* is to *ocean* as *soldier* is to 2._____
   A. river   B. sailor   C. shore   D. uniform   E. sailing

3. *Sugar* is to *candy* as *flour* is to 3._____
   A. eat   B. cook   C. candy   D. bread   E. sweet

4. *Sorrow* is to *joy* as *laugh* is to 4._____
   A. amuse   B. tears   C. fun   D. weep   E. cry

5. *Heat* is to *fire* as *pain* is to 5._____
   A. injury   B. wind   C. weather   D. cool   E. summer

6. *Grass* is to *cattle* as *milk* is to 6._____
   A. growing   B. lawn   C. baby   D. green   E. sun

7. *Winter* is to *spring* as *autumn* is to 7._____
   A. summer   B. winter   C. warm   D. cold   E. flower

8. *Rising* is to *falling* as *smile* is to 8._____
   A. climbing   B. baking   C. scolding
   D. frown   E. laughing

9. *Day* is to *night* as *succeed* is to 9._____
   A. fail   B. sunshine   C. evening
   D. afternoon E. morning

10. *Apple* is to *fruit* as *corn* is to 10._____
    A. orange   B. eat   C. grain   D. cereal   E. food

161

KEY (CORRECT ANSWERS)

1. D
2. B
3. D
4. E
5. A

6. C
7. B
8. D
9. A
10. C

TEST 4

DIRECTIONS: In Questions 1 to 10, the first two *italicized* words have a relationship to each other. Determine that relationship, and then match the third *italicized* word with the one of the lettered choices with which it has the same relationship as the words of the first pair have to each other. *PRINT THE LETTER OF THE CORRECT ANSWER IN THE SPACE AT THE RIGHT.*

1. *Robin* is to *feathers* as *cat* is to   1.____
   A. sing   B. fur   C. eat   D. bird   E. fly

2. *Late* is to *end* as *early* is to   2.____
   A. prompt   B. enter   C. begin   D. start   E. end

3. *Beginning* is to *end* as *horse* is to   3.____
   A. cart   B. automobile   C. wagon
   D. travel   E. ride

4. *Kitten* is to *cat* as *baby* is to   4.____
   A. rabbit   B. mother   C. dog   D. cow   E. lamb

5. *Little* is to *weak* as *big* is to   5.____
   A. boy   B. man   C. tall   D. baby   E. strong

6. *Arm* is to *hand* as *leg* is to   6.____
   A. knee   B. toe   C. elbow   D. foot   E. finger

7. *Alive* is to *dead* as *well* is to   7.____
   A. grow   B. sick   C. decay   D. sleep   E. play

8. *In* is to *out* as *bad* is to   8.____
   A. up   B. open   C. good   D. shut   E. on

9. *Dust* is to *dry* as *mud* is to   9.____
   A. wet   B. blow   C. splash   D. fly   E. settle

10. *Width* is to *wide* as *height* is to   10.____
    A. high   B. low   C. tall   D. brief   E. short

163

KEY (CORRECT ANSWERS)

1. B
2. C
3. A
4. B
5. E

6. D
7. B
8. C
9. A
10. C

TEST 5

DIRECTIONS: In Questions 1 to 10, the first two *italicized* words have a relationship to each other. Determine that relationship, and then match the third *italicized* word with the one of the lettered choices with which it has the same relationship as the words of the first pair have to each other. *PRINT THE LETTER OF THE CORRECT ANSWER IN THE SPACE AT THE RIGHT.*

1. *Above* is to *below* as *before* is to

    A. beyond   B. behind   C. beside   D. between   E. after

    1._____

2. *Start* is to *stop* as *begin* is to

    A. go   B. run   C. wait   D. finish   E. work

    2._____

3. *Everything* is to *nothing* as *always* is to

    A. forever   B. usually   C. never
    D. sometimes   E. something

    3._____

4. *Search* is to *find* as *question* is to

    A. answer   B. reply   C. study
    D. problem   E. explain

    4._____

5. *Top* is to *spin* as *spear* is to

    A. bottom   B. roll   C. throw   D. sharp   E. pin

    5._____

6. *Scale* is to *weight* as *thermometer* is to

    A. weather   B. temperature   C. pounds
    D. spring   E. chronometer

    6._____

7. *Congress* is to *senator* as *convention* is to

    A. election   B. chairman   C. delegate
    D. nominee   E. representative

    7._____

8. *Dividend* is to *investor* as *wage* is to

    A. employee   B. salary   C. consumer
    D. price   E. employer

    8._____

9. *Terminate* is to *commence* as *adjourn* is to

    A. enact   B. convene   C. conclude
    D. veto   E. prorogue

    9._____

10. *Administrator* is to *policy* as *clerk* is to

    A. subornation   B. organization   C. coordination
    D. direction   E. application

    10._____

165

KEY (CORRECT ANSWERS)

1. E
2. D
3. C
4. A
5. C

6. B
7. C
8. A
9. B
10. E

VERBAL ANALOGIES
EXAMINATION SECTION

DIRECTIONS: Each question or incomplete statement is followed by several suggested answers or completions. Select the one that BEST answers the question or completes the statement. *PRINT THE LETTER OF THE CORRECT ANSWER IN THE SPACE AT THE RIGHT.*

Questions 1-10.

DIRECTIONS: In each of Questions 1 through 10, a pair of related words written in capital letters is followed by four other pairs of words. For each question, select the pair of words which MOST closely expresses a relationship similar to that of the pair in capital letters.

SAMPLE QUESTION:

BOAT - DOCK
- A. airplane - hangar
- B. rain - snow
- C. cloth - cotton
- D. hunger - food

Choice A is the answer to this sample question since of the choices given, the relationship between airplane and hangar is most similar to the relationship between boat and dock.

1. AUTOMOBILE - FACTORY
    - A. tea - lemon
    - B. wheel - engine
    - C. pot - flower
    - D. paper - mill

2. GIRDER - BRIDGE
    - A. petal - flower
    - B. street - sidewalk
    - C. meat - vegetable
    - D. sun - storm

3. RADIUS - CIRCLE
    - A. brick - building
    - B. tie - tracks
    - C. spoke - wheel
    - D. axle - tire

4. DISEASE - RESEARCH
    - A. death - poverty
    - B. speech - audience
    - C. problem - conference
    - D. invalid - justice

5. CONCLUSION - INTRODUCTION
    - A. commencement - beginning
    - B. housing - motor
    - C. caboose - engine
    - D. train - cabin

6. SOCIETY - LAW
    - A. baseball - rules
    - B. jury - law
    - C. cell - prisoner
    - D. sentence - jury

7. PLAN - ACCOMPLISHMENT

   A. deed - fact
   B. method - success
   C. graph - chart
   D. rules - manual

8. ORDER - GOVERNMENT

   A. chaos - administration
   B. confusion - pandemonium
   C. rule - stability
   D. despair - hope

9. TYRANNY - FREEDOM

   A. despot - mob
   B. wealth - poverty
   C. nobility - commoners
   D. dictatorship - democracy

10. TELEGRAM - LETTER

    A. hare - tortoise
    B. lie - truth
    C. number - word
    D. report - research

Questions 11-30.

DIRECTIONS: In Questions 11 through 30, the first two capitalized words have a relationship to each other. Determine the relationship, and then match the third capitalized word with the one of the lettered choice with which it has the same relationship as the words of the first pair have to each other.

11. CONGRESS is to SENATOR as CONVENTION is to

    A. election   B. chairman   C. delegate   D. nominee

12. DIVIDEND is to INVESTOR as WAGE is to

    A. employee   B. salary   C. consumer   D. price

13. TERMINATE is to COMMENCE as ADJOURN is to

    A. enact   B. convene   C. conclude   D. veto

14. SANITATION is to HEALTH as EDUCATION is to

    A. school   B. hygiene   C. knowledge   D. teacher

15. ADMINISTRATOR is to POLICY as CLERK is to

    A. subordinate
    B. organization
    C. coordination
    D. procedure

16. ALLEGIANCE is to LOYALTY as TREASON is to

    A. felony   B. faithful   C. obedience   D. rebellion

17. DIAMOND is to GLASS as PLATINUM is to

    A. jewelry   B. metal   C. aluminum   D. mine

18. WATER is to AQUEDUCT as ELECTRICITY is to

    A. meter   B. battery   C. fuse   D. wire

19. ORATORY is to FILIBUSTER as REIGN is to   19.____
    A. tyranny   B. terror   C. government   D. empire

20. GRAVITY is to GAIETY as TAUNT is to   20.____
    A. ridicule   B. console   C. avoid   D. amuse

21. ELECTRON is to ATOM as EARTH is to   21.____
    A. sun   B. solar system   C. moon   D. planet

22. FLATTERY is to PRAISE as CRUELTY is to   22.____
    A. pain   B. punishment   C. pleasantry   D. favoritism

23. ROWBOAT is to OAR as AUTOMOBILE is to   23.____
    A. land   B. engine   C. driver   D. passenger

24. FRICTION is to OIL as WAR is to   24.____
    A. conference   B. peace   C. munitions   D. satellite

25. DISEASE is to INFECTION as REACTION is to   25.____
    A. control   B. injury   C. relapse   D. stimulus

26. PERSECUTION is to MARTYR as SWINDLE is to   26.____
    A. embezzler   B. refugee   C. victim   D. bank

27. PHYSICIAN is to PATIENT as ATTORNEY is to   27.____
    A. court   B. client   C. counsel   D. judge

28. JUDGE is to SENTENCE as JURY is to   28.____
    A. court   B. foreman   C. defendant   D. verdict

29. REVERSAL is to AFFIRMANCE as CONVICTION is to   29.____
    A. appeal   B. acquittal   C. error   D. mistrial

30. GENUINE is to TRUE as SPURIOUS is to   30.____
    A. correct   B. conceived   C. false   D. speculative

KEY (CORRECT ANSWERS)

1.	D	16.	D
2.	A	17.	C
3.	C	18.	D
4.	C	19.	A
5.	C	20.	B
6.	A	21.	B
7.	B	22.	B
8.	C	23.	B
9.	D	24.	A
10.	A	25.	D
11.	C	26.	C
12.	A	27.	B
13.	B	28.	D
14.	C	29.	B
15.	D	30.	C

VERBAL ANALOGIES
EXAMINATION SECTION

DIRECTIONS: Each question or incomplete statement is followed by several suggested answers or completions. Select the one that BEST answers the question or completes the statement. *PRINT THE LETTER OF THE CORRECT ANSWER IN THE SPACE AT THE RIGHT.*

Questions 1-10.

DIRECTIONS: In each of Questions 1 through 10, a pair of related words written in capital letters is followed by four other pairs of words. For each question, select the pair of words which MOST closely expresses a relationship similar to that of the pair in capital letters.

SAMPLE QUESTION:

BOAT - DOCK
    A. airplane - hangar   B. rain - snow
    C. cloth - cotton   D. hunger - food

Choice A is the answer to this sample question since of the choices given, the relationship between airplane and hangar is most similar to the relationship between boat and dock.

1. AUTOMOBILE - FACTORY   1.____
    A. tea - lemon   B. wheel - engine
    C. pot - flower   D. paper - mill

2. GIRDER - BRIDGE   2.____
    A. petal - flower   B. street - sidewalk
    C. meat - vegetable   D. sun - storm

3. RADIUS - CIRCLE   3.____
    A. brick - building   B. tie - tracks
    C. spoke - wheel   D. axle - tire

4. DISEASE - RESEARCH   4.____
    A. death - poverty   B. speech - audience
    C. problem - conference   D. invalid - justice

5. CONCLUSION - INTRODUCTION   5.____
    A. commencement - beginning   B. housing - motor
    C. caboose - engine   D. train - cabin

6. SOCIETY - LAW   6.____
    A. baseball - rules   B. jury - law
    C. cell - prisoner   D. sentence - jury

7. PLAN - ACCOMPLISHMENT
   - A. deed - fact
   - B. method - success
   - C. graph - chart
   - D. rules - manual

8. ORDER - GOVERNMENT
   - A. chaos - administration
   - B. confusion - pandemonium
   - C. rule - stability
   - D. despair - hope

9. TYRANNY - FREEDOM
   - A. despot - mob
   - B. wealth - poverty
   - C. nobility - commoners
   - D. dictatorship - democracy

10. TELEGRAM - LETTER
    - A. hare - tortoise
    - B. lie - truth
    - C. number - word
    - D. report - research

Questions 11-30.

DIRECTIONS: In Questions 11 through 30, the first two capitalized words have a relationship to each other. Determine the relationship, and then match the third capitalized word with the one of the lettered choice with which it has the same relationship as the words of the first pair have to each other.

11. CONGRESS is to SENATOR as CONVENTION is to
    - A. election
    - B. chairman
    - C. delegate
    - D. nominee

12. DIVIDEND is to INVESTOR as WAGE is to
    - A. employee
    - B. salary
    - C. consumer
    - D. price

13. TERMINATE is to COMMENCE as ADJOURN is to
    - A. enact
    - B. convene
    - C. conclude
    - D. veto

14. SANITATION is to HEALTH as EDUCATION is to
    - A. school
    - B. hygiene
    - C. knowledge
    - D. teacher

15. ADMINISTRATOR is to POLICY as CLERK is to
    - A. subordinate
    - B. organization
    - C. coordination
    - D. procedure

16. ALLEGIANCE is to LOYALTY as TREASON is to
    - A. felony
    - B. faithful
    - C. obedience
    - D. rebellion

17. DIAMOND is to GLASS as PLATINUM is to
    - A. jewelry
    - B. metal
    - C. aluminum
    - D. mine

18. WATER is to AQUEDUCT as ELECTRICITY is to
    - A. meter
    - B. battery
    - C. fuse
    - D. wire

19. ORATORY is to FILIBUSTER as REIGN is to 19.____
    A. tyranny   B. terror   C. government   D. empire

20. GRAVITY is to GAIETY as TAUNT is to 20.____
    A. ridicule   B. console   C. avoid   D. amuse

21. ELECTRON is to ATOM as EARTH is to 21.____
    A. sun   B. solar system   C. moon   D. planet

22. FLATTERY is to PRAISE as CRUELTY is to 22.____
    A. pain   B. punishment C. pleasantry   D. favoritism

23. ROWBOAT is to OAR as AUTOMOBILE is to 23.____
    A. land   B. engine   C. driver   D. passenger

24. FRICTION is to OIL as WAR is to 24.____
    A. conference B. peace   C. munitions   D. satellite

25. DISEASE is to INFECTION as REACTION is to 25.____
    A. control   B. injury   C. relapse   D. stimulus

26. PERSECUTION is to MARTYR as SWINDLE is to 26.____
    A. embezzler   B. refugee   C. victim   D. bank

27. PHYSICIAN is to PATIENT as ATTORNEY is to 27.____
    A. court   B. client   C. counsel   D. judge

28. JUDGE is to SENTENCE as JURY is to 28.____
    A. court   B. foreman   C. defendant   D. verdict

29. REVERSAL is to AFFIRMANCE as CONVICTION is to 29.____
    A. appeal   B. acquittal   C. error   D. mistrial

30. GENUINE is to TRUE as SPURIOUS is to 30.____
    A. correct   B. conceived   C. false   D. speculative

KEY (CORRECT ANSWERS)

1.	D	16.	D
2.	A	17.	C
3.	C	18.	D
4.	C	19.	A
5.	C	20.	B
6.	A	21.	B
7.	B	22.	B
8.	C	23.	B
9.	D	24.	A
10.	A	25.	D
11.	C	26.	C
12.	A	27.	B
13.	B	28.	D
14.	C	29.	B
15.	D	30.	C

VERBAL ANALOGIES – 2 BLANKS
EXAMINATION SECTION
TEST 1

DIRECTIONS: Each question in this part consists of two capitalized words which have a certain relationship to each other, followed by four lettered pairs of words. Choose the letter of the pair of words which are related to each other in the SAME way as the words of the capitalized pair are related to each other. *PRINT THE LETTER OF THE CORRECT ANSWER IN THE SPACE AT THE RIGHT.*

1. BLUE : SKY ::

   A. new : path
   C. green : grass
   B. tiny : mountain
   D. glad : bear

   1.____

2. EATING : DINING ROOM ::

   A. waiting : restaurant
   C. sleeping : barn
   B. cooking : kitchen
   D. running : bedroom

   2.____

3. WASH : CLEAN ::

   A. iron : clothes
   C. wipe : dry
   B. scrub : repair
   D. rinse : dirty

   3.____

4. HOT : COLD ::

   A. slow : easy
   C. big : fat
   B. asleep : awake
   D. funny : quick

   4.____

5. LISTEN : RECORDS ::

   A. open : floor
   C. meet : mile
   B. jump : table
   D. watch : television

   5.____

6. LEAD : PENCIL ::

   A. match : pipe
   C. ink : pen
   B. water : pail
   D. chalk : slate

   6.____

7. DWARF : SMALL ::

   A. witch : stupid
   C. gnome : jolly
   B. clown : sad
   D. giant : tall

   7.____

8. HOME RUN : BASEBALL ::

   A. round : wrestling
   C. foul : basketball
   B. touchdown : football
   D. drive : golf

   8.____

9. CHICKEN : HATCHED ::

   A. baby : born
   C. tree : planted
   B. puppy : lost
   D. lawn : mowed

   9.____

10. REMEMBER : FORGET ::

    A. find : lose
    C. arrive : stay
    B. buy : own
    D. borrow : rent

    10.____

11. PIANO : KEY ::

    A. drum : bugle
    B. guitar : string
    C. trumpet : band
    D. violin : case

12. KNAPSACK : HIKE ::

    A. suitcase : trip
    B. sneaker : stroll
    C. canteen : journey
    D. bearer : safari

13. HEALTHY : SICK ::

    A. huge : large
    B. rapid : sudden
    C. strong : weak
    D. complete : empty

14. TENNIS : RACKET ::

    A. golf : club
    B. chess : pawn
    C. checkers : board
    D. boxing : ring

15. DORMITORY : SLEEPING ::

    A. theater : applauding
    B. classroom : learning
    C. truck : traveling
    D. market : storing

16. SQUIRREL : NUTS ::

    A. termite : wood
    B. grasshopper : sugar
    C. goat : milk
    D. mouse : cheese

17. NEEDLE : SEW ::

    A. knife : carve
    B. spoon : drink
    C. hammer : break
    D. iron : steam

18. CORN : HUSK ::

    A. pea : pod
    B. weed : flower
    C. spinach : leaf
    D. plant : stem

19. MOTOR : GASOLINE ::

    A. bicycle : spoke
    B. sailboat : wind
    C. engine : smoke
    D. sled : ice

20. WALLET : MONEY ::

    A. notebook : paper
    B. magazine : cover
    C. briefcase : leather
    D. newspaper : print

21. FISH : CAT ::

    A. worm : bird
    B. hoot : owl
    C. giraffe : beast
    D. duck : goose

22. COFFEE : BEAN ::

    A. soda : flavor
    B. cocoa : sugar
    C. tea : leaf
    D. milk : cream

23. ABSENCE : ATTENDANCE ::   23.____

    A. emptiness : fullness   B. peace : tranquility
    C. solemnity : gloom   D. happiness : cheer

24. HAMMER : CARPENTER ::   24.____

    A. saw : janitor   B. shovel : electrician
    C. wrench : plumber   D. ladle : gardener

25. TIPTOE : STAMP ::   25.____

    A. practice : play   B. sneak : attack
    C. whisper : shout   D. hum : harmonize

26. WATER : LIQUID ::   26.____

    A. wood : hard   B. cloth : pretty
    C. sand : yellow   D. rock : solid

27. BRACELET : WRIST ::   27.____

    A. crutch : leg   B. tooth : mouth
    C. lace : neck   D. ring : finger

28. FLIGHT : AIRPLANE ::   28.____

    A. track : train   B. garage : automobile
    C. voyage : ship   D. destination : bus

29. ELEPHANT : TUSK ::   29.____

    A. rabbit : hare   B. turtle : mud
    C. elk : antler   D. alligator : swamp

30. DAIRY : MILK ::   30.____

    A. farm : egg   B. bakery : bread
    C. factory : tool   D. garden : tomato

31. FIRST : LAST ::   31.____

    A. today : tomorrow   B. attempt : failure
    C. beginning : end   D. length : width

32. TEMPERATURE : THERMOMETER ::   32.____

    A. year : calendar   B. hour : second
    C. size : shape   D. weight : scale

33. BOAT : CANAL ::   33.____

    A. yacht : anchor   B. airplane : mechanic
    C. car : street   D. bus : stop

34. FUDGE : CANDY ::   34.____

    A. rice : potato   B. tuna : salmon
    C. fruit : vegetable   D. lamb : meat

35. COLLAR : DOG ::

    A. fur : fox
    B. wing : sparrow
    C. bridle : horse
    D. cage : rabbit

36. WOUND : HEAL ::

    A. bottle : break
    B. rip : mend
    C. wool : knit
    D. bump : hit

37. CATERPILLAR : BUTTERFLY ::

    A. tadpole : frog
    B. ox : antelope
    C. pony : stallion
    D. mule : zebra

38. ADMIRE : PRAISE ::

    A. dislike : criticize
    B. enjoy : memorize
    C. pretend : impress
    D. favor : persuade

39. REFEREE : ROUND ::

    A. captain : team
    B. umpire : inning
    C. swimmer : pool
    D. player : match

40. GROCER : VEGETABLES ::

    A. optometrist : eyes
    B. machinist : nails
    C. pharmacist : drugs
    D. typist : papers

41. STOVE : HEATS ::

    A. refrigerator : cools
    B. sink : drains
    C. pot : boils
    D. toaster : burns

42. GALE : WIND ::

    A. storm : weather
    B. downpour : rain
    C. humidity : moisture
    D. report : forecast

43. KNEE : FOOT ::

    A. eye : ear
    B. fist : finger
    C. knuckle : nail
    D. elbow : hand

44. BLUEPRINT : HOUSE ::

    A. script : theater
    B. map : globe
    C. skeleton : body
    D. pattern : dress

45. TREE : FOREST ::

    A. gate : wall
    B. flower : bouquet
    C. house : street
    D. oil : drop

46. GOOSE : FOWL ::

    A. crab : shellfish
    B. cow : calf
    C. eel : octopus
    D. worm : snake

47. MUSIC : HEAR ::

    A. telephone : talk   B. piano : touch
    C. quiz : solve   D. picture : see

48. ZOO : MONKEY ::

    A. carnival : balloon   B. aquarium : goldfish
    C. ranch : cowboy   D. jungle : camel

49. PAINTER : BRUSH ::

    A. sculptor : chisel   B. actor : script
    C. musician : baton   D. architect : building

50. CHUM : FRIEND ::

    A. school : vacation   B. hobby : interest
    C. game : enjoyment   D. porch : house

KEY (CORRECT ANSWERS)

1. C	11. B	21. A	31. C	41. A
2. B	12. A	22. C	32. D	42. B
3. C	13. C	23. A	33. C	43. D
4. B	14. A	24. C	34. D	44. D
5. D	15. B	25. C	35. C	45. B
6. C	16. D	26. D	36. B	46. A
7. D	17. A	27. D	37. A	47. D
8. B	18. A	28. C	38. A	48. B
9. A	19. B	29. C	39. B	49. A
10. A	20. A	30. B	40. C	50. B

TEST 2

DIRECTIONS: Each question in this part consists of two capitalized words which have a certain relationship to each other, followed by four lettered pairs of words. Choose the letter of the pair of words which are related to each other in the SAME way as the words of the capitalized pair are related to each other. *PRINT THE LETTER OF THE CORRECT ANSWER IN THE SPACE AT THE RIGHT.*

1. LEAD : PENCIL :: 1.___

    A. match : pipe   B. water : pail
    C. ink : pen   D. chalk : slate

2. DWARF : SMALL :: 2.___

    A. witch : stupid   B. clown : sad
    C. gnome : jolly   D. giant : tall

3. BOOK : WRITE :: 3.___

    A. puzzle : add   B. picture : draw
    C. building : wreck   D. road : fix

4. AIRPLANE : BIRD :: 4.___

    A. truck : eagle   B. railroad : mule
    C. submarine : fish   D. computer : owl

5. KANGAROO : HOP :: 5.___

    A. cat : wander   B. snake : crawl
    C. spider : fly   D. crow : perch

6. TENNIS : RACKET :: 6.___

    A. golf : club   B. chess : pawn
    C. croquet : wicket   D. boxing : ring

7. DINNER : BANQUET :: 7.___

    A. car : limousine   B. bus : motorcycle
    C. boat : sail   D. train : track

8. CHARIOT : HORSE :: 8.___

    A. den : bear   B. wagon : cart
    C. hutch : rabbit   D. automobile : engine

9. HEALTHY : SICK :: 9.___

    A. huge : large   B. rapid : sudden
    C. strong : weak   D. complete : empty

10. DINING ROOM : EAT :: 10.___

    A. kitchen : sit   B. porch : read
    C. bedroom : sleep   D. closet : hide

11. FOUL : FAIR :: 11.___

    A. unlawful : legal   B. good : better
    C. complex : complicated   D. near : close

12. DAGGER : SWORD ::

    A. pistol : rifle
    B. bow : arrow
    C. shell : bullet
    D. trigger : gun

    12.____

13. CAT : TIGER ::

    A. lizard : turtle
    B. dog : wolf
    C. bird : insect
    D. mare : cow

    13.____

14. DRAMATICS : THEATER ::

    A. acoustics : auditorium
    B. pediatrics : playground
    C. athletics : gymnasium
    D. economics : bank

    14.____

15. HAND BEATER : ELECTRIC MIXER ::

    A. broom : vacuum cleaner
    B. flashlight : light bulb
    C. sink : dishwasher
    D. wrench : vise

    15.____

16. COAST : OCEAN ::

    A. sand : beach
    B. grass : island
    C. tunnel : mountain
    D. bank : river

    16.____

17. PRESCRIPTION : MEDICINE ::

    A. recipe : cake
    B. food : meal
    C. pill : powder
    D. petition : name

    17.____

18. COCONUT : MILK ::

    A. grapefruit : juice
    B. peach : fuzz
    C. plum : jelly
    D. almond : nut

    18.____

19. CLASP : NECKLACE ::

    A. brooch : pin
    B. buckle : belt
    C. seam : garment
    D. thong : sandal

    19.____

20. MANUFACTURE : REFRIGERATORS ::

    A. publish : newspapers
    B. edit : manuscripts
    C. dye : fabrics
    D. repair : watches

    20.____

21. NUMB : FEELING ::

    A. blind : knowing
    B. deaf : hearing
    C. stiff : touching
    D. ill : tasting

    21.____

22. BASKETBALL : COURT ::

    A. target : revolver
    B. archery : range
    C. baseball : bleachers
    D. hockey : stick

    22.____

23. INITIATION : CLUB MEMBER ::

    A. introduction : letter
    B. imitation : mimic
    C. inauguration : president
    D. implication : speaker

    23.____

24. SAVE : WASTE ::
    A. deny : disprove   B. hoard : withhold
    C. acquire : inherit   D. accumulate : disperse

25. PRICK : PIN ::
    A. break : dish   B. cut : knife
    C. rip : scissors   D. punch : paper

26. VACATION : SCHOOL ::
    A. finale : opera   B. recess : yard
    C. margin : book   D. intermission : performance

27. LEGIBLE : WRITING ::
    A. clear : thinking   B. swift : walking
    C. soft : speaking   D. pretty : seeing

28. ORDER : DELIVER ::
    A. prepare : destroy   B. wonder : think
    C. ask : answer   D. find : lose

29. EXTORTIONIST : BLACKMAIL ::
    A. arsonist : bail   B. kidnapper : crime
    C. kleptomaniac : theft   D. bandit : reward

30. SNOWPLOW : SNOW ::
    A. crane : rocks   B. tractor : farm
    C. bulldozer : earth   D. tank : army

31. JAVELIN : THROW ::
    A. stadium : sit   B. discus : weigh
    C. rope : swing   D. hurdle : jump

32. TWINKLE : EYE ::
    A. frown : wrinkle   B. grin : mouth
    C. chuckle : laugh   D. anger : tears

33. KAYAK : CANOE ::
    A. igloo : tepee   B. bow : arrow
    C. child : papoose   D. blubber : wampum

34. BEDROCK : TOPSOIL ::
    A. cellar : garage   B. house : porch
    C. foundation : roof   D. fireplace : chimney

35. WETNESS : MONSOON ::
    A. coldness : famine   B. mildness : season
    C. windiness : rain   D. dryness : drought

36. QUARRY : GRANITE ::   36._____

    A. pond : brook   B. mine : coal
    C. granary : wheat   D. cliff : rock

37. TURPENTINE : PAINT ::   37._____

    A. polish : varnish   B. soap : dirt
    C. cleaner : floor   D. mop : rag

38. SPIKE : STAKE ::   38._____

    A. timber : lumber   B. leather : hide
    C. nail : peg   D. nut : bolt

39. BRIEFCASE : FILE CABINET ::   39._____

    A. letter : envelope   B. wallet : vault
    C. satchel : pouch   D. suitcase : luggage

40. AMATEUR : PROFESSIONAL ::   40._____

    A. teacher : professor   B. writer : editor
    C. beginner : veteran   D. prompter : understudy

41. MIRAGE : ILLUSION ::   41._____

    A. object : reality   B. happiness : tragedy
    C. plan : obstacle   D. pain : relief

42. HUSK : CORN ::   42._____

    A. seed : flower   B. leaf : stem
    C. cob : stalk   D. pod : pea

43. BUTTON : HOLE ::   43._____

    A. zipper : lining   B. snap : fastener
    C. hook : eye   D. stitch : hem

44. ATTIC : HOUSE ::   44._____

    A. peak : mountain   B. bush : tree
    C. top : bottom   D. hill : slope

45. STOMACH : DIGESTION ::   45._____

    A. blood : circulation   B. gland : sensation
    C. skeleton : posture   D. lung : respiration

46. SHIELD : PROTECTION ::   46._____

    A. armor : insulation   B. disguise : deception
    C. flag : attention   D. war : duration

47. FLICKER : FLAME ::   47._____

    A. nod : head   B. break : wave
    C. quench : fire   D. quaver : voice

48. BURLAP : SILK ::
    A. material : velvet
    C. pottery : china
    B. needle : thread
    D. plate : bowl

49. SKYSCRAPER : URBAN ::
    A. highway : metropolitan
    C. garage : surburban
    B. apartment : local
    D. silo : rural

50. CINNAMON : SPICE ::
    A. mustard : condiment
    C. liqueur : appetizer
    B. sauce : herb
    D. icing : dessert

48. ___
49. ___
50. ___

KEY (CORRECT ANSWERS)

1. C	11. A	21. B	31. D	41. A
2. D	12. A	22. B	32. B	42. D
3. B	13. B	23. C	33. C	43. C
4. C	14. C	24. D	34. C	44. A
5. B	15. A	25. B	35. D	45. D
6. A	16. A	26. D	36. B	46. B
7. A	17. A	27. A	37. B	47. B
8. D	18. A	28. A	38. C	48. C
9. C	19. A	29. C	39. B	49. D
10. C	20. A	30. C	40. C	50. A

TEST 3

DIRECTIONS: Each question in this part consists of two capitalized words which have a certain relationship to each other, followed by four lettered pairs of words. Choose the letter of the pair of words which are related to each other in the SAME way as the words of the capitalized pair are related to each other. *PRINT THE LETTER OF THE CORRECT ANSWER IN THE SPACE AT THE RIGHT.*

1. COMMA : PERIOD ::   1._____

   A. begin : cease   B. cut : sever
   C. delay : hinder   D. pause : stop

2. IRON : RUST ::   2._____

   A. steel : bend   B. silver : tarnish
   C. wood : crumble   D. gold : melt

3. RACETRACK : BET ::   3._____

   A. opera : sing   B. circus : perform
   C. auction : bid   D. bazaar : display

4. COPYRIGHT : PUBLISHED ::   4._____

   A. requirement : completed   B. patent : manufactured
   C. plaque : remembered   D. deed : purchased

5. CANARY : CAGE ::   5._____

   A. bear : cave   B. squirrel : tree
   C. horse : racecourse   D. goldfish : aquarium

6. PURITY : TAINTED ::   6._____

   A. hardiness : healthy   B. tastiness : aged
   C. freshness : stale   D. coldness : icy

7. GERM : DISINFECT ::   7._____

   A. insect : exterminate   B. fat : saturate
   C. vapor : fumigate   D. root : cultivate

8. RINK : SKATE ::   8._____

   A. stadium : sit   B. arena : cheer
   C. pool : swim   D. snow : ski

9. SKIRMISH : BATTLE ::   9._____

   A. tiff : fight   B. soldier : company
   C. advance : retreat   D. camp : fort

10. IDENTICAL : DIFFERENCES ::   10._____

    A. dynamic : exceptions   B. symmetrical : details
    C. perfect : flaws   D. intact : parts

185

11. DOCTOR : SURGEON ::

    A. artist : sculptor
    B. lawyer : official
    C. actor : director
    D. clerk : supervisor

11.____

12. FORGE : SIGNATURE ::

    A. repeat : order
    B. sketch : illustration
    C. gamble : dice
    D. counterfeit : money

12.____

13. ALMOND : NUT ::

    A. honey : flower
    B. leaf : branch
    C. apricot : fruit
    D. corn : kernel

13.____

14. FOURSOME : GOLF ::

    A. team : playing
    B. band : marching
    C. singles : serving
    D. quartet : singing

14.____

15. BUCK : DOE ::

    A. panther : cub
    B. calf : bull
    C. ram : ewe
    D. raven : crow

15.____

16. PROTECT : RESCUE ::

    A. preserve : waste
    B. procure : receive
    C. prevent : cure
    D. promote : deter

16.____

17. IRONING : WRINKLES ::

    A. dusting : mops
    B. cleaning : stains
    C. sewing : seams
    D. cooking : odors

17.____

18. BEAUTICIAN : HAIR ::

    A. barber : chin
    B. speaker : tongue
    C. manicurist : nails
    D. chiropodist : toes

18.____

19. TICK : CLOCK ::

    A. buzzer : doorbell
    B. ring : telephone
    C. tap : step
    D. pitch : voice

19.____

20. IMPOUND : DOG ::

    A. levy : revenue
    B. license : hunter
    C. imprison : person
    D. inspect : baggage

20.____

21. HAZY : SIGHT ::

    A. salty : taste
    B. pungent : smell
    C. shiny : touch
    D. muffled : sound

21.____

22. STUDENT : TUITION ::

    A. minister : collection
    B. employee : taxation
    C. traveler : trip
    D. tenant : rent

22.____

23. UMPIRE : BASEBALL :: 23._____

    A. center : basketball   B. jockey : racing
    C. referee : boxing   D. goalie : soccer

24. TOOL : HAMMER :: 24._____

    A. ornament : ribbon   B. metal : structure
    C. needle : scissors   D. velvet : sheen

25. IMPORTED : DOMESTIC :: 25._____

    A. alien : native   B. senator : enactment
    C. musician : performer   D. deacon : congregation

26. THIEF : STEALS :: 26._____

    A. perjurer : lies   B. pirate : sails
    C. murderer : hides   D. saboteur : kidnaps

27. COW : BOVINE :: 27._____

    A. kennel : canine   B. trout : aquatic
    C. cat : feline   D. bird : aerial

28. THIMBLE : FINGER :: 28._____

    A. ankles : shins   B. goggles : eyes
    C. bracelet : wrist   D. belt : waist

29. BASE : PYRAMID :: 29._____

    A. angle : corner   B. floor : room
    C. height : house   D. pot : flower

30. THEORY : APPLICATION :: 30._____

    A. thought : action   B. experiment : apparatus
    C. research : finding   D. machine : production

31. ENCYCLOPEDIA : INFORMATION :: 31._____

    A. verse : reference   B. index : definition
    C. manual : instruction   D. textbook : activity

32. CREDIBLE : CERTAIN :: 32._____

    A. possible : actual   B. indefinite : undecided
    C. careless : thoughtful   D. factual : real

33. SOPORIFIC : SLEEPINESS :: 33._____

    A. stimulant : alertness   B. tranquilizer : nervousness
    C. medicine : disease   D. aspirin : headache

34. APOLOGIZE : SORRY :: 34._____

    A. complain : discontent   B. rationalize : emotional
    C. submit : recalcitrant   D. antagonize : placid

35. INVITATION : GUEST ::

    A. mortgage : owner
    B. subpoena : witness
    C. certificate : notary
    D. diploma : graduate

    35.____

36. RUSHED : TIME ::

    A. frantic : motion
    B. busy : idea
    C. cramped : space
    D. nimble : position

    36.____

37. WARDEN : PRISON ::

    A. porter : depot
    B. janitor : office
    C. painter : gallery
    D. curator : museum

    37.____

38. ESSAY : WORD ::

    A. code : letter
    B. sonata : note
    C. graph : number
    D. algebra : line

    38.____

39. MIND : CLEVER ::

    A. soul : unseen
    B. body : agile
    C. form : slender
    D. notion : fanciful

    39.____

40. BLIGHT : PLANTS ::

    A. famine : crops
    B. drought : land
    C. plague : people
    D. fire : timber

    40.____

41. VOCALIST : SONGS ::

    A. musician : compositions
    B. engineer : highways
    C. athlete : teams
    D. orator : speeches

    41.____

42. TRIBUTE : PRAISE ::

    A. criticism : admiration
    B. denouncement : censure
    C. drama : action
    D. poetry : prose

    42.____

43. FOWL : TURKEY ::

    A. carnivore : beef
    B. legume : bean
    C. carrot : stalk
    D. head : lettuce

    43.____

44. PRIDE : CONCEIT ::

    A. humility : vanity
    B. weakness : strength
    C. prejudice : dislike
    D. caution : cowardice

    44.____

45. EQUAL : EXCEED ::

    A. colleague : friend
    B. runner-up : winner
    C. peer : superior
    D. helper : partner

    45.____

46. NATURALIZATION : CITIZENSHIP ::

    A. conversion : religion
    B. change : chameleon
    C. representation : statehood
    D. vote : franchise

    46.____

47. PIOUS : SANCTIMONIOUS ::

    A. dignified : pompous
    B. intelligent : witty
    C. skillful : nimble
    D. curious : uninformed

48. INSERT : DELETE ::

    A. approve : edit
    B. alter : revise
    C. whiten : darken
    D. lengthen : shorten

49. SHAWL : COAT ::

    A. kerchief : hat
    B. hood : cape
    C. scarf : glove
    D. boot : shoe

50. INFRACTION : LAW ::

    A. ignorance : rule
    B. faith : belief
    C. learning : education
    D. crudity : propriety

KEY (CORRECT ANSWERS)

1. D	11. A	21. D	31. C	41. A
2. B	12. D	22. D	32. A	42. B
3. C	13. C	23. C	33. A	43. B
4. D	14. D	24. A	34. A	44. D
5. D	15. C	25. A	35. D	45. C
6. C	16. C	26. A	36. C	46. A
7. A	17. B	27. C	37. D	47. A
8. C	18. C	28. B	38. B	48. D
9. A	19. B	29. B	39. B	49. B
10. C	20. C	30. A	40. A	50. A

READING COMPREHENSION
UNDERSTANDING AND INTERPRETING WRITTEN MATERIAL

STRATEGIES

SURVEYING PASSAGES, SENTENCES AS CUES

While individual readers develop unique reading styles and skills, there are some known strategies which can assist any reader in improving his or her reading comprehension and performance on the reading subtest. These strategies include understanding how single paragraphs and entire passages are structured, how the ideas in them are ordered, and how the author of the passage has connected these ideas in a logical and sequential way for the reader.

The section that follows highlights the importance of reading a passage through once for meaning, and provides instruction on careful reading for context cues within the sentences before and after the missing word.

SURVEY THE ENTIRE PASSAGE

To get a sense of the topic and the organization of ideas in a passage, it is important to survey each passage initially in its entirety and to identify the main idea. (The first sentence of a paragraph usually states the main idea.) Do not try to fill in the blanks initially. The purpose or surveying a passage is to prepare for the more careful reading which will follow. You need a sense of the big picture before you start to fill in the details; for example, a quick survey of the passage on page 11 indicate that the topic is the early history of universities. The paragraphs are organized to provide information on the origin of the first universities, the associations formed by teachers and students, the early curriculum, and graduation requirements.

READ PRECEDING SENTENCES CAREFULLY

The missing words in a passage cannot be determined by reading and understanding only the sentences in which the deletions occur. Information from the sentences which precede or follow can provide important cues to determine the correct choice. For example, if you read the first sentence from the passage about universities which contains a blank, you will notice that all the alternatives make sense if this one sentence is read in isolation:

    Nobody actually _____ them.
      A. started   B. guarded   C. blamed
      D. compared   E. remembered

The only way that you can make the correct word choice is to read the preceding sentences. In the excerpt below, notice that the first sentence tells the reader what the passage will be about: how universities developed. A key word in the first sentence is *emerged*, which is closely related in meaning to one of the five choices for the first blank. The second sentence explains the key word *emerged*, by pointing out that we have no historical record of a decree or a date indicating when the first university was established. Understanding the ideas in the first two sentences makes it possible to select the correct word for the blank. Look at the sentence with the deleted word in the context of the preceding sentences and think about why you are now able to make the correct choice.

> The first universities emerged at the end of the 11th century and beginning of the 12th. These institutions were not founded on any particular date or created by any formal action. Nobody actually _____ them.
> A. started   B. guarded   C. blamed
> D. compared   E. remembered

Started is the best choice because it fits the main idea of the passage and is closely related to the key word *emerged*.

READ THE SENTENCE WHICH FOLLOWS TO VERIFY YOUR CHOICE

The sentences which follow the one from which a word has been deleted may also provide cues to the correct choice. For example, look at an excerpt from the passage about universities again, and consider how the sentence which follows the one with the blank helps to reinforce the choice of the word *started*.

> The first universities emerged at the end of the 11th century and the beginning of the 12th. These institutions were not founded on any particular date or created by any formal action. Nobody actually _____ them. Instead, they developed gradually in places like Paris, Oxford, and Bologna, where scholars had long been teaching students.
> A. started   B. guarded   C. blamed
> D. compared   E. remembered

The words *developed gradually* mean the same as the key word *emerged*. The signal word *instead* helps to distinguish the difference between starting on a specific date as a result of some particular act or event and emerging over a period of time as a result of various factors.

Here is another example of how the sentence which follows the one from which a word is deleted might help you decide which of two good alternatives is the correct choice. This excerpt is from the practice passage about bridges (page 10).

> Bridges are built to allow a continuous flow of highway and railway traffic across water lying in their paths. But engineers cannot forget that river traffic, too, is essential to our economy. The role of _____ is important. To keep these vessels moving freely, bridges are built big enough, when possible, to let them pass underneath.
> A. wind   B. boats   C. weight
> D. wires   E. experience

After the first two sentences, the reader may be uncertain about the direction the writer intended to take in the rest of the paragraph. If the writer intended to continue the paragraph with information concerning how engineers make choices about the relative importance and requirements of land traffic and rive traffic, *experience* might be the appropriate choice for the missing word. However, the sentence following the one in which the deletion occurs makes it clear that *boats* is the correct choice. It provides the synonym *vessels*, which in the noun phrase *these vessels* must refer back to the previous sentence or sentences. The phrase *to let them pass underneath* also helps make it clear that *boats* is the appropriate choice. *Them* refers back to *these vessels* which, in turn, refers back to *boats* when the word *boats* is placed in the previous sentence. Thus, the reader may use these cohesive ties (the pronoun referents) to verify the final choice.

Even when the text following a sentence with a deletion is not necessary to choose the best alternative, it may be helpful in other ways. Specifically, complete sentences provide important transitions into a related topic which is developed in the rest of the paragraph or in the next paragraph of the same passage. For example, the first paragraph in the passage about universities ends with a sentence which introduces the term *guilds*: *But, over time, they joined together to form guilds.* Prior to this sentence, information about the slow emergence of universities and about how independently scholars had acted was introduced. The next paragraph begins with two sentences about guilds in general. Someone who had not read the last sentence in the first paragraph might have missed the link between guilds and scholars and universities and, thus, might have been unnecessarily confused.

COHESIVE TIES AS CUES

Sentences in a paragraph may be linked together by several devices called cohesive ties. Attention to these ties may provide further cues about missing words. This section will describe the different types of cohesive ties and show how attention to them can help you to select the correct word.

PERSONAL PRONOUNS

Personal pronouns (e.g., he, she, they, it, its) are often used in adjoining sentences to refer back to an already mentioned person, place, thing, or idea. The word to which the pronoun refers is called the antecedent.

Tools used in farm work changed very slowly from ancient times to the eighteenth century, and the changes were minor. Since the eighteenth century *they* have changed quickly and dramatically.

The word *they* refers back to *tools* in the example above.

In the examination reading subtest, a deleted word sometimes occurs in a sentence in which the sentence subject is a pronoun that refers back to a previously mentioned noun. You must correctly identify the referent for the particular pronoun in order to interpret the sentence and select the correct answer. Here is an example from the passage about bridges.

An ingenious engineer designed the bridge so that it did not have to be raised above traffic. Instead it was _____.
  A. burned   B. emptied   C. secured
  D. shared   E. lowered

Q. What is the antecedent of *it* in both cases in the example?
A. The antecedent, of course, is *bridge*.

DEMONSTRATIVE PRONOUNS

Demonstrative pronouns (e.g., this, that, these) are also used to refer to a specific, previously mentioned noun. They may occur alone as noun replacements, or they may accompany and modify nouns.

I like jogging, swimming, and tennis. *These* are the only sports I enjoy.

In the sentence above, the word *these* is a replacement noun. However, demonstrative pronouns may also occur as adjectives modifying nouns.

I like jogging, swimming, and tennis. *These* sports are the only ones I enjoy.

The word *these* in the example above is an adjective modifier. The word *these* in each of the two previous examples refers to *jogging, swimming,* and *tennis.*

Here is an example from the passage about universities on page 11.

Undergraduates took classes in Greek philosophy, Latin grammar, arithmetic, music, and astronomy. These were the only _____ available.
  A. rooms   B. subjects   C. clothes
  D. pens   E. company

Q. Which word is a noun replacement?
A. The word *these* is the replacement for *Greek philosophy, Latin grammar, arithmetic, music,* and *astronomy.*

Here is another example from the same passage.

The concept of a fixed program of study leading to a degree first evolved in Medieval Europe. This _____ had not appeared before.
  A. idea   B. desk   C. library   D. capital

Q. What is the antecedent of *this*?
A. The antecedent is *the concept of a fixed program of study leading to a degree*.

COMPARATIVE ADJECTIVES AND ADVERBS

When comparative adjectives and adverbs (e.g., so, such, better, more) occur, they refer to something else in the passage, otherwise a comparison could not be made.

The hotels in the city were all full; so were the motels and boarding houses.

Q. To what in the first sentence does the word *so* refer?
A. *So* tells us to compare the *motels* and *boarding houses* to the *hotels in the city*.

Q. In what way are the *hotels, motels,* and *boarding houses* similar to each other?
A. The *hotels, motels,* and *boarding houses* are similar in that they were all *full*.

Look at an example from the passage about universities.

Guilds were groups of tradespeople, somewhat akin to modern trade unions. In the Middle Ages, all the crafts had such
  A. taxes   B. secrets   C. products
  D. problems   E. organizations

Q. To what in the first sentence does the word *such* refer?
A. *Such* refers to *groups of tradespeople*.

SUBSTITUTIONS

Substitution is another form of cohesive tie. A substitution occurs when one linguistic item (e.g., a noun) is replaced by another. Sometimes the substitution provides new or contrasting information. The substitution is not identical to the original, or antecedent, idea. A frequently occurring substitution involves the use of *one*. A noun substitution may involve another member of the same class as the original one.

My car is falling apart. I need a new one.

Q. What in the first sentence is replaced in the second sentence with *one*?
A. *One* is a substitute for the specific car mentioned in the first sentence. The contrast comes from the fact that the *new one* isn't the writer's current car.

The substitution may also pinpoint a specific member of a general class.

1. There are many unusual courses available at the university this summer. The *one* I am taking is called *Death and Dying*.
2. There are many unusual courses available at the university this summer. *Some* have never been offered before.

Q. In these examples, what is the general class in the first sentence that is replaced by *one* and by *some*?
A. In both cases the words *one* and *some* replace *many unusual* courses.

SYNONYMS

Synonyms are words that have similar meaning. In the examination reading subtest, a synonym of a deleted word is sometimes found in one of the sentences before and/or after the sentence with the deletion. Examine the following excerpt from the passage about bridges again.

But engineers cannot forget that river traffic, too, is essential to our economy. The role of _____ is important. To keep these vessels moving freely, bridges are built high enough, when possible, to let them pass underneath.
  A. wind   B. boats   C. weight
  D. wires   E. experience

Q. Can you identify synonyms in the sentences, before and after the sentence containing the deletion, which are cues to the correct deleted word?

A. If you identified the correct words, you probably noticed that *river traffic* is not exactly a synonym since it is a slightly more general term than the word *boats* (the correct choice). But the word *vessels* is a direct synonym. Demonstrative pronouns (this, that, these, those) are sometimes used as modifiers for synonymous nouns in sentences which follow those containing deletions. The word *these* in *these vessels* is the demonstrative pronoun (modifier) for the synonymous noun *vessels*.

ANTONYMS

Antonyms are words of opposite meaning. In the examination reading subtest passages, antonyms may be cues for missing words. A contrasting relationship, which calls for the use of an antonym, is often signaled by the connective words *instead, however, but*, etc. Look at an excerpt from the passage about bridges.

An ingenious engineer designed the bridges so that it did not have to be raised above traffic. Instead it was
  A. burned   B. emptied   C. secured
  D. shared   E. lowered

Q: Can you identify an antonym in the first sentence for one of the five alternatives?
A. The word *raised* is an antonym for the word *lowered*.

SUBORDINATE-SUBORDINATE WORDS

In the examination reading subtest, a passage sometimes contains a general term which provides a cue that a more specific term is the appropriate alternative. At other times, the passage may contain a specific term which provides cues that a general term is the appropriate alternative for a particular deletion. The general and more specific words are said to have superordinate-subordinate relationships.

Look at Example 1 below. The more specific word *boy* in the first sentence serves as the antecedent for the more general word *child* in the second sentence. In Example 2, the relationship is reversed. In both examples, the words *child* and *boy* reflect a superordinate-subordinate relationship.

1. The *boy* climbed the tree. Then the *child* fell.
2. The *child* climbed the tree. Then the *boy* fell.

In the practice passage about bridges on Page 11, the phrase *river traffic* is a general term that is superordinate to the alternative *boats* (Item 1). Later in the passage about bridges the following sentences also contain superordinate-subordinate words:

A lift bridge was desired, but there were wartime shortages of steel and machinery needed for the towers. It was hard to find enough _____.
  A. work   B. material   C. time
  D. power   E. space

Q. Can you identify two words in the first sentence that are specific examples for the correct response in the second sentence?
A. Of course, the words *steel* and *machinery* are the specific examples for the more general term *material*.

WORDS ASSOCIATED BY ENTAILMENT

Sometimes the concept described by one word within the context of the passage entails, or implies, the concept described by another word. For example, consider again Item 7 in the practice passage about bridges. Notice how the follow-up sentence to Item 7 provides a cue to the correct response.

An ingenious engineer designed the bridge so that it did not have to be raised above traffic. Instead it was _____. It could be submerged seven meters below the surface of the river.
 A. burned B. emptied C. secured
 D. shared E. lowered

Q. What word in the sentence after the blank implies the concept of an alternative?
A. *Submerged* implies *lowered*. The concept of submerging something implies the idea of lowering the object beneath the surface of the water.

WORDS ASSOCIATED BY PART-WHOLE RELATIONSHIPS

Words may be related because they involve part of a whole and the whole itself; for example, *nose* and *face*. Words may also be related because they involve two parts of the same whole; for example, *radiator* and *muffler* both refer to parts of a car.

The captain of the ship was nervous. The storm was becoming worse and worse. The hardened man paced the _____.
 A. floor B. hall C. deck D. court

Q. Which choice has a part-whole relationship with a word in the sentences above?
A. A *deck* is a part of a *ship*. Therefore, *deck* has a part-whole relationship with *ship*.

CONJUNCTIVE AND CONNECTIVE WORDS AND PHRASES

Conjunctions or connectives are words or phrases that connect parts of sentences or parts of a passage to each other. Their purpose is to help the reader understand the logical and conceptual relationships between ideas and events within a passage. Examples of these words and phrases include coordinate conjunctions (e.g., and, but, yet), subordinate conjunctions (e.g., because, although, since, after), and other connective words and phrases (e.g., too, also, on the other hand, as a result).

Listed below are types of logical relationships expressed by conjunctive, or connective words. Also listed are examples of words used to cue relationships to the reader.

Additive and comparative words and phrases: and, in addition to, too, also, furthermore, similarly.

Adversative and contrastive words and phrases: yet, though, only, but, however, instead, rather, on the other hand, conversely.

Causal words or phrases: so, therefore, because, as a result, if…then, unless, except, in that case, under the circumstances.

Temporal words and phrases: before, after, when, while, initially, lastly, finally, until.

Examples

1. I enjoy fast-paced sports like tennis and volleyball, but my brother prefers _____ sports.
   A. running   B. slower   C. team   D. active

   Q. What is the connective word that tells you to look for a contrast relationship between the two parts of the sentence?
   A. The connective word *but* signals that a contrast relationship exists between the two parts of the sentence.

   Q. Of the four options, what is the best choice for the blank?
   A. The word *slower* is the best response here.

2. The child stepped to close to the edge of the brook. As a result, he _____ in.
   A. fell   B. waded   C. ran   D. jumped

   Q. What is the connective phrase that links the two sentences?
   A. The connective phrase *as a result* links the two sentences.

   Q. Of the four relationships of words and phrases listed previously, what kind of relationship between the two sentences does the connective phrase in the example signal to the reader?
   A. The phrase *as a result* signals that a cause and effect relationship exists between the two sentences.

   Q. Identify the correct response which makes the second sentence reflect and cause and effect relationship.
   A. The correct response is *fell*.

Understanding connectives is very important to success on the examination reading subtest. Sentences with deletions are often very closely related to adjacent sentences in meaning, and the relationships often signaled by connective words or phrases. Here is an example from the practice passage about universities.

At first, these tutors had not been associated with one another. Rather, they had been _____. But, over time, they joined together to form guilds.
   A. curious   B. poor   C. religious
   D. ready   E. independent

Q. Identify the connective and contrastive words and phrases in the example.
A. *At first* and *over time* are connective phrases that set up temporal progression. *Rather* and *but* are contrastive items. The use of *rather* in the sentence with the deletion tells the reader that the missing word has to convey a meaning in contrast to *associated with one another*. (Notice also that *rather* occurs after a negative statement.) The use of *but* in the sentence after the one with the deletion indicates that the deleted word in the previous sentence has to reflect a meaning that contrasts with *joined together*. Thus, the reader is given two substantial cues to the meaning of the missing word. *Independent* is the only choice that meets the requirement for contrastive meaning.

SAMPLE QUESTIOINS

DIRECTIONS: There are two passages on the following pages. In each passage some words are missing. Wherever a word is missing, there is a blank line with a number on it. Below the passage you will find the same number and five words. Choose the word that makes the best sense in the blank. You may not be sure of the answer to a question until you read the sentences that come after the blank, so be sure to read enough to answer the questions. As you work on these passages, you will find that the second passage is harder to read than the first. Answer as many questions as you can.

    Bridges are built to allow a continuous flow of highway and railway traffic across water lying in their paths. But engineers cannot forget that river traffic, too, is essential to our economy. The role of __1__ is important. To keep these vessels moving freely, bridges are built high enough, when possible, to let them pass underneath. Sometimes, however, channels must accommodate very tall ships. It may be uneconomical to build a tall enough bridge. The __2__ would be too high. To save money, engineers build movable bridges.

    In the swing bridge, the middle part pivots or swings open. When the bridge is closed, this section joins the two ends of the bridge, blocking tall vessels. But this section __3__. When swung open, it is perpendicular to the ends of the bridge, creating two free channels for river traffic. With swing bridges channel width is limited by the bridge's piers. The largest swing bridge provides only a 75-meter channel. Such channels are sometimes __4__. In such cases, a bascule bridge may be built.

    Bascule bridges are drawbridges with two arms that swing upward. They provide an opening as wide as the span. They are also versatile. These bridges are not limited to being fully opened or fully closed. They can be __5__ in many ways. They can be fixed at different angles to accommodate different vessels.

    In vertical lift bridges, the center remains horizontal. Towers at both ends allow the center to be lifted like an elevator. One interesting variation of this kind of bridge was built during World War II. A lift bridge was desired, but there were wartime shortages of the steel and machinery needed for the towers. It was hard enough to find enough __6__. An ingenious engineer designed the bridge so that it did not have to be raised above traffic. Instead it was __7__. It could be submerged seven meters below the surface of the river. Ships sailed over it.

1.   A. wind   B. boats   C. experience   1._____
     D. wires   E. experience

2.   A. levels   B. cost   C. standards   2._____
     D. waves   E. deck

3.   A. stands   B. floods   C. wears   3._____
     D. turns   E. supports

4.   A. narrow   B. rough   C. long   4._____
     D. deep   E. straight

5.   A. crossed   B. approached   C. lighted   5._____
     D. planned   E. positioned

6. A. work   B. material   C. time   6._____
    D. power   E. space

7. A. burned   B. emptied   C. secured   7._____
    D. shared   E. lowered

The first universities emerged at the end of the 11th century and beginning of the 12th. These institutions were not founded on any particular date or created by any formal action. Nobody actually __8__ them. Instead, they developed gradually in places like Paris, Oxford, and Bologna, where scholars had long been teaching students. At first, these tutors had not been associated with one another. Rather, they had been __9__. But, over time, they joined together to form guilds.

Guilds were groups of tradespeople, somewhat akin to modern unions. In the Middle Ages, all the crafts had such __10__. The scholars' guilds built school buildings and evolved an administration which charged fees and set standards for the curriculum. It set prices for members' services and fixed requirements for entering the profession.

Professors were not the only schoolpeople forming associations. In Italy, students joined guilds to which teachers had to swear obedience. The students set strict rules, fining professors for beginning class a minute late. Teachers had to seek their students' permission to marry, and such permission was not always granted. Sometimes the students __11__. Even if they said yes, the teacher got only one day's honeymoon.

Undergraduates took classes in Greek philosophy, Latin grammar, arithmetic, music, and astronomy. These were the only __12__ available. More advanced study was possible in law, medicine, and theology, but one could not earn such postgraduate degrees quickly. It took a long time to __13__. Completing the requirements in theology, for example, took at least 13 years.

The concept of a fixed program of study leading to a degree first evolved in medieval Europe. This __14__ had not appeared before, in earlier academic settings, notions about *meeting requirements meeting requirements* and *graduating* had been absent. Since the middle ages, though, we have continued to view education as a set curriculum culminating in a degree.

8. A. started   B. guarded   C. blamed   8._____
    D. compared   E. remembered

9. A. curious   B. poor   C. religious   9._____
    D. ready   E. independent

10. A. taxes   B. secrets   C. products   10._____
    D. problems   E. organizations

11. A. left   B. copied   C. refused   11._____
    D. paid   E. prepared

12. A. rooms   B. subjects   C. clothes   12._____
    D. pens   E. markets

13. A. add   B. answer   C. forget   13._____
    D. finish   E. travel

14. A. idea   B. desk   C. library   14.____
    D. capital   E. company

KEY (CORRECT ANSWERS)

1.	B	6.	B	11.	C
2.	B	7.	E	12.	B
3.	D	8.	A	13.	D
4.	A	9.	E	14.	A
5.	E	10.	E		

READING COMPREHENSION
UNDERSTANDING AND INTERPRETING WRITTEN MATERIAL
EXAMINATION SECTION
TEST 1

DIRECTIONS: Each question has five suggested answers, lettered A to E. Decide which one is the BEST answer. *PRINT THE LETTER OF THE CORRECT ANSWER IN THE SPACE AT THE RIGHT.*

1. Some specialists are willing to give their services to the Government entirely free of charge; some feel that a nominal salary, such as will cover traveling expenses, is sufficient for a position that is recognized as being somewhat honorary in nature; many other specialists value their time so highly that they will not devote any of it to public service that does not repay them at a rate commensurate with the fees that they can obtain from a good private clientele.
   The paragraph BEST supports the statement that the use of specialists by the Government
   A. is rare because of the high cost of securing such persons
   B. may be influenced by the willingness of specialists to serve
   C. enables them to secure higher salaries in private fields
   D. has become increasingly common during the past few years
   E. always conflicts with private demands for their services

   1.____

2. The fact must not be overlooked that only about one-half of the international trade of the world crosses the oceans. The other half is merely exchanges of merchandise between countries lying alongside each other or at least within the same continent.
   The paragraph BEST supports the statement that
   A. the most important part of any country's trade is transoceanic
   B. domestic trade is insignificant when compared with foreign trade
   C. the exchange of goods between neighboring countries is not considered international trade
   D. foreign commerce is not necessarily carried on by water
   E. about one-half of the trade of the world is international

   2.____

3. Individual differences in mental traits assume importance in fitting workers to jobs because such personal characteristics are persistent and are relatively little influenced by training and experience.
   The paragraph BEST supports the statement that training and experience
   A. are limited in their effectiveness in fitting workers to jobs
   B. do not increase a worker's fitness for a job
   C. have no effect upon a person's mental traits
   D. have relatively little effect upon the individual's chances for success
   E. should be based on the mental traits of an individual

   3.____

4. The competition of buyers tends to keep prices up, the competition of sellers to send them down. Normally, the pressure of competition among sellers is stronger than that among buyers since the seller has his article to sell and must get rid of it, whereas the buyer is not committed to anything.
The paragraph BEST supports the statement that low prices are caused by
   A. buyer competition
   B. competition of buyers with sellers
   C. fluctuations in demand
   D. greater competition among sellers than among buyers
   E. more sellers than buyers

5. In seventeen states, every lawyer is automatically a member of the American Bar Association. In some other states and localities, truly representative organizations of the Bar have not yet come into being, but are greatly needed.
The paragraph IMPLIES that
   A. representative Bar Associations are necessary in states where they do not now exist
   B. every lawyer is required by law to become a member of the Bar
   C. the Bar Association is a democratic organization
   D. some states have more lawyers than others
   E. every member of the American Bar Association is automatically a lawyer in seventeen states

KEY (CORRECT ANSWERS)

1. B
2. D
3. A
4. D
5. A

TEST 2

DIRECTIONS: Each question has five suggested answers, lettered A to E. Decide which one is the BEST answer. *PRINT THE LETTER OF THE CORRECT ANSWER IN THE SPACE AT THE RIGHT.*

1. We hear a great deal about the new education, and see a great deal of it in action. But the school house, though prodigiously magnified in scale, is still very much the same old school house.
   The paragraph IMPLIES
   A. the old education was, after all, better than the new
   B. although the modern school buildings are larger than the old ones, they have not changed very much in other respects
   C. the old school houses do not fit in with modern educational theories
   D. a fine school building does not make up for poor teachers
   E. schools will be schools

   1.____

2. No two human beings are of the same pattern—not even twins and the method of bringing out the best in each one necessarily according to the nature of the child.
   The paragraph IMPLIES that
   A. individual differences should be considered in dealing with children
   B. twins should be treated impartially
   C. it is an easy matter to determine the special abilities of children
   D. a child's nature varies from year to year
   E. we must discover the general technique of dealing with children

   2.____

3. Man inhabits today a world very different from that which encompassed even his parents and grandparents. It is a world geared to modern machinery—automobiles, airplanes, power plants; it is linked together and served by electricity.
   The paragraph IMPLIES that
   A. the world has no changed much during the last few generations
   B. modern inventions and discoveries have brought about many changes in man's way of living
   C. the world is run more efficiently today than it was in our grandparents' time
   D. man is much happier today than he was a hundred years ago
   E. we must learn to see man as he truly is, underneath the veneers of man's contrivances

   3.____

4. Success in any study depends largely upon the interest taken in that particular subject by the student. This being the case, each teacher earnestly hopes that her students will realize at the vey onset that shorthand can be made an intensely fascinating study.
   The paragraph IMPLIES that
   A. Everyone is interested in shorthand
   B. success in a study is entirely impossible unless the student finds the study very interesting

   4.____

205

C. if a student is eager to study shorthand, he is likely to succeed in it
D. shorthand is necessary for success
E. anyone who is not interested in shorthand will not succeed in business

5. The primary purpose of all business English is to move the reader to agreeable and mutually profitable action. This action may be indirect or direct, but in either case a highly competitive appeal for business should be clothed with incisive diction tending to replace vagueness and doubt with clarity, confidence, and appropriate action.
The paragraph IMPLIES that the
   A. ideal business letter uses words to conform to the reader's language level
   B. business correspondent should strive for conciseness in letter writing
   C. keen competition of today has lessened the value of the letter as an appeal for business
   D. writer of a business letter should employ incisive diction to move the reader to compliant and gainful action
   E. the writer of a business letter should be himself clear, confident, and forceful

5.____

KEY (CORRECT ANSWERS)

1. B
2. A
3. B
4. C
5. D

TEST 3

DIRECTIONS: Each question has five suggested answers, lettered A to E. Decide which one is the BEST answer. *PRINT THE LETTER OF THE CORRECT ANSWER IN THE SPACE AT THE RIGHT.*

1. To serve the community best, a comprehensive city plan must coordinate all physical improvements, even at the possible expense of subordinating individual desires, to the end that a city may grow in a more orderly way and provide adequate facilities for its people
   The paragraph IMPLIES that
   A. city planning provides adequate facilities for recreation
   B. a comprehensive city plan provides the means for a city to grow in a more orderly fashion
   C. individual desires must always be subordinated to civic changes
   D. the only way to serve a community is to adopt a comprehensive city plan
   E. city planning is the most important function of city government

   1.____

2. Facility in writing letters, the knack of putting into these quickly written letters the same personal impression that would mark an interview, and the ability to boil down to a one-page letter the gist of what might be called a five- or ten-minute conversation —all these are essential to effective work under conditions of modern business organization.
   The paragraph IMPLIES that
   A. letters are of more importance in modern business activities than ever before
   B. letters should be used in place of interviews
   C. the ability to write good letters is essential to effective work in modern business organization
   D. business letters should never be more than one page in length
   E. the person who can write a letter with great skill will get ahead more readily than others

   2.____

3. The general rule is that it is the city council which determines the amount to be raised by taxation and which therefore determines, within the law, the tax rates. As has been pointed out, however, no city council or city authority has the power to determine what kind of taxes should be levied.
   The paragraph IMPLIES that
   A. the city council has more authority than any other municipal body
   B. while the city council has a great deal of authority in the levying of taxes, its power is not absolute
   C. the kinds of taxes levied in different cities vary greatly
   D. the city council appoints the tax collectors
   E. the mayor determines the kinds of taxes to be levied

   3.____

4. The growth of modern business has made necessary mass production, mass distribution, and mass selling. As a result, the problems of personnel and industrial relations have increased so rapidly that grave injustice in the handling of personal relationships have frequently occurred. Personnel administration is complex because, as in all human problems, many intangible elements are involved. Therefore a thorough, systematic, and continuous study of the psychology of human behavior is essential to the intelligent handling of personnel.
   The paragraph IMPLIES that
   A. complex modern industry makes impossible the personal relationships which formerly existed between employer and employee
   B. mass decisions are successfully applied to personnel problems
   C. the human element in personnel administration makes continuous study necessary to is intelligent application
   D. personnel problems are less important than the problems of mass production and mass distribution
   E. since personnel administration is so complex and costly, it should be subordinated to the needs of good industrial relations

4.____

5. The Social Security Act is striving toward the attainment of economic security for the individual and for his family. It was stated, in outlining this program, that security for the individual and for the family concerns itself with three factors: (1) decent homes to live in; (2) development of the natural resources of the country so as to afford the fullest opportunity to engage in productive work; and (3) safeguards against the major misfortunes of life. The Social Security Act is concerned with the third of these factors —"safeguards against misfortunes which cannot be wholly eliminated in this man-made world of ours."
   The paragraph IMPLIES that the
   A. Social Security Act is concerned primarily with supplying to families decent homes in which to live
   B. development of natural resources is the only means of offering employment to the masses of the unemployed
   C. Social Security Act has attained absolute economic security for the individual and his family
   D. Social Security Act deals with the first (1) factor as stated in the paragraph above
   E. Social Security Act deals with the third (3) factor as stated in the paragraph above

5.____

KEY (CORRECT ANSWERS)

1. B
2. C
3. B
4. C
5. E

TEST 4

DIRECTIONS: Each question has five suggested answers, lettered A to E. Decide which one is the BEST answer. *PRINT THE LETTER OF THE CORRECT ANSWER IN THE SPACE AT THE RIGHT.*

PASSAGE 1

Free unrhymed verse has been practiced for some thousands of years and reaches back to the incantation which linked verse with the ritual dance. It provided a communal emotion; the aim of the cadenced phrases was to create a state of mind. The general coloring of free rhythms in the poetry of today is that of speech rhythm, composed in the sequence of the musical phrase, not in the sequence of the metronome, the regular beat. In the twenties, conventional rhyme fell into almost complete disuse. This liberation from rhyme became as well a liberation of rhyme. Freed of its exacting task of supporting lame verse, it would be applied with greater effect where wanted for some special effect. Such break in the tradition of rhymed verse had the healthy effect of giving it a fresh start, released from the hampering convention of too familiar cadences. This refreshing and subtilizing of the use of rhythm can be seen everywhere in the poetry today.

1. The title below that BEST expresses the ideas of this paragraph is:
   A. Primitive Poetry
   B. The Origin of Poetry
   C. Rhyme and Rhythm in Modern Verse
   D. Classification of Poetry
   E. Purposes in All Poetry

2. Free verse had its origin in primitive
   A. fairytales   B. literature   C. warfare
   D. chants   E. courtship

3. The object of early free verse was to
   A. influence the mood of the people   B. convey ideas
   C. produce mental pictures   D. create pleasing sounds
   E. provide enjoyment

PASSAGE 2

Control of the Mississippi had always been goals of nations having ambitions in the New World. LaSalle claimed it for France in 1682. Iberville appropriated it to France when he colonized Louisiana in 1700. Bienville founded New Orleans, its principal port, as a French city in 1718. The fleur-de-lis were the blazon of the delta country until 1762. Then Spain claimed all of Louisiana. The Spanish were easy neighbors. American products from western Pennsylvania and the Northwest Territory were barged down the Ohio and Mississippi to New Orleans; here they were reloaded on ocean-going vessels that cleared for the great seaports of the world.

4. The title below that BEST expresses the ideas of this paragraph is:
   A. Importance of Seaports
   B. France and Spain in the New World
   C. Early Control of the Mississippi
   D. Claims of European Nations
   E. American Trade on the Mississippi

5. Until 1762, the lower Mississippi area was held by
   A. England   B. Spain   C. the United States
   D. France   E. Indians

6. In doing business with Americans, the Spaniards were
   A. easy to outsmart
   B. friendly to trade
   C. inclined to charge high prices for use of their ports
   D. shrewd
   E. suspicious

PASSAGE 3

Our humanity is by no means so materialistic as foolish talk is continually asserting it to be. Judging by what I have learned about men and women, I am convinced that there is far more in them of idealistic willpower than ever comes to the surface of the world. Just as the water of streams is small in amount compared to that which flows underground, so the idealism which becomes visible is small in amount compared with that which men and women bear locked in their hearts, unreleased or scarcely released. To unbind what is bound, to bring the underground waters to the surface—mankind is waiting and longing for men who can do that.

7. The title below that BEST expresses the ideas of the paragraph is:
   A. Releasing Underground Riches
   B. The Good and Bad in Man
   C. Materialism in Humanity
   D. The Surface and the Depths of Idealism
   E. Unreleased Energy

8. Human beings are more idealistic than
   A. the water in underground streams
   B. their waiting and longing proves
   C. outward evidence shows
   D. the world
   E. other living creatures

PASSAGE 4

The total impression made by any work of fiction cannot be rightly understood without a sympathetic perception of the artistic aims of the writer. Consciously or unconsciously, he has accepted certain facts, and rejected or suppressed other facts, in order to give unity to the particular aspect of human life which he is depicting. No novelist possesses the impartiality, the indifference, the infinite tolerance of nature. Nature displays to use, with complete unconcern, the beautiful and the ugly, the precious and the trivial, the pure and the impure. But a writer must select the aspects of nature and human nature which are demanded by the work in hand. He is forced to select, to combine, to create.

9. The title below that BEST expresses the ideas of this paragraph is: 9.____
   A. Impressionists in Literature
   B. Nature as an Artist
   C. The Novelist as an Imitator
   D. Creative Technic of the Novelist
   E. Aspects of Nature

10. A novelist rejects some facts because they 10.____
    A. are impure and ugly
    B. would show he is not impartial
    C. are unrelated to human nature
    D. would make a bad impression
    E. mar the unity of his story

11. It is important for a reader to know 11.____
    A. the purpose of the author
    B. what facts the author omits
    C. both the ugly and the beautiful
    D. something about nature
    E. what the author thinks of human nature

PASSAGE 5

If you watch a lamp which is turned very rapidly on and off, and you keep your eyes open, "persistence of vision" will bridge the gaps of darkness between the flashes of light, and the lamp will seem to be continuously lit. This "topical afterglow" explains the magic produced by the stroboscope, a new instrument which seems to freeze the swiftest motions while they are still going on, and to stop time itself dead in its tracks. The "magic" is all in the eye of the beholder.

12. The "magic" of the stroboscope is due to 12.____
    A. continuous lighting
    B. intense cold
    C. slow motion
    D. behavior of the human eye
    E. a lapse of time

13. "Persistence of vision" is explained by 13.____
    A. darkness
    B. winking
    C. rapid flashes
    D. gaps
    E. after impression

KEY (CORRECT ANSWERS)

1.	C	6.	B	11.	A
2.	D	7.	D	12.	D
3.	A	8.	C	13.	E
4.	C	9.	D		
5.	D	10.	E		

TEST 5

DIRECTIONS: Each question has five suggested answers, lettered A to E. Decide which one is the BEST answer. *PRINT THE LETTER OF THE CORRECT ANSWER IN THE SPACE AT THE RIGHT.*

PASSAGE 1

During the past fourteen years, thousands of top-lofty United States elms have been marked for death by the activities of the tiny European elm bark beetle. The beetles, however, do not do fatal damage. Death is caused by another importation, Dutch elm disease, a fungus infection which the beetles carry from tree to tree. Up to 1941, quarantine and tree-sanitation measures kept the beetles and the disease pretty well confined within 510 miles around metropolitan New York. War curtailed these measures and made Dutch elm disease a wider menace. Every household and village that prizes an elm-shaded lawn or commons must now watch for it. Since there is as yet no cure for it, the infected trees must be pruned or felled, and the wood must be burned in order to protect other healthy trees.

1. The title below that BEST expresses the ideas of this paragraph is: 1.____
   A. A Menace to Our Elms
   B. Pests and Diseases of the Elm
   C. Our Vanishing Elms
   D. The Need to Protect Dutch Elms
   E. How Elms are Protected

2. The danger of spreading the Dutch elm disease was increased by 2.____
   A. destroying infected trees   B. the war
   C. the lack of a cure   D. a fungus infection
   E. quarantine measures

3. The European elm bark beetle is a serious threat to our elms because it 3.____
   A. chews the bark
   B. kills the trees
   C. is particularly active on the eastern seaboard
   D. carries infection
   E. cannot be controlled

PASSAGE 2

It is elemental that the greater the development of man, the greater the problems he has to concern him. When he lived in a cave with stone implements, his mind no less than his actions was grooved into simple channels. Every new invention, every new way of doing things posed fresh problems for him. And, as he moved along the road, he questioned each step, as indeed he should, for he trod upon the beliefs of his ancestors. It is equally elemental to say that each step upon this later road posed more questions than the earlier ones. It is only the educated man who realizes the results of his actions; it is only the thoughtful one who questions his own decisions.

4. The title below that BEST expresses the ideas of this paragraph is:
   A. Channels of Civilization
   B. The Mark of a Thoughtful Man
   C. The Cave Man in Contrast with Man Today
   D. The Price of Early Progress
   E. Man's Never-Ending Challenge

PASSAGE 3

Spring is one of those things that man has no hand in, any more than he has a part in sunrise or the phases of the moon. Spring came before man was here to enjoy it, and it will go right on coming even if man isn't here some time in the future. It is a matter of solar mechanics and celestial order. And for all our knowledge of astronomy and terrestrial mechanics, we haven't yet been able to do more than bounce a radar beam off the moon. We couldn't alter the arrival of the spring equinox by as much as one second, if we tried.

Spring is a matter of growth, of chlorophyll, of bud and blossom. We can alter growth and change the time of blossoming in individual plants; but the forests still grow in nature's way, and the grass of the plains hasn't altered its nature in a thousand years. Spring is a magnificent phase of the cycle of nature; but man really hasn't any guiding or controlling hand in it. He is here to enjoy it and benefit by it. And April is a good time to realize it; by May perhaps we will want to take full credit.

5. The title below that BEST expresses the ideas of this passage is:
   A. The Marvels of the Spring Equinox
   B. Nature's Dependence on Mankind
   C. The Weakness of Man Opposed to Nature
   D. The Glories of the World
   E. Eternal Growth

6. The author of the passage states that
   A. man has a part in the phases of the moon
   B. April is a time for taking full-credit
   C. April is a good time to enjoy nature
   D. man has a guiding hand in spring
   E. spring will cease to be if civilization ends

PASSAGE 4

The walled medieval town was as characteristic of its period as the cut of a robber baron's beard. It sprang out of the exigencies of war, and it was not without its architectural charm, whatever is hygienic deficiencies may have been. Behind its high, thick walls not only the normal inhabitants but the whole countryside fought and cowered in an hour of need. The capitals of Europe now forsake the city when the sirens scream and death from the sky seems imminent. Will the fear of bombs accelerate the slow decentralization which began with the automobile and the wide distribution of electrical energy and thus reverse the medieval flow to the city?

7. The title below that BEST expresses the ideas in this paragraph is: 7.____
   A. A Changing Function of the Town
   B. The Walled Medieval Town
   C. The Automobile's Influence on City Life
   D. Forsaking the City
   E. Bombs Today and Yesterday

8. Conditions in the Middle Ages made the walled town 8.____
   A. a natural development
   B. the most dangerous of all places
   C. a victim of fires
   D. lacking in architectural charm
   E. healthful

9. Modern conditions may 9.____
   A. make cities larger
   B. make cities more hygienic
   C. protect against floods
   D. cause people to move from population centers
   E. encourage good architecture

PASSAGE 5

The literary history of this nation began when the first settler from abroad of sensitive mind paused in his adventure long enough to feel that he was under a different sky, breathing new air and that a New World was all before him with only his strength and Providence for guides. With him began a new emphasis upon an old theme in literature, the theme of cutting loose and faring forth, renewed, under the powerful influence of a fresh continent for civilized literature, whose other flow has come from a nostalgia for the rich culture of Europe, so much of which was perforce left behind.

10. The title below that BEST expresses the ideas of this paragraph is: 10.____
    A. America's Distinctive Literature   B. Pioneer Authors
    C. The Dead Hand of the Past   D. Europe's Literary Grandchild
    E. America Comes of Age

11. American writers, according to the author, because of their colonial experiences 11.____
    A. were antagonistic to European writers
    B. cut loose from Old World influences
    C. wrote only on New World events and characters
    D. created new literary themes
    E. gave fresh interpretation to an old literary idea

KEY (CORRECT ANSWERS)

1. A
2. B
3. D
4. E
5. C
6. C
7. A
8. A
9. D
10. A
11. E

TEST 6

DIRECTIONS: Each question has five suggested answers, lettered A to E. Decide which one is the BEST answer. *PRINT THE LETTER OF THE CORRECT ANSWER IN THE SPACE AT THE RIGHT.*

1. Any business not provided with capable substitutes to fill all important positions is a weak business. Therefore, a foreman should train each man not on to perform his own particular duties but also to do those of two or three positions.
The paragraph BEST supports the statement that
    A. dependence on substitutes is a sign of weak organization
    B. training will improve the strongest organization
    C. the foreman should be the most expert at any particular job under him
    D. every employee can be trained to perform efficiency work other than his own
    E. vacancies in vital positions should be provided for in advance

    1.____

2. The coloration of textile fabrics composed of cotton and wool generally requires two processes, as the process used in dyeing wool is seldom capable of fixing the color upon cotton. The usual method is to immerse the fabric in the requisite baths to dye the wool and then to treat the partially dyed material in the manner found suitable for cotton.
The paragraph BEST supports the statement that the dyeing of textile fabrics composed of cotton and wool is
    A. less complicated than the dyeing of wool alone
    B. more successful when the material contains more cotton than wool
    C. not satisfactory when solid colors are desired
    D. restricted to two colors for any one fabric
    E. usually based upon the methods required for dyeing the different materials

    2.____

3. The serious investigator must direct his whole effort toward success in his work. If he wishes to succeed in each investigation, his work will be by no means easy, smooth, or peaceful; on the contrary, he will have to devote himself completely and continuously to a task that requires all his ability.
The paragraph BEST supports the statement that an investigator's success depends most upon
    A. ambition to advance rapidly in the service
    B. persistence in the face of difficulty
    C. training and experience
    D. willingness to obey orders without delay
    E. the number of investigations which he conducts

    3.____

4. Honest people in one nation find it difficult to understand the viewpoint of honest people in another. State departments and their ministers exist for the purpose of explaining the viewpoints of one nation in terms understood by another. Some of their most important work lies in this direction.

    4.____

217

The paragraph BEST supports the statement that
- A. people of different nations may not consider matters in the same light
- B. it is unusual for many people to share similar ideas
- C. suspicion prevents understanding between nations
- D. the chief work of state departments is to guide relations between nations united by a common cause
- E. the people of one nation must sympathize with the viewpoints of others

5. Economy once in a while is just not enough. I expect to find it at every level of responsibility, from cabinet member to the newest and youngest recruit. Controlling waste is something like bailing a boat; you have to keep at it. I have no intention of easing up on my insistence on getting a dollar of value for each dollar we spend.
The paragraph BEST supports the statement that
- A. we need not be concerned about items which cost less than a dollar
- B. it is advisable to buy the cheaper of two items
- C. the responsibility of economy is greater at high levels than at low levels
- D. economy becomes easy with practice
- E. economy is a continuing responsibility

KEY (CORRECT ANSWERS)

1. E
2. E
3. B
4. A
5. E

TEST 7

DIRECTIONS: Each question has five suggested answers, lettered A to E. Decide which one is the BEST answer. *PRINT THE LETTER OF THE CORRECT ANSWER IN THE SPACE AT THE RIGHT.*

1. On all permit imprint mail the charge for postage has been printed by the mailer before he presents it for mailing and pays the postage. Such mail of any class is mailable only at the post office that issued a permit covering it. Since the postage receipts for such mail represent only the amount of permit imprint mail detected and verified, employees in receiving, handling, and outgoing sections must be alert constantly to route such mail to the weighing section before it is handled or dispatched.
   The paragraph BEST supports the statement that, at post offices where permit mail is received for dispatch,
   A. dispatching units make a final check on the amount of postage payable on permit imprint mail
   B. employees are to check the postage chargeable on mail received under permit
   C. neither more nor less postage is to be collected than the amount printed on permit imprint mail
   D. the weighing section is primarily responsible for failure to collect postage on such mail
   E. unusual measures are taken to prevent unstamped mail from being accepted

1.____

2. Education should not stop when the individual has been prepared to make a livelihood and to live in modern society. Living would be mere existence were there were no appreciation and enjoyment of the riches of art, literature, and science.
   The paragraph BEST supports the statement that true education
   A. is focused on the routine problems of life
   B. prepares one for full enjoyment of life
   C. deals chiefly with art, literature, and science
   D. is not possible for one who does not enjoy scientific literature
   E. disregards practical ends

2.____

3. Insured and c.o.d. air and surface mail is accepted with the understanding that the sender guarantees any necessary forwarding or return postage. When such mail is forwarded or returned, it shall be rated up for collection of postage; except that insured or c.o.d. air mail weighing 8 ounces or less and subject to the 40 cents an ounce rate shall be forwarded by air if delivery will be advanced, and returned by surface means without additional postage.
   The paragraph BEST supports the statement that the return postage for undeliverable insured mail is
   A. included in the original prepayment on air mail parcels
   B. computed but not collected before dispatching surface patrol post mail to sender

3.____

219

C. not computed or charged for any air mail that is returned by surface transportation
D. included in the amount collected when the sender mails parcel post
E. collected before dispatching for return if any amount due has been guaranteed

4. All undeliverable first-class mail, except first-class parcels and parcel post paid with first-class postage, which cannot be returned to the sender, is sent to a dead-letter branch. Undeliverable matter of the third- and fourth-classes of obvious value for which the sender does not furnish return postage and undeliverable first-class parcels and parcel-post matter bearing postage of the first-class, which cannot be returned, is sent to a dead parcel-post branch.
The paragraph BEST supports the statement that matter that is sent to a dead parcel-post branch includes all undeliverable
   A. mail, except for first-class letter mail, that appears to be valuable
   B. mail, except that of the first-class, on which the sender failed to prepay the original mailing costs
   C. parcels on which the mailer prepaid the first-class rate of postage
   D. third- and fourth-class matter on which the required return postage has not been paid
   E. parcels on which first-class postage has been prepaid, when the sender's address is not known

5. Civilization started to move rapidly when man freed himself of the shackles that restricted his search for truth.
The passage BEST supports the statement that the progress of civilization
   A. came as a result of man's dislike for obstacles
   B. did not begin until restrictions on learning were removed
   C. has been aided by man's efforts to find the truth
   D. is based on continually increasing efforts
   E. continues at a constantly increasing rate

KEY (CORRECT ANSWERS)

1. B
2. B
3. B
4. E

TEST 8

DIRECTIONS: Each question has five suggested answers, lettered A to E. Decide which one is the BEST answer. *PRINT THE LETTER OF THE CORRECT ANSWER IN THE SPACE AT THE RIGHT.*

1. E-mails should be clear, concise, and brief. Omit all unnecessary words. The parts of speech most often used in e-mails are nouns, verbs, adjectives, and adverbs. If possible, do without pronouns, prepositions, articles, and copulative verbs. Use simple sentences, rather than complex and compound.
    The paragraph BEST supports the statement that in writing e-mails one should always use
    A. common and simple words
    B. only nouns, verbs, adjectives, and adverbs
    C. incomplete sentences
    D. only words essential to the meaning
    E. the present tense of verbs

    1.____

2. The function of business is to increase the wealth of the country and the value and happiness of life. It does this by supplying the material needs of men and women. When the nation's business is successfully carried on, it renders public service of the highest value.
    The paragraph BEST supports the statement that
    A. all businesses which render public service are successful
    B. human happiness is enhanced only by the increase of material wants
    C. the value of life is increased only by the increase of wealth
    D. the material needs of men and women are supplied by well-conducted business
    E. business is the only field of activity which increases happiness

    2.____

3. In almost every community, fortunately, there are certain men and women known to be public-spirited. Others, however, may be selfish and act only as their private interests seem to require.
    The paragraph BEST supports the statement that those citizens who disregard others are
    A. fortunate   B. needed
    C. found only in small communities   D. not known
    E. not public spirited

    3.____

KEY (CORRECT ANSWERS)

1. D
2. D
3. E

READING COMPREHENSION
UNDERSTANDING AND INTERPRETING WRITTEN MATERIAL
EXAMINATION SECTION
TEST 1

DIRECTIONS: Each question or incomplete statement is followed by several suggested answers or completions. Select the one that BEST answers the question or completes the statement. *PRINT THE LETTER OF THE CORRECT ANSWER IN THE SPACE AT THE RIGHT.*

Question 1.
DIRECTIONS: Question 1 is to be answered on the basis of the following passage.

    Skiing has recently become one of the more popular sports in the United States. Because of its popularity, thousands of winter vacationers are flying north rather than south. In many areas, reservations are required months ahead of time.
    I discovered the accommodation shortage through an unfortunate experience. On a sunny Saturday morning, I set out from Denver for the beckoning slopes of Aspen, Colorado. After passing signs for other ski areas, I finally reached my destination. Naturally, I lost no time in heading for the nearest tow. After a stimulating afternoon of miscalculated stem turns, I was famished. Well, one thing led to another, and it must have been eight o'clock before I concerned myself with a bed for my bruised and aching bones.
    It took precisely one phone call to ascertain the lack of lodgings in the Aspen area. I had but one recourse. My auto and I started the treacherous jaunt over the pass and back towards Denver. Along the way, I went begging for a bed. Finally, a jolly tavernkeeper took pity, and for only thirty dollars a night allowed me the privilege of staying in a musty, dirty, bathless room above his tavern.

1. The author's problem would have been avoided if he had
   A. not tired himself out skiing
   B. taken a bus instead of driving
   C. arranged for food as soon as he arrived
   D. arranged for accommodations well ahead of his trip
   E. answer cannot be determined from the information given

1.____

Question 2.
DIRECTIONS: Question 2 is to be answered on the basis of the following passage.

    Helen Keller was born in 1880 in Tuscumbia, Alabama. When she was two years old, she lost her sight and hearing as the result of an illness. In 1886, she became the pupil of Anne Sullivan, who taught Helen to see with her fingertips, to *hear* with her feet and hands, and to communicate with other people. Miss Sullivan succeeded in arousing Helen's curiosity and interest by spelling the names of objects into her hand. At the end of three years, Helen had mastered the manual and the braille alphabet and could read and write.

2. When did Helen Keller lose her sight and hearing?

2.____

Question 3.
DIRECTIONS: Question 3 is to be answered on the basis of the following passage.

Sammy got to school ten minutes after the school bell had rung. He was breathing hard and had a black eye. His face was dirty and scratched. One leg of his pants was torn.

Tommy was late to school, too; however, he was only five minutes late. Like Sammy, he was breathing hard, but he was happy and smiling.

3. Sammy and Tommy had been fighting.   3.____
    Who probably won?
       A. Sammy   B. Tommy
       C. Cannot tell from story   D. The teacher
       E. The school

Question 4.
DIRECTIONS: Question 4 is to be answered on the basis of the following passage.

This is like a game to see if you can tell what the nonsense word in the paragraph stands for. The nonsense word is just a silly word for something that you know very well. Read the paragraph and see if you can tell what the underlined nonsense word stands for.

You can wash your hands and face in zup. You can even take a bath in it. When people swim, they are in the zup. Everyone drinks zup.

4. Zup is PROBABLY
       A. milk   B. pop   C. soap   D. water   E. soup

Question 5.
DIRECTIONS: Question 5 is to be answered on the basis of the following passage.

After two weeks of unusually high-speed travel, we reached Xeno, a small planet whose population, though never before visited by Earthmen, was listed as *friendly* in the INTERSTELLAR GAZETTEER.

On stepping lightly (after all, the gravity of Xeno is scarcely more than twice that of our own moon) from our spacecraft, we saw that *friendly* was an understatement. We were immediately surrounded by Frangibles of various colors, mostly pinkish or orange, who held out their *hands* to us. Imagine our surprise when their *hands* actually merged with ours as we tried to shake them!

Then, before we could stop them (how could we have stopped them?), two particularly pink Frangibles simply stepped right into two eminent scientists among our party, who immediately lit up with the same pink glow. While occupied in this way, the scientists reported afterwards they suddenly discovered they *knew* a great deal about Frangibles and life on Xeno..

Apparently, Frangibles could take themselves apart atomically and enter right into any other substance. They communicated by thought waves, occasionally merging *heads* for greater clarity. Two Frangibles who were in love with each other would spend most of their time merged into one; they were a bluish-green color unless they were having a love's quarrel, when they turned gray.

5. In order to find out about an object which interested him, what would a Frangible MOST likely do?   5._____
    A. Take it apart
    B. Enter into it
    C. Study it scientifically
    D. Ask earth scientists about it
    E. Wait to see if it would change color

Question 6.
DIRECTIONS: Question 6 is to be answered on the basis of the following passage.

This is like a game to see if you can tell what the nonsense word in the paragraph stands for. The nonsense word is just a silly word for something that you know very well. Read the paragraph and see if you can tell what the underlined nonsense word stands for.

Have you ever smelled a <u>mart</u>? They smell very good. Bees like <u>marts</u>. They come inn many colors. <u>Marts</u> grow in the earth, and they usually bloom in the spring.

6. <u>Marts</u> are PROBABLY
    A. bugs   B. flowers   C. perfume   D. pies   E. cherries

Question 7.
DIRECTIONS: Question 7 is to be answered on the basis of the following passage.

Christmas was only a few days away. The wind was strong and cold. The walks were covered with snow. The downtown streets were crowded with people. Their faces were hidden by many packages as they went in one store after another. They all tried to move faster as they looked at the clock.

7. When did the story PROBABLY happen?   7._____
    A. November 28   B. December 1   C. December 21
    D. December 25   E. December 2

Question 8.
DIRECTIONS: Question 8 is to be answered on the basis of the following passage.

<u>THE WAYFARER</u>

The Wayfarer,
Perceiving the pathway to truth,
Was struck with astonishment.
It was thickly grown with weeds.
Ha, he said,
I see that no one has passed here
In a long time.
Later he saw that each weed
Was a singular knife,
Well, he mumbled at last,
Doubtless there are other roads.

8. *I see that no one has passed here in a long time.* 8._____
What do the above lines from the poem mean?
   A. The way of truth is popular.
   B. People are fascinated by the truth.
   C. Truth comes and goes like the wind.
   D. The truth is difficult to recognize.
   E. Few people are searching for the truth.

Question 9.
DIRECTIONS: Question 9 is to be answered on the basis of the following passage.

Any attempt to label an entire generation is unrewarding, and yet the generation which went through the last war, or at least could get a drink easily once it was over, seems to possess a uniform, general quality which demands an adjective. It was John Kerouac, the author of a fine, neglected novel, THE TOWN AND THE CITY, who final came up with it. It was several years ago, when the face was harder to recognize, but he had a sharp, sympathetic eye, and one day he said, *You know, this is really a beat generation.* The origins of the word *beat* are obscure, but the meaning is only too clear to most Americans. More than mere weariness, it implies the feeling of having been used, of being raw. It involves a sort of nakedness of mind, and, ultimately of soul; a feeling of being reduced to the bedrock of consciousness. In short, it means being undramatically pushed up against the wall of oneself. A man is beat whenever he goes for broke and waters the sum of his resources on a single number; and the young generation has done that continually from early youth.

9. What does the writer suggest when he mentions a *fine, neglected novel*? 9._____
   A. Kerouac had the right idea about the war.
   B. Kerouac had a clear understanding of the new post-war generation.
   C. Kerouac had not received the recognition of THE TOWN AND THE CITY that was deserved.
   D. Kerouac had the wrong idea about the war.
   E. All of the above

Questions 10-11.
DIRECTIONS: Questions 10 and 11 are to be answered on the basis of the following passage.

One spring, Farmer Brown had an unusually good field of wheat. Whenever he say any birds in this field, he got his gun and shot as many of them as he could. In the middle of the summer, he found that his wheat was being ruined by insects. With no birds to feed on them, the insects had multiplied very fast. What Farmer Brown did not understand was this: A bird is not simply an animal that eats food the farmer may want for himself. Instead, it is one of many links in the complex surroundings, or environment, in which we live.

How much grain a farmer can raise on an acre of ground depends on many factors. All of these factors can be divided into two big groups. Such things as the richness of the soil, the amount of rainfall, the amount of sunlight, and the temperature belong together in one of these groups. This group may be called nonliving factors. The second group may be called living factors. The living factors in any plant's environment are animals and other plants. Wheat, for example, may be damaged by wheat rust, a tiny plant that feeds on wheat, or it may be eaten by plant-eating animals such as birds or grasshoppers…

It is easy to see that the relations of plants and animals to their environment are very complex, and that any change in the environment is likely to bring about a whole series of changes.

10. What does the passage suggest a good farmer should understand about nature? 10._____
    A. Insects are harmful to plants.
    B. Birds are not harmful to plants.
    C. Wheat may be damaged by both animals and other plants.
    D. The amount of wheat he can raise depends on two factors: birds and insects.
    E. A change in one factor of plants' surroundings may cause other factors to change.

11. What important idea about nature does the writer want us to understand? 11._____
    A. Farmer Brown was worried about the heavy rainfall.
    B. Nobody needs to have such destructive birds around.
    C. Farmer Brown did not want the temperature to change.
    D. All insects need not only wheat rust but grasshoppers.
    E. All living things are dependent on other living things.

Question 12.
DIRECTIONS: Question 12 is to be answered on the basis of the following passage.

For a 12-year-old, I've been around a lot because my father's in the Army. I have been to New York and to Paris. When I was nine, my parents took me to Rome. I didn't like Europe very much because the people don't speak the same language as I do. When I am older, my mother says I can travel by myself. I think I will like that. Ever since I was 13, I have wanted to go to Canada.

12. Why can't everything this person said be TRUE? 12._____
    A. 12-year-olds can't travel alone.
    B. No one can travel that much in 12 years.
    C. There is a conflict in the ages used in the passage.
    D. 9-year-olds can't travel alone.
    E. He is a liar.

Question 13.
DIRECTIONS: Question 13 is to be answered on the basis of the following passage.

Between April and October, the Persian Gulf is dotted with the small boats of pearl divers. Some seventy-five thousand of them are busy diving down and bringing up pearl-bearing oysters. These oysters are not the kind we eat. The edible oyster produces pearls of little or no value. You may have heard tales of divers who discovered pearls and sold them for great sums of money. These stories are entertaining but not accurate.

13. The Persian Gulf has many 13.____
    A. large boats of pearl divers
    B. pearl divers who eat oysters
    C. edible oysters that produce pearls
    D. non-edible oysters that produce pearls
    E. edible oysters that do not produce pearls

Question 14.
DIRECTIONS: Question 14 is to be answered on the basis of the following passage.

Art says that the polar ice cap is melting at the rate of 3% per year. Bert says that this isn't true because the polar ice cap is really melting at the rate of 7% per year.

14. We know for certain that 14.____
    A. Art is wrong.   B. Bert is wrong.
    C. they are both wrong   D. they both might be right
    E. they can't both be right

Question 15.
DIRECTIONS: Question 15 is to be answered on the basis of the following passage.

FORTUNE AND MEN'S EYES
                                                Shakespeare

When, in disgrace with fortune and men's eyes,
I all alone beweep my outcast state,
And trouble deaf heaven with my bootless cries,
And look upon myself and curse my fate,
Wishing me like to one more rich in hope,
Featured like him, like him with friends possessed
Desiring this man's art, and that man's scope,
With what I most enjoy contented least;
Yet in these thoughts myself almost despising,
Haply I think on thee; and then my state,
Like to the lark at break of day arising
From sullen earth, sings hymns at heaven's gate;
For thy sweet love remembered, such wealth brings
That then I scorn to change my state with kings.

15. What saves this man from wishing to be different than he is? 15.____
    A. Such wealth brings   B. Hymns at heaven's gate
    C. The lark at break of day   D. Thy sweet love remembered
    E. Change my state with kings

Question 16.
DIRECTIONS: Question 16 is to be answered on the basis of the following passage.

My name is Gregory Gotrocks, and I live in Peoria, Illinois. I sell tractors. In June 1952, the Gotrocks Tractor Company (my dad happens to be the president) sent me to Nepal-Tibet to check on our sales office there.

Business was slow, and I had a lot of time to kill. I decided to see Mt. Everest so that I could tell everyone back in Peoria that I had seen it.

It was beautiful; I was spellbound. I simply had to see what the view looked like from the top. So I started up the northwest slope. Everyone know that this is the best route to take. It took me three long hours to reach the top, but the climb was well worth it.

16. Gregory Gotrocks went to see Mt. Everest so that he could 16.____
    A. see some friends
    B. sell some tractors
    C. take a picture of it
    D. plant a flag at its base
    E. entertain his friends back home

Questions 17-18.
DIRECTIONS: Questions 17 and 18 are to be answered on the basis of the following passage.

Suburbanites are not irresponsible. Indeed, what is striking about the young couples' march along the abyss is the earnestness and precision with which they go about it. They are extremely budget-conscious. They can rattle off most of their monthly payments down to the last penny; one might say that even their impulse buying is deliberately planned. They are conscientious in meeting obligations and rarely do they fall delinquent in their accounts.

They are exponents of what could be called budgetism. This does not mean that they actually keep formal budgets—quite the contrary. The beauty of budgetism is that one doesn't have to keep a budget at all. It's done automatically. In the new middle-class rhythms of life, obligations are homogenized, for the overriding aim is to have oneself precommitted to regular, unvarying monthly payments on all the major items,

Americans used to be divided into three sizable groups: those who thought of money obligations in terms of the week, of the month, and of the year. Many people remain at both ends of the scale; but with the widening of the middle class, the mortgage payments are firmly geared to a thirty-day cycle, and any dissonant peaks and valleys are anathema. Just as young couples are now paying winter fuel bills in equal monthly fractions through the year, so they seek to spread out all the other heavy seasonal obligations they can anticipate. If vendors will not oblige by accepting equal monthly installments, the purchasers will smooth out the load themselves by floating loans.

It is, suburbanites cheerfully explain, a matter of psychology. They don't trust themselves. In self-entrapment is security. They try to budget so tightly that there is no unappropriated funds, for they know these would burn a hole in their pocket. Not merely out of greed for goods, then, do they commit themselves; it is protection they want, too. And though it would be extreme to say that they go into debt to be secure, carefully chartered debt does give them a certain peace of mind—and in suburbia this is more coveted than luxury itself.

17. What is the *abyss* along which the young couples are marching? 17.____
    A. Nuclear war
    B. Unemployment
    C. Mental breakdown
    D. Financial disaster
    E. Catastrophic illness

18. What conclusion does the author reach concerning carefully chartered debt 18.____
    among young couples in the United States today?
    It
    A. is a symbol of love
    B. bring marital happiness
    C. helps them to feel secure
    D. enables them to acquire wealth
    E. provides them with material goods

Question 19.
DIRECTIONS: Question 19 is to be answered on the basis of the following passage. Read the verse and fill in the space at the right the object described in the verse.

You see me when I'm right or wrong;
My face I never hide.
My hands move slowly round and round
And o'er me minutes glide.

19.   A. Book   B. Clock   C. Record   D. Table   E. Lock   19.____

Question 20-22.
DIRECTIONS: Questions 20 through 22 are to be answered on the basis of the following passage.

Until about thirty years ago, the village of Nayon seems to have been a self-sufficient agricultural community with a mixture of native and sixteenth century Spanish customs. Lands were abandoned when too badly eroded. The balance between population and resources allowed a minimum subsistence. A few traders exchanged goods between Quito and the villages in the tropical barrancas, all within a radius of ten miles. Houses had dirt floors, thatched roofs, and pole walls that were sometimes plastered with mud. Guinea pigs ran freely about each house and were the main meat source. Most of the population spoke no Spanish. Men wore long hair and concerned themselves chiefly with farming.

The completion of the Guayaquil-Quito railway in 1908 brought the first real contacts with industrial civilization to the high inter-Andean valley. From this event gradually flowed not only technological changes but new ideas and social institutions. Feudal social relationships no longer seemed right and immutable; medicine and public health improved; elementary education became more common; urban Quito began to expand; and finally, and perhaps least important so far, modern industries began to appear, although even now on a most modest scale.

In 1948-49, the date of our visit, only two men wore their hair long; and only to old-style houses remained. If guinea pigs were kept, they were penned; their flesh was now a luxury food, and beef the most common meat. Houses were of adobe or fired brick, usually with tile roofs, and often contained five or six rooms, some of which had plank or brick floors. Most of the population spoke Spanish. There was no resident priest, but an appointed government official and a policeman represented authority. A six-teacher school provided education. Clothing was becoming citified; for men it often included overalls for work and a tailored suit, white shirt, necktie, and felt hat for trips to Quito. Attendance at church was low, and many festivals had been abandoned. Volleyball or soccer was played weekly in the plaza by young men who sometimes wore shorts, blazers, and berets. There were few shops, for most purchases were made in Quito, and from there came most of the food, so that there was a far more varied diet than twenty-five years ago. There were piped water and sporadic health services; in addition, most families patronized Quito doctors in emergencies.

The crops and their uses had undergone change. Maize, or Indian corn, was still the primary crop, but very little was harvested as grain. Almost all was sold in Quito as green corn to eat boiled on the cob, and a considerable amount of the corn eaten as grain in Nayon was imported. Beans, which do poorly here, were grown on a small scale for household consumption. Though some squash was eaten, most was exported. Sweet potatoes, tomatoes, cabbage, onions, peppers, and, at lower elevations, sweet yucca, and arrowroot were grown extensively for export; indeed, so export-minded was the community that it was almost impossible to buy locally grown produce in the village. People couldn't be bothered with retail scales.

20. Why was there primitiveness and self-containment in Nayon before 1910? 20.____
    A. Social mores
    B. Cultural tradition
    C. Biological instincts
    D. Geographical factors
    E. Religious regulations

21. By 1948, the village of Nayon was 21.____
    A. a self-sufficient village
    B. out of touch with the outside world
    C. a small dependent portion of a larger economic unit
    D. a rapidly growing and sound social and cultural unit
    E. a metropolis

22. Why was Nayon originally separated from its neighbors? 22.____
    A. Rich arable land
    B. Long meandering streams
    C. Artificial political barriers
    D. Broad stretches of arid desert
    E. Deep rugged gorges traversed by rock trails

Question 23.
DIRECTIONS: Question 23 is to be answered on the basis of the following passage. Read the verse and fill in the space at the right the object described in the verse.

I have two eyes and when I'm worn
I give the wearer four.
I'm strong or weak or thick or thin
Need I say much more?

23. A. Clock   B. Eyeglasses   C. Piano   23.____
    D. Thermometer   E. I don't know

Question 24.
DIRECTIONS: Question 24 is to be answered on the basis of the following passage.

Scarlet fever begins with fever, chills, headache, and sore throat. A doctor diagnoses the illness as scarlet fever when a characteristic rash erupts on the skin. This rash appears on the neck and chest in three to five days after the onset of the illness and spreads rapidly over the body. Sometimes the skin on the palm of the hands and soles of the feet shreds in flakes.
Scarlet fever is usually treated with penicillin and, in severe cases, a convalescent serum. The disease may be accompanied by infections of the ear and throat, inflammation of the kidneys, pneumonia, and inflammation of the heart.

24. How does the author tell us that scarlet fever may be a serious disease? 24.____
    A. He tells how many people die of it.
    B. He tells that he once had the disease.
    C. He tells that hands and feet may fall off.

D. He tells how other infections may come with scarlet fever.
E. None of the above

Question 25.
DIRECTIONS: Question 25 is to be answered on the basis of the following passage. Read the verse and fill in the space at the right the object described in the verse.

I have no wings but often fly;
I come in colors many.
From varied nationalities
Respect I get a-plenty.

25. A. Deck of cards B. Eyeglasses C. Flag 25.____
    D. Needles   E. None of the above

KEY (CORRECT ANSWERS)

1. D   11. E
2. B   12. C
3. B   13. D
4. D   14. E
5. B   15. D

6. B   16. E
7. C   17. D
8. E   18. C
9. C   19. B
10. E   20. D

21. C
22. E
23. B
24. D
25. C

READING COMPREHENSION
UNDERSTANDING WRITTEN MATERIALS
COMMENTARY

The ability to read and understand written materials—texts, publications, newspapers, orders, directions, expositions—is a skill basic to a functioning democracy and to an efficient business or viable government.

That is why almost all examinations—for beginning, middle, and senior levels—test reading comprehension, directly or indirectly.

The reading test measures how well you understand what you read. This is how it is done: You read a passage followed by several statements. From these statements, you choose the one statement, or answer, that is BEST supported by, or BEST matches, what is said in the paragraph. PRINT THE LETTER OF THE CORRECT ANSWER IN THE SPACE AT THE RIGHT.

SAMPLE QUESTION

DIRECTIONS: Answer Question 1 ONLY according to the information given in the following passage.

1. A cashier has to make many arithmetic calculations in connection with his work. Skill in arithmetic comes readily with practice; no special talent is needed.
   On the basis of the above statement, it is MOST accurate to state that
   A. the most important part of a cashier's job is to make calculations
   B. few cashiers have the special ability needed to handle arithmetic problems easily
   C. without special talent, cashiers cannot learn to do the calculations they are required to do in their work
   D. a cashier can, with practice, learn to handle the computations he is required to make

   1.____

The CORRECT answer is D.

EXAMINATION SECTION
TEST 1

DIRECTIONS: Questions 1 through 5 are to be answered on the basis of the following reading passage. *PRINT THE LETTER OF THE CORRECT ANSWER IN THE SPACE AT THE RIGHT.*

The size of each collection route will be determined by the amount of waste per stop, distance between stops, speed of loading, speed of truck, traffic conditions during loading time, etc.

Basically, the route should consist of a proper amount of work for a crew for the daily work period. The crew should service all properties eligible for this service in their area. Routes should, whenever practical, be compact, with a logical progression through the area. Unnecessary travel should be avoided. Traffic conditions on the route should be thoroughly studied to prevent lost time in loading, to reduce hazards to employees, and to minimize tying up of regular traffic movements by collection forces. Natural and physical barriers and arterial streets should be used as route boundaries wherever possible to avoid lost time in travel.

Routes within a district should be laid out so that the crews start at the point farthest from the disposal area and, as the day progresses, move toward that area, thus reducing the length of the haul. When possible, the work of the crews in a district should be parallel as they progress throughout the day, with routes finishing up within a short distance of each other. This enables the supervisor to be present when crews are completing their work and enables him to shift crews to trouble spots to complete the day's work.

1. Based on the above passage, an advantage of having collection routes end near one another is that
    A. routes can be made more compact
    B. unnecessary travel is avoided, saving manpower
    C. the length of the haul is reduced
    D. the supervisor can exercise better manpower control

1.____

2. Of the factors mentioned above which affect the size of a collection route, the two over which the sanitation forces have LEAST control are
    A. amount of waste; traffic conditions
    B. speed of loading; amount of waste
    C. speed of truck; distance between stops
    D. traffic conditions; speed of truck

2.____

3. According to the above passage, the size of a collection route is probably good if
    A. it is a fair day's work for a normal crew
    B. it is not necessary for the trucks to travel too fast
    C. the amount of waste collected can be handled properly
    D. the distance between stops is approximately equal

3.____

4. Based on the above passage, it is reasonable to assume that a sanitation officer laying out collection routes should NOT try to have
   A. an arterial street as a route boundary
   B. any routes near the disposal area
   C. the routes overlap a little
   D. the routes run in the same direction

4._____

5. The term "logical progression," as used in the second paragraph of the passage refers MOST NEARLY to
   A. collecting from street after street in order
   B. numbering streets one after the other
   C. rotating crew assignments
   D. using logic as a basis for assigned crews

5._____

KEY (CORRECT ANSWERS)

1. D
2. A
3. A
4. C
5. A

TEST 2

DIRECTIONS: Questions 1 through 3 are to be answered on the basis of the following reading passage. *PRINT THE LETTER OF THE CORRECT ANSWER IN THE SPACE AT THE RIGHT.*

In an open discussion designed to arrive at solutions to community problems, the person leading the discussion group should give the members a chance to make their suggestions before he makes his. He must not be afraid of silence; if he talks just to keep things going, he will find he can't stop, and good discussion will not develop. In other words, the more he talks, the more the group will depend on him. If he finds, however, that no one seems ready to begin the discussion, his best "opening" is to ask for definitions of terms which form the basis of the discussion. By pulling out as many definitions or interpretations as possible, he can get the group started "thinking out load," which is essential to good discussion.

1. According to the above passage, good group discussion is MOST likely to result if the person leading the discussion group
   A. keeps the discussion going by speaking whenever the group stops speaking
   B. encourages the group to depend on him by speaking more than any other group member
   C. makes his own suggestions before the group has a chance to make theirs
   D. encourages discussion by asking the group to interpret the terms to be discussed

1.____

2. According to the above passage, "thinking out loud" by the discussion group is
   A. *good* practice, because "thinking out loud" is important to good discussion
   B. *poor* practice, because group members should think out their ideas before discussing them
   C. *good* practice, because it will encourage the person leading the discussion to speak more
   D. *poor* practice, because it causes the group to fear silence during discussion

2.____

3. According to the above passage, the one of the following which is LEAST desirable at an open discussion is having
   A. silent periods during which none of the group members speaks
   B. differences of opinion among the group members concerning the definition of terms
   C. a discussion leader who uses "openings" to get the discussion started
   D. a discussion leader who provides all suggestions and definitions for the group

3.____

KEY (CORRECT ANSWERS)

1. D
2. A
3. D

TEST 3

DIRECTIONS: Questions 1 through 4 are to be answered on the basis of the following reading passage. *PRINT THE LETTER OF THE CORRECT ANSWER IN THE SPACE AT THE RIGHT.*

The insects you will control are just a minute fraction of the millions which inhabit the world. Man does well to hold his own in the face of the constant pressures that insects continue to exert upon him. Not only are the total numbers tremendous, but the number of individual kinds, or species, certainly exceeds 800,000—number greater than that of all other animals combined. Many of these are beneficial but some are especially competitive with man. Not only are insects numerous, but they are among the most adaptable of all animals. In their many forms, they are fitted for almost any specific way of life. Their adaptability, combined with their tremendous rate of reproduction, gives insects an unequaled potential for survival!

The food of insects includes almost anything that can be eaten by any other animal as well as many things which cannot even be digested by any other animals. Most insects do not harm the products of man or carry diseases harmful to him; however, many do carry diseases and others feed on his food and manufactured goods. Some are adapted to living only in open areas while others are able to live in extremely confined spaces. All of these factor combined make the insects a group of animals having many members which are a nuisance to man and thus of great importance.

The control of insects requires an understanding of their way of life. Thus, it is necessary to understand the anatomy of the insect, its method of growth, the time it takes for the insect to grow from egg to adult, its habits, the stage of its life history in which it causes damage, its food, and its common living places. In order to obtain the best control, it is especially important to be able to identify correctly the specific insect involved because, without this knowledge, it is impossible to prescribe a proper treatment.

1. Which one of the following is a CORRECT statement about the insect population of the world, according to the above passage? The
    A. total number of insects is less than the total number of all other animals combined
    B. number of species of insects is greater than the number of species of all other animals combined
    C. total number of harmful insects is less than the number of species of those which are harmful
    D. number of species of harmless insects is less than the number of species of those which are harmful

1.____

2. Insects will be controlled MOST efficiently if you
    A. understand why the insects are so numerous
    B. know what insects you are dealing with
    C. see if the insects compete with man
    D. are able to identify the food which the insects digest

2.____

3. According to the above passage, insects are of importance to a scientist PRIMARILY because they 3.____
   A. can be annoying, destructive, and harmful to man
   B. are able to thrive in very small spaces
   C. cause damage during their growth stages
   D. are so adaptable that they can adjust to any environment

4. According to the above passage, insects can eat 4.____
   A. everything that any other living thing can eat
   B. man's food and thing which he makes
   C. anything which other animals can't digest
   D. only food and food products

KEY (CORRECT ANSWERS)

1. B
2. B
3. A
4. B

TEST 4

DIRECTIONS: Questions 1 through 3 are to be answered on the basis of the following reading passage. *PRINT THE LETTER OF THE CORRECT ANSWER IN THE SPACE AT THE RIGHT.*

Telephone service in a government agency should be adequate and complete with respect to information given or action taken. It must be remembered that telephone contacts should receive special consideration since the caller cannot see the operator. People like to feel that they are receiving personal attention and that their requests or criticisms are receiving individual rather than routine consideration. All this contributes to what has come to be known as *tone of service*. The aim is to use standards which are clearly very good or superior. The factors to be considered in determining what makes good tone of service are speech, courtesy, understanding, and explanations. A caller's impression of tone of service will affect the general public attitude toward the agency and city services in general.

1. The above passage states that people who telephone a government agency like to feel that they are
    A. creating a positive image of themselves
    B. being given routine consideration
    C. receiving individual attention
    D. setting standards for telephone service

    1._____

2. Which one of the following is NOT mentioned in the above passage as a factor in determining good tone of service?
    A. Courtesy   B. Education   C. Speech   D. Understanding

    2._____

3. The above passage implies that failure to properly handle telephone calls is MOST likely to result in
    A. a poor impression of city agencies by the public
    B. a deterioration of courtesy toward operators
    C. an effort by operators to improve the Tone of Service
    D. special consideration by the public of operator difficulties

    3._____

KEY (CORRECT ANSWERS)

1. C
2. B
3. A

TEST 5

DIRECTIONS: Questions 1 through 5 are to be answered on the basis of the following reading passage. *PRINT THE LETTER OF THE CORRECT ANSWER IN THE SPACE AT THE RIGHT.*

For some office workers it is useful to be familiar with the four main classes of domestic mail; for others, it is essential. Each class has a different rate of postage and some have requirements concerning wrapping, sealing, or special information to be placed on the package.

First-class mail, the class which may not be opened for postal inspection, includes letters, postcards, business reply cards, and other kinds of written matter. There are different rates for some of the kinds of cards which can be sent by first-class mail. The maximum weight for an item sent by first-class mail is 70 pounds. An item which is not letter size should be marked "First Class: on all sides.

Although office workers most often come into contact with first-class mail, they may find it helpful to know something about the other classes. Second-class mail is generally used for mailing newspapers and magazines. Publishers of these articles must meet certain U.S. Postal Service requirements in order to obtain a permit to use second-class mailing rates. Third-class mail, which must weigh less than 1 pound, includes printed materials and merchandise parcels. There are two rate structure for this class, a single-piece rate and a bulk rate. Fourth-class mail, also known as parcel post, includes packages weighing from one to 40 pounds. For more information about these classes of mail and the actual mailing rates, contact our local post office.

1. According to this passage, first-class mail is the only class which 1.____
   A. has a limit on the maximum weight of an item
   B. has different rates for items within the class
   C. may not be opened for postal inspection
   D. should be used by office workers

2. According to this passage, the one of the following items which may CORRECTLY 2.____
   be sent by fourth-class mail is a
   A. magazine weighing one-half pound
   B. package weighing one-half pound
   C. package weighing two pounds
   D. postcard

3. According to this passage, there are different postage rates for 3.____
   A. a newspaper sent by second-class mail and a magazine sent by second-class mail
   B. each of the classes of mail
   C. each pound of fourth-class mail
   D. printed material sent by third-class mail and merchandise parcels sent by third-class mail

4. In order to send a newspaper by second-class mail, a publisher must　　　　4.____
    A. have met certain postal requirements and obtained a permit
    B. indicate whether he wants to use the single-piece or the bulk rate
    C. make certain that the newspaper weighs less than one pound
    D. mark the newspaper "Second Class" on the top and bottom of the wrapper

5. Of the following types of information, the one which is NOT mentioned in the passage is the　　　　5.____
    A. class of mail to which parcel post belongs
    B. kinds of items which can be sent by each class of mail
    C. maximum weight for an item sent by fourth-class mail
    D. postage rate for each of the four classes of mail

KEY (CORRECT ANSWERS)

1. C
2. C
3. B
4. A
5. D

TEST 6

DIRECTIONS: Questions 1 through 5 are to be answered on the basis of the following reading passage. *PRINT THE LETTER OF THE CORRECT ANSWER IN THE SPACE AT THE RIGHT.*

The thickness of insulation necessary for the most economical results varies with the steam temperature. The standard covering consists of 85 percent magnesia with 10 percent of long-fibre asbestos as a binder. Both magnesia and laminated asbestos-felt and other forms of mineral wool including glass wool are also used for heat insulation. The magnesia and laminated-asbestos coverings may be safely used at temperatures up to 600°F. Pipe insulation is applied in molded sections 3 feet long; the sections are attached to the pipe by means of galvanized iron wire or netting. Flanges and fittings can be insulated by direct application of magnesia cement to the metal without *reinforcement*. Insulation should always be maintained inn good condition because it saves fuel. Routine maintenance of warm-pipe insulation should include prompt repair of damaged surfaces. Steam and hot-water leaks concealed by insulation will be difficult to detect. Underground steam or hot-water pipes are best insulated using a concrete trench with removable cover.

1. The word *reinforcement*, as used above, means MOST NEARLY
   A. resistance
   B. strengthening
   C. regulation
   D. removal

2. According to the above paragraph, magnesia and laminated asbestos coverings may be safely used at temperatures up to
   A. 800°F
   B. 720°F
   C. 675°F
   D. 600°F

3. According to the above paragraph, insulation should *always* be maintained in good condition because it
   A. is laminated
   B. saves fuel
   C. is attached to the pipe
   D. prevents leaks

4. According to the above paragraph, pipe insulation sections are attached to the pipe by means of
   A. binders
   B. mineral wool
   C. netting
   D. staples

5. According to the above paragraph, a leak in a hot-water pipe may be difficult to detect because, when insulation is used, the leak is
   A. underground
   B. hidden
   C. routine
   D. cemented

KEY (CORRECT ANSWERS)

1. B
2. D
3. B
4. C
5. B

TEST 7

DIRECTIONS: Questions 1 through 4 are to be answered on the basis of the following reading passage. *PRINT THE LETTER OF THE CORRECT ANSWER IN THE SPACE AT THE RIGHT.*

Cylindrical surfaces are the most common form of finished surfaces found on machine parts, although flat surfaces are also very common; hence, many metal-cutting processes are for the purpose of producing either cylindrical or flat surfaces. The machines used for cylindrical or flat shapes may be, and often are, utilized also for forming the various irregular or special shapes required on many machine parts. Because of the prevalence of cylindrical and flat surfaces, the student of manufacturing practice should learn first about the machines and methods employed to produce these surfaces. The cylindrical surfaces may be internal as in holes and cylinders. Any one part may, of course, have cylindrical sections of different diameters and lengths and include flat ends or shoulders and, frequently, there is a threaded part or, possibly, some finished surface that is not circular in cross-section. The prevalence of cylindrical surfaces on machine parts explains why lathes are found in all machine shops. It is important to understand the various uses of the lathes because many of the operations are the same fundamentally as those performed on other types of machine tools.

1. According to the above passage, the MOST common form of finished surfaces found on machine parts is
    A. cylindrical   B. elliptical   C. flat   D. square   1.____

2. According to the above passage, any one part of cylindrical surfaces may have
    A. chases   B. shoulders   C. keyways   D. splines   2.____

3. According to the above passage, lathes are found in all machine shops because cylindrical surfaces on machine parts are
    A. scarce   B. internal   C. common   D. external   3.____

4. As used in the above paragraph, the word *processes* means
    A. operations   B. purposes   C. devices   D. tools   4.____

KEY (CORRECT ANSWERS)

1. A
2. B
3. C
4. A

TEST 8

DIRECTIONS: Questions 1 and 2 are to be answered on the basis of the following reading passage. *PRINT THE LETTER OF THE CORRECT ANSWER IN THE SPACE AT THE RIGHT.*

The principle of interchangeability requires manufacture to such specification that component parts of a device may be selected at random and assembled to fit and operate satisfactorily. Interchangeable manufacture, therefore, requires that parts be made to definite limits of error, and to fit gages instead of mating parts. Interchangeability does not necessarily involve a high degree of precision; stove lids, for example, are interchangeable but are not particularly accurate, and carriage bolts and nuts are not precision products but are completely interchangeable. Interchangeability may be employed in unit-production as well as mass-production systems of manufacture.

1. According to the above paragraph, in order for parts to be interchangeable, they must be
   - A. precision-machined
   - B. selectively-assembled
   - C. mass-produced
   - D. made to fit gages

   1.____

2. According to the above paragraph, carriage bolts are interchangeable because they are
   - A. precision-made
   - B. sized to specific tolerances
   - C. individually matched products
   - D. produced in small units

   2.____

KEY (CORRECT ANSWERS)

1. D
2. B

READING COMPREHENSION
UNDERSTANDING AND INTERPRETING WRITTEN MATERIAL
EXAMINATION SECTION
TEST 1

DIRECTIONS: All questions are to be answered SOLELY on the basis of the information contained in the passage. Each question or incomplete statement is followed by several suggested answers or completions. Select the one that BEST answers the question or completes the statement. *PRINT THE LETTER OF THE CORRECT ANSWER IN THE SPACE AT THE RIGHT.*

Questions 1-3.

The equipment in a mail room may include a mail-metering machine. This machine simultaneously stamps, postmarks, seals, and counts letters as fast as the operator can feed them. It can also print the proper postage directly on a gummed strip to be affixed to bulky items. It is equipped with a meter which is removed from the machine and sent to the postmaster to be set for a given number of stampings of any denomination. The setting of the meter must be paid for in advance. One of the advantages of metered mail is that it bypasses the cancellation operation and, thereby, facilitates handling by the post office. Mail metering also makes the pilfering of stamps impossible, but does not prevent the passage of personal mail in company envelopes through the meters unless there is established a rigid control or censorship over outgoing mail.

1. According to this statement, the postmaster
   A. is responsible for training new clerks in the use of mail-metering machines
   B. usually recommends that both large and small firms adopt the use of mail metering machines
   C. is responsible for setting the meter to print a fixed number of stampings
   D. examines the mail-metering machines to see that they are properly installed in the mail room

1.____

2. According to this statement, the use of mail-metering machines
   A. requires the employment of more clerks in a mail room than does the use of postage stamps
   B. interferes with the handling of large quantities of outgoing mail
   C. does not prevent employees from sending their personal letters at company expense
   D. usually involves smaller expenditures for mail room equipment than does the use of postage stamps

2.____

3. On the basis of this statement, it is MOST accurate to state that
   A. mail-metering machines are often used for opening envelopes
   B. postage stamps are generally used when bulky packages are to be mailed
   C. the use of metered mail tends to interfere with rapid mail handling by the post office
   D. mail-metering machines can seal and count letters at the same time

3.____

Questions 4-8.

It is the Housing Administration's policy that all tenants, whether new or transferring from one housing development to another, shall be required to pay a standard security deposit of one month's rent based on the rent at the time of admission. There are, however, certain exceptions to this policy. Employees of the Administration shall not be required to pay a security deposit if they secure an apartment in an Administration development. Where the payment of a full security deposit may present a hardship to a tenant, the development's manager may allow a tenant to move into an apartment upon payment of only part of the security deposit. In such cases, however, the tenant must agree to gradually pay the balance of the deposit. If a tenant transfers from one apartment to another within the same project, the security deposit originally paid by the tenant for his former apartment will be acceptable for his new apartment, even if the rent in the new apartment is greater than the rent in the former one. Finally, tenants who receive public assistance need not pay a security deposit before moving into an apartment if the appropriate agency states, in writing, that it will pay the deposit. However, it is the responsibility of the development's manager to make certain that payment shall be received within one month of the date the tenant moves into the apartment.

4. According to the above passage, when a tenant transfers from one apartment to another in the same development, the Housing Administration will
   A. accept the tenant's old security deposit as the security deposit for his new apartment
   B. refund the tenant's old security deposit and not require him to pay a new deposit
   C. keep the tenant's old security deposit and require him to pay a new deposit
   D. require the tenant to pay a new security deposit based on the difference between his old rent and his new rent

4.____

5. On the basis of the above passage, it is INCORREC to state that a tenant who receives public assistance may move into an Administration development if
   A. he pays the appropriate security deposit
   B. the appropriate agency gives a written indication that it will pay the security deposit before the tenant moves in
   C. the appropriate agency states, by telephone, that it will pay the security deposit
   D. the appropriate agency writes the manager to indicate that the security deposit will be paid within one month but not less than two weeks from the date the tenant moves into the apartment

5.____

6. On the basis of the above passage, a tenant who transfers from an apartment in one development to an apartment in a different department will
   A. forfeit his old security deposit and be required to pay another deposit
   B. have his old security deposit refunded and not have to pay a new deposit
   C. pay the difference between his old security deposit and the new one
   D. have to pay a security deposit based on the new apartment's rent

6.____

7. The Housing Administration will NOT require payment of a security deposit if a tenant
   A. is an Administration employee
   B. is receiving public assistance
   C. claims that payment will present a hardship
   D. indicates, in writing, that he will be responsible for any damage done to his apartment

8. Of the following, the BEST title for the above passage is:
   A. Security Deposits – Transfers
   B. Security Deposits – Policy
   C. Exemptions and Exceptions – Security Deposits
   D. Amounts – Security Deposits

Questions 9-11.

Terrazzo flooring will last a very long time if it is cared for properly. Lacquers, shellac or varnish preparations should never be used on terrazzo. Soap cleaners are not recommended, since they dull the appearance of the floor. Alkaline solutions are harmful, so neutral cleaner or non-alkaline synthetic detergents will give best results. If the floor is very dirty, it may be necessary to scrub it. The same neutral cleaning solution should be used for scrubbing as for mopping. Scouring powder may be sprinkled at particularly dirty spots. Do not use steel wool for scrubbing. Small pieces of steel filings left on the floor will rust and discolor the terrazzo. Non-woven nylon or open-mesh fabric abrasive pads are suitable for scrubbing terrazzo floors.

9. According to the above passage, the BEST cleaning agent for terrazzo flooring is a(n)
   A. soap cleaner   B. varnish preparation
   C. neutral cleaner   D. alkaline solution

10. According to the above passage, terrazzo floors should NOT be scrubbed with
    A. non-woven nylon abrasive pads   B. steel wool
    C. open-mesh fabric abrasive pads   D. scouring powder

11. As used in the above passage, the word *discolor* means MOST NEARLY
    A. crack   B. scratch   C. dissolve   D. stain

Questions 12-15.

Planning for the unloading of incoming trucks is not easy since generally little or no advance notice of truck arrivals is received. The height of the floor of truck bodies and loading platforms sometimes are different; this makes necessary the use of special unloading methods. When available, hydraulic ramps compensate for the differences in platform and truck floor levels. When hydraulic ramps are not available, forklift equipment can sometimes be used, if the truck sprigs are strong enough to support such equipment. In a situation like this, the unloading operation does not differ much from unloading a railroad box car in the cases where the forklift truck or a hydraulic pallet jack cannot be used inside the truck, a pallet dolly should be placed inside the truck, so that the empty pallet can be loaded close to the truck contents and rolled easily to the truck door and platform.

12. According to the above passage, unloading trucks are 12.____
    A. easy to plan since the time of arrival is usually known beforehand
    B. the same as loading a railroad box car
    C. hard to plan since trucks arrive without notice
    D. a very normal thing to do

13. According to the above passage, which materials-handling equipment can 13.____
    make up for the difference in platform and truck floor levels?
    A. Hydraulic jacks   B. Hydraulic ramps
    C. Forklift trucks   D. Conveyors

14. According to the above passage, what materials-handling equipment can be 14.____
    used when a truck cannot support the weight of forklift equipment?
    A. A pallet dolly   B. A hydraulic ramp
    C. Bridge plates   D. A warehouse tractor

15. Which of the following is the BEST title for the above passage? 15.____
    A. Unloading Railroad Box Cars   B. Unloading Motor Trucks
    C. Loading Rail Box   D. Loading Motor Trucks

Questions 16-19.

Ventilation, as used in firefighting operations, means opening up a building or structure in which a fire is burning to release the accumulated heat, smoke, and gases. Lack of knowledge of the principle of ventilation on the part of firemen may result in unnecessary punishment due to ventilation being neglected or improperly handled. While ventilation itself extinguishes no fires, when used in an intelligent manner, it allows firemen to get at the fire more quickly, easily, and with less danger and hardship.

16. According to the above passage, the MOST important result of failure to apply 16.____
    the principles of ventilation at a fire may be
    A. loss of public confidence   B. disciplinary action
    C. waste of water   D. excessive use of equipment
    E. injury to fireman

17. It may be inferred from the above passage that the CHIEF advantage of 17.____
    ventilation is that it
    A. eliminates the need for gas masks
    B. reduces smoke damage
    C. permits firemen to work closer to the fire
    D. cools the fire
    E. enables firemen to use shorter hose lines

18. Knowledge of the principles of ventilation, as defined in the above passage, 18.____
    would be LEAST important in a fire in a
    A. tenement house   B. grocery store   C. ship's hold
    D. lumberyard   E. office building

19. We may conclude from the above passage that, for the well-trained and equipped fireman, ventilation is   19.____
    A. a simple matter
    B. rarely necessary
    C. relatively unimportant
    D. a basic tool
    E. sometimes a handicap

Questions 20-22.

Many public service and industrial organizations are becoming increasingly insistent that supervisors at the work level be qualified instructors. The reason for this is that technological improvements and overall organizational growth require the acquisition of new skills and knowledge by workers. These skills and knowledge can be acquired in two ways. They can be gained either by absorption-rubbing shoulders with the job or through planned instruction. Permitting the acquisition of new skills and knowledge is to be haphazard and uncertain is too costly. At higher supervisory levels, the need for instructing subordinate is not so obvious, but it is just as important as at the lowest work level. A high-ranking supervisor accomplishes the requirements of his position only if his subordinate supervisors perform their work efficiently. Regardless of one's supervisory position, the ability to instruct easily and efficiently helps to insure well-qualified and thoroughly-trained subordinates. There exists an unfounded but rather prevalent belief that becoming a competent instructor is a long, arduous, and complicated process. This belief arises partially as a result of the requirement of a long period of college preparation involved in preparing teachers for our school system. This time is necessary because teachers must learn a great deal of subject matter. The worker who advances to a supervisory position generally has superior skill and knowledge; therefore, he has only to learn the techniques by which he can impart his knowledge in order to become a competent instructor.

20. According to the above passage, a prolonged period of preparation for instructing is NOT generally necessary for a worker who is advanced to a supervisory position because   20.____
    A. he may already possess some of the requirements of a competent instructor
    B. his previous job knowledge is generally sufficient to enable him to begin instructing immediately
    C. in his present position there is less need for the specific job knowledge of the ordinary worker
    D. the ability to instruct follows naturally from superior skill and knowledge

21. According to the above passage, it is important for the higher-level supervisor to be a good instructor because   21.____
    A. at this level there is a tendency to overlook the need for instruction of both subordinate supervisors and workers
    B. good training practices will then be readily adopted by lower-level supervisors
    C. the need for effective training is more critical at the higher levels of responsibility
    D. training can be used to improve the supervisory performance of his subordinate supervisors

22. According to the above passage, the acquisition of new skills and knowledge by workers is BEST accomplished when
    A. the method of training allows for the use of absorption
    B. organizational growth and technological improvement indicate a need for further training
    C. such training is the result of careful planning
    D. the cost factor involved in training can be readily justified

Questions 23-25.

The organization of any large agency falls into three broad general zones: top management, middle management, and rank-and-file operations. The normal task of middle management is to supervise, direct, and control the performance of operations within the scope of law, policy, and regulations already established. Where policy is settled and well defined, middle management is basically a set of standard operations, although they may call for high-developed skills. Where, however, policy is not clearly stated, is ambiguous, or is rapidly shifting, middle management is likely to have an important influence upon emergency policy trends. Persons working in the zone of middle management usually become specialists. They need specialist knowledge of law, rules, and regulations, and court decisions governing their organization if they are to discharge their duties effectively. They will also have acquired specialist knowledge of relationships and sequences in the normal flow of business. Further, their attention is brought to bear on a particular administrative task, in a particular jurisdiction, with a particular clientele. The importance of middle management is obviously great. The reasons for such importance are not difficult to find: Here it is that the essential action of government in behalf of citizens is taken; here it is that citizens deal with government when they pass beyond their first contacts; here is a training ground from which a considerable part of top management emerges; and here it is that the spirit and temper of the public service and its reputation are largely made.

23. According to the above passage, the critical importance of middle management is due to the fact that it is at this level that
    A. formal executive training can be most useful
    B. the greatest amount of action is taken on the complaints of the general public
    C. the official actions taken have the greatest impact on general attitudes towards the public service
    D. the public most frequently comes in contact with governmental operations and agencies

24. According to the above passage, the one of the following statements which is NOT offered as an explanation of the tendency for middle management responsibility to produce specialists is that
    A. middle-management personnel frequently feel that their work is the most important in an organization
    B. specialized knowledge is acquired during the course of everyday work
    C. specialized knowledge is necessary for effective job performance
    D. their work assignments are directed to specific problems in specific situations

25. According to the above passage, the GREATEST impact of middle management in policy determination would be likely to be felt in the situation in which
    A. middle management possesses highly developed operational skills
    B. several policy directives from top management are subject to varying interpretations
    C. the authority of middle management to supervise, direct, and control operations has been clearly established
    D. top management has neglected to consider the policy views of middle management

KEY (CORRECT ANSWERS)

1.	C		11.	D
2.	C		12.	C
3.	D		13.	B
4.	A		14.	A
5.	C		15.	B
6.	D		16.	E
7.	A		17.	C
8.	B		18.	D
9.	C		19.	D
10.	B		20.	A

21.	D
22.	C
23.	C
24.	A
25.	B

TEST 2

DIRECTIONS: All questions are to be answered SOLELY on the basis of the information contained in the passage. Each question or incomplete statement is followed by several suggested answers or completions. Select the one that BEST answers the question or completes the statement. *PRINT THE LETTER OF THE CORRECT ANSWER IN THE SPACE AT THE RIGHT.*

Questions 1-2.

Metal spraying is used for many purposes. Worn bearings on shafts and spindles can be readily restored to original dimensions with any desired metal or alloy. Low-carbon steel shafts may be supplied with high-carbon steel journal surfaces, which can then be ground to size after spraying. By using babbitt wire, bearings can be lined or babbited while rotating. Pump shafts and impellers can be coated with any desired metal to overcome wear and corrosion. Valve seats may be re-surfaced. Defective castings can be repaired by filling in blowholes and checks. The application of metal spraying to the field of corrosion resistance is growing, although the major application in this field is in the use of sprayed zinc. Tin, lead, and aluminum have been used considerably. The process is used for structural and tank applications in the field as well as in the shop.

1. According to the above passage, worn bearing surface on shafts are metal-sprayed in order to
   A. prevent corrosion of the shaft
   B. fit them into larger-sized impellers
   C. returns them to their original sizes
   D. replaces worn babbitt metal

1.____

2. According to the above passage, rotating bearings can be metal-sprayed using
   A. babbitt wire
   B. high-carbon steel
   C. low-carbon steel
   D. any desired metal

2.____

Questions 3-5.

The method of cleaning which should generally be used is the space assignment method. Under this method, the buildings to be cleaned are divided into different sections. Within each section, each crew of Custodial Assistants is assigned to do one particular cleaning job. For example, within a section, one crew may be assigned to cleaning offices, another to scrubbing floors, a third to collecting trash, and so on. Other methods which may be used are the post-assignment methods and the gang-cleaning method. Under the post-assignment method, a Custodial Assistant is assigned to one area of a building and performs all cleaning jobs in that area. This method is seldom used except where buildings are so small and distant from each other that it is not economical to use the space-assigned method. Under the gang-cleaning method, a Custodial Foreman takes a number of Custodial Assistants through a section of the building. These Custodial Assistants work as a group and complete the various cleaning jobs as they go. This method is generally used only where the building contains very large open areas.

2 (#2)

3. According to the above passage, under the space-assignment method, each crew generally
   A. works as a group and does a variety of different cleaning jobs
   B. is assigned to one area and performs all cleaning jobs in that area
   C. does one particular cleaning job within a section of a building
   D. follows the Custodial Foreman through a building containing large, open areas

3.____

4. According to the above passage, the post-assignment method is used mostly where the buildings to be cleaned are _____ in size and situated _____.
   A. large; close together
   B. small; close together
   C. large; far apart
   D. small; far apart

4.____

5. As used in the above passage, the word *economical* means MOST NEARLY
   A. thrifty   B. agreed   C. unusual   D. wasteful

5.____

Questions 6-9.

The desirability of complete refuse collection by municipalities is becoming generally accepted. In many cases, however, such ideal service is economically impractical and certain limits must be imposed. Some municipal authorities find it necessary to regulate the quantity of refuse, by weight or volume, which will be collected from a single residence or place of business at one collection. The purpose of the regulations is twofold: First, to maintain the degree of service rendered on a somewhat uniform basis; and, second, to insure a more or less constant collection from week to week. If left unregulated, careless producers might permit large quantities of refuse to accumulate on their premises over long periods and place abnormal amounts out for collection at irregular intervals, thus upsetting the collection schedule. Regulation is especially applied to large wholesale, industrial, and manufacturing enterprises which, in the great majority of cases, are required to dispose of all or part of their refuse themselves, at their own expense. The maximum quantities permitted by regulation should obviously be sufficient to take care of a normal accumulation at a household over the established interval between regular collections. In commercial districts, the maximum quantity limitations are often fixed on arbitrary bases rather than on normal production.

6. According to the above passage, many municipalities do not have complete refuse collections because
   A. it costs too much
   B. it is difficult to regulate
   C. it is not a municipal function
   D. they don't consider it desirable

6.____

7. According to the above passage, regulation by municipalities of the amount of refuse collected per collection from any one place of business does NOT contribute to
   A. accumulation of refuse by careless producers
   B. maintenance of collection schedules
   C. steady collection from one week to the next
   D. uniform service

7.____

8. According to the above passage, regulations by municipalities of refuse collection from certain enterprises helps to cut down
   A. accumulation of refuse for private collection
   B. the amount of refuse produced
   C. variation in the volume of refuse produced
   D. variation in collection service

9. According to the above passage, municipalities limit the amount of refuse collected in commercial districts on an arbitrary basis rather than on the basis of a normal accumulation. This is probably done because
   A. arbitrary standards are easy to establish and enforce
   B. normal accumulation is different for each district
   C. normal accumulation would require the collection of too much refuse
   D. there is no such thing as a normal accumulation

Questions 10-13.

The following passage is adapted from an old office manual:

Modern office methods, geared to ever higher speeds and aimed at ever greater efficiency, are largely the result of the typewriter. The typewriter is a substitute for handwriting and, in the hands of a skilled typist, not only turns out letters and other documents at least three times faster than a penman can do the work, but turns out the greater volume more uniformly and legibly. With the use of carbon paper and onionskin paper, identical copies can be made at the same time.
The typewriter, besides its effect on the conduct of business and government, has had a very important effect on the position of women. The typewriter has done much to bring women into business and government and today there are vastly more women than men typists. Many women have used the keys of the typewriter to climb the ladder to responsible managerial positions.
The typewriter, as its name implies, employs type to make an ink impression on paper. For many years, the manual typewriter was the standard machine used. Today, the electric typewriter is dominant, and completely automatic typewriters are coming into wider use.
The mechanism of the office manual typewriter includes a set of keys arranged systematically in rows; a semicircular frame of type, connected to the keys by levers; the carriage, or paper carrier; a rubber roller, called a platen, against which the type strikes; and an inked ribbon which makes the impression of the type character when the key strikes it.

10. The above passage mentions a number of good features of the combination of a skilled typist and a typewriter. Of the following, the feature which is NOT mentioned in the passage is
    A. speed   B. uniformity   C. reliability   D. legibility

11. According to the above passage, a skilled typist can
    A. turn out at least five carbon copies of typed matter
    B. type at least three times faster than a penman can write
    C. type more than 80 words a minute
    D. readily move into a managerial position

12. According to the above passage, which of the following is NOT part of the mechanism of a manual typewriter?   12.____
    A. Carbon paper   B. Paper carrier
    C. Platen   D. Inked ribbon

13. According to the above passage, the typewriter has helped   13.____
    A. men more than women in business
    B. women in career advancement into management
    C. men and women equally, but women have taken better advantage of it
    D. more women than men, because men generally dislike routine typing work

Questions 14-18.

Reductions in pipe size of a building heating system are made with eccentric fittings and are pitched downward. The ends of mains with gravity return shall be at least 18" above the water line of the boiler. As condensate flows opposite to the steam, run outs are one size larger than the vertical pipe and are pitched upward. In a one-pipe system, an automatic air vent must be provided at each main to relieve air pressure and to let steam enter the radiator. As steam enters the radiator, a *thermal* device causes the vent to close, thereby holding the steam. Steam mains should not be less than two inches in diameter. The end of the steam main should have a minimum size of one-half of its greatest diameter. Small steam systems should be sized for a 2-oz. pressure drop. Large steam systems should be sized for a 4-oz. pressure drop.

14. The word *thermal*, as used in the above passage, means MOST NEARLY   14.____
    A. convector   B. heat   C. instrument   D. current

15. According to the above passage, the one of the following that is one size larger than the vertical pipe is the   15.____
    A. steam main   B. valve   C. water line   D. run out

16. According to the above paragraph, small steam systems should be sized for a pressure drop of _____ oz.   16.____
    A. 2   B. 3   C. 4   D. 5

17. According to the above passage, ends of mains with gravity return shall be AT LEAST   17.____
    A. 18" above the water line of the boiler
    B. one-quarter of the greatest diameter of the main
    C. twice the size of the vertical pipe in the main
    D. 18" above the steam line of the boiler

18. According to the above passage, the one of the following that is provided at each main to relieve air pressure is a(n)   18.____
    A. gravity return   B. convector   C. eccentric   D. vent

Questions 19-21.

The bearings of all electrical equipment should be subjected to careful inspection at scheduled periodic intervals in order to secure maximum life. The newer type of sleeve bearing requires very little attention since the oil does not become contaminated and oil leakage is negligible. Maintenance of the correct oil level is frequently the only upkeep required for years of service with this type of bearing.

19. According to the above passage, the MAIN reason for making periodic inspections of electrical equipment is to 19.____
    A. reduce waste of lubricants
    B. prevent injury to operators
    C. make equipment last longer
    D. keeps operators "on their toes"

20. According to the above passage, the bearings of electrical equipment should be inspected 20.____
    A. whenever the equipment isn't working properly
    B. whenever there is time for inspections
    C. at least once a year
    D. at regular times

21. According to the above passage, when using the newer type of sleeve bearings, 21.____
    A. oil leakage is slight
    B. the oil level should be checked every few years
    C. oil leakage is due to carelessness
    D. oil soon becomes dirty

Questions 22-25.

There is hardly a city in the country that is not short of fire protection in some areas within its boundaries. These municipalities have spread out and have re-shuffled their residential, business, and industrial districts without readjusting the existing protective fire forces; or creating new protection units. Fire stations are still situated according to the needs of earlier times and have not been altered or improved to house modern firefighting equipment. They are neither efficient for carrying out their tasks nor livable for the men who must occupy them.

22. Of the following, the title which BEST describes the central idea of the above passage is: 22.____
    A. The Dynamic Nature of Contemporary Society
    B. The Cost of Fire Protection
    C. The Location and Design of Fire Stations
    D. The Design and Use of Firefighting Equipment
    E. The Growth of American Cities

23. According to the above passage, fire protection is inadequate in the United Sates in 23.____
    A. most areas of some cities
    B. some areas of most cities
    C. some areas in all cities
    D. all areas in some cities
    E. most areas in most cities

6 (#2)

24. The one of the following criteria for planning of fire stations which is NOT mentioned in the above passage is: 24.____
    A. Comfort of Firemen
    B. Proper Location
    C. Design for Modern Equipment
    D. Efficiency of Operation
    E. Cost of Construction

25. Of the following suggestions for improving the fire service, the one which would BEST deal with the problem discussed in the above passage would involve   25.____
    A. specialized training in the use of modern fire apparatus
    B. replacement of obsolete fire apparatus
    C. revision of zoning laws
    D. longer basic training for probationary firemen
    E. reassignment of fire districts

Questions 26-30.

Stopping, standing, and parking of motor vehicles is regulated by law to keep the public highways open for a smooth flow of traffic, and to keep stopped vehicles from blocking intersections, driveways, signs, fire hydrants, and other areas that must be kept clear. These established regulations apply in all situations, unless otherwise indicated by signs. Other local restrictions are posted in the areas to which they apply. Three examples of these other types of restrictions, which may apply singly or in combination with one another are:
NO STOPPING: This means that a driver may not stop a vehicle for any purpose except when necessary to avoid interference with other vehicles, or in compliance with directions of a police officer or signal.
NO STANDING: This means that a driver may stop a vehicle only temporarily to actually receive or discharge passengers.
NO PARKING: This means that a driver may stop a vehicle only temporarily to actually load or unload merchandise or passengers. When stopped, it is advisable to turn on warning flashers, if equipped with them. However, one should never use a directional signal for this purpose, because it may confuse other drivers. Some NO PARKING signs prohibit parking between certain hours on certain days. For example, the sign may read NO PARKING 8 A.M. to 11 A.M., MONDAY, WEDNESDAY, FRIDAY. These signs are usually utilized on streets where cleaning operations take place on alternate days.

26. The parking regulation that applies to fire hydrants is an example of _____ regulations.   26.____
    A. local   B. established   C. posted   D. temporary

27. When stopped in a NO PARKING zone, it is advisable to   27.____
    A. turn on the right directional signal to indicate to other drivers that you will remain stopped
    B. turn on the left directional signal to indicate to other drivers that you may be leaving the curb after a period of time
    C. turn on the warning flashers if your car is equipped with them
    D. put the vehicle in reverse so that the backup lights will be on to warn approaching cars that you have temporarily stopped

28. You may stop a vehicle temporarily to discharge passengers in an area under the restriction of a _____ zone.
    A. NO STOPPING – NO STANDING
    B. NO STANDING – NO PARKING
    C. NO PARKING – NO STOPPING
    D. NO STOPPING – NO STANDING – NO PARKING

29. A sign reads "NO PARKING 8 A.M. to 11 A.M., MONDAY, WEDNESDAY, FRIDAY."
    Based on this sign, an enforcement officer would issue a summons to a car that is parked on a
    A. Tuesday at 9:30 A.M.
    B. Wednesday at 12:00 A.M.
    C. Friday at 10:30 A.M.
    D. Saturday at 8:00 A.M.

30. NO PARKING signs prohibiting parking between certain hours, on certain days, are usually utilized on streets where
    A. vehicles frequently take on and discharge passengers
    B. cleaning operations take place on alternate days
    C. NO STOPPING signs have been ignored
    D. commercial vehicles take on and unload merchandise

KEY (CORRECT ANSWERS)

1. C	11. B	21. A
2. A	12. A	22. C
3. C	13. B	23. B
4. D	14. B	24. E
5. A	15. D	25. E
6. A	16. A	26. B
7. A	17. A	27. C
8. D	18. D	28. B
9. C	19. C	29. C
10. C	20. D	30. B

ARITHMETIC

EXAMINATION SECTION

TEST 1

DIRECTIONS: Each question or incomplete statement is followed by several suggested answers or completions. Select the one that BEST answers the question or completes the statement. *PRINT THE LETTER OF THE CORRECT ANSWER IN THE SPACE AT THE RIGHT.*

1. The result of a computation using only the numbers 8 and 7 is 15. In this computation, the number 15 is the
   A. product
   B. sum
   C. quotient
   D. difference
   E. average

   1.____

2. Which statement describes how to find the average of a group of scores?
   A. Find the sum of the scores and divide by 2.
   B. Find the sum of the scores and divide by the number of scores.
   C. Arrange the scores from lowest to highest and select the middle one.
   D. Take half the difference between the highest score and the lowest score.
   E. None of the above

   2.____

3. 6428
   974
   86
   7280
   763
   5407

   A. 19,838   B. 20,828   C. 20,838   D. 20,928   E. 20,938

   3.____

4. What is the inverse operation used to check division?
   A. Addition
   B. Subtraction
   C. Multiplication
   D. Division
   E. None of the above

   4.____

5. What is the ratio of 1 inch to 1 yard?
   A. 1   B. 3   C. 12   D. 24   E. 36

   5.____

6. Which of the following is NOT evenly divisible by 8?
   A. 6   B. 8   C. 40   D. 72   4. 104

   6.____

7. Each of the numerals listed below represents a number of feet. Which numeral MOST NEARLY represents the height of an average American man?
   A. .059   B. 0.59   C. 5.90   D. 59.0   E. 590

   7.____

Questions 8-9.

DIRECTIONS: Questions 8 and 9 are to be answered on the basis of the following line.

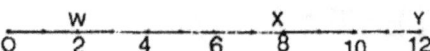

8. The point halfway between W and X would correspond to 8.____
   A. 4   B. 4 ½   C. 5   D. 5 ½   E. 6

9. What number would correspond to point P if it is placed on the number line 9.____
   so that P is between X and Y, and W is between P and X?
   A. 6
   B. 7 ½
   C. 9
   D. 10
   E. No such point can exist

10. What is the GREATEST common divisor of 24, 40, and 120? 10.____
    A. 2   B. 4   C. 8   D. 10   E. 12

11. Which of these is NOT equal to 4/9? 11.____
    A. 2/3   B. 20/45   C. 8/18   D. 16/36   E. 12/27

12. For which pair of the following operations are the rules for placing the 12.____
    decimal point in the answer the SAME?
    I. Addition   II. Subtraction
    III Multplication   IV. Division
    The CORRECT answer is:
    A. I and II
    B. I and III
    C. II and IV
    D. III and IV
    E. The rules are different for each operation

13. Three of four identical measuring containers are filled as shown at the right. All the liquid in the three containers is poured into the empty container on the right. What fractional part of this container will be filled? 13.____
    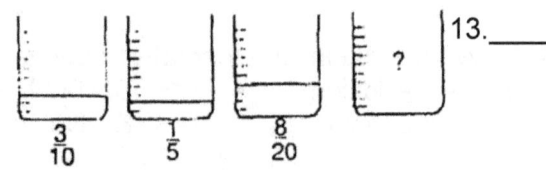
    A. 1/10   B. 12/35   C. 7/10   D. 9/10   E. 1

14. 1/2 of 20 is the same as 1/4 of 14.____
    A. 5   B. 10   C. 40   D. 60   E. 80

15. What is the SMALLEST number which can be divided evenly by each of 15.____
    the following numbers: 4, 6, 8?
    A. 48   B. 32   C. 24   D. 16   E. 12

16. $(2/3 \div 1/2) \times \frac{1}{2} =$
    A. 1/6   B. 3/8   C. 2/3   D. 3/2   E. 8/3

17. A bank clerk reported that the number of $100 bills in the vault was 10,003. About how much money is this?
    A. $1,000,
    B. $10,000
    C. $100,000
    D. $1,000,000
    E. $10,000,000

18. 3/40 is the same as
    A. .0075   B. .0133   C. .075   D. .1333   E. .75

19.   94/5
    +131 1/4

    A. 22 5/9   B. 22 9/20   C. 23   D. 23 1/20   E. 23 15

20.   36
    52)1872
    To make the answer in the above example four times as large as it is, you could change the number 1872 to
    A. 208   B. 468   C. 936   D. 3944   E. 7488

21. Which of these will produce an even whole number no matter what whole number is put in place of A?
    I. $2 \times \triangle + 1$
    II. $2 \times \triangle + 2$
    III. $2 \times \triangle + 3$
    The CORRECT answer is:
    A. I only
    B. II only
    C. III only
    D. I and II only
    E. I and III only

22. Which of these shows the CORRECT meaning of 407?
    A. (4 × ten) + (7 × one)
    B. (4 × ten × ten) + (0 × ten) + (7 × one)
    C. (4+0+7) × (one hundred)
    D. (4 × one) + (0 × ten) + (7 × ten × ten)
    E. (4 × one) + (7 × ten)

23. If the scale length of 4 ½ inches represents an actual distance of 72 miles, how many miles does the scale length of 7 inches represent?
    A. 2   B. 56   C. 74 ½   D. 112   E. 504

24. 4 5 6 . 7 2 3 8
    ↑ ↑   ↑ ↑ ↑
    F G   H J K

    In the above numeral, which arrow points to the hundreds place?
    A. F   B. G   C. H   D. J   E. K

16._____

17._____

18._____

19._____

20._____

21._____

22._____

23._____

24._____

25._____

25. Which of these is between 5/6 and 7/8?
    A. 2/3   B. 3/4   C. 4/5   D. 6/7   E. 8/9

26. 340.292 ÷ 48.2 =
    A. 706   B. 76   C. 70.6   D. 7.6   E. 7.06

27. Jim started mowing the grass at 1:45 P.M. and finished at 2:15 P.M. How many minutes did Jim take to mow the grass?
    A. 30   B. 70   C. 90   D. 180   E. 240

28. To reduce a fraction to LOWEST terms, what should be done to both numerator and denominator?
    A. Each should be divided by 2.
    B. Each should be multiplied by 2.
    C. Each should be multiplied by the least common multiple.
    D. Each should be divided by the greatest common divisor.
    E. The same number should be subtracted from each.

29. $3 + \sqrt{64}$ =
    A. 11   B. 19   C. 24   D. 35   E. $\sqrt{73}$

30. Between 8 A.M. and 3 P.M., the temperature rose 25°. The temperature at 8 A.M. was 10° below zero.
    At 3 P.M., the temperature was _____ zero.
    A. 26° above   B. 15° above   C. 5° above
    D. 5° below   E. 35° below

31. A boy saves 18 dollars in 8 weeks. He continues to save at the same rate. How many weeks will it take him to save 81 dollars?
    A. 13   B. 36   C. 40   D. 71   E. 181 ¼

32. One whole number is divided by another whole number. It is ALWAYS TRUE that the
    A. divisor is smaller than the quotient
    B. remainder is smaller than the divisor
    C. quotient is smaller than the divisor
    D. remainder is smaller than the quotient
    E. dividend is smaller than the remainder

33. Which of these will NEVER change the value of a number?
    I. Multiplying it by 1
    II. Dividing it by 1
    III. Multiplying it by its reciprocal
    The CORRECT answer is:
    A. I only   B. II only   C. III only
    D. I and II only   E. I and III only

5 (#1)

34. Which of the following equals 7 × (3+9)? 34.____
    A. (7×3) + (7×9)
    B. (7×9) + (3×9)
    C. (7×3) + (7×9)
    D. 7 × 27
    E. 21 + 9

35. 35.____

```
       1
       ─
A      2      B
       3
       ─
C      4      D
```

In the above figure $\dfrac{\text{length of AB}}{\text{length of CD}} =$

    A. 1/2   B. 1/3   C. 2/3   D. 3/2   E. 5/3

36. Which series is NOT in descending order? 36.____
    A. 4.04, 4.004, 404
    B. 2.1, 1.2, 2.12
    C. .06, .009, .10
    D. 13.2, 12/3, 12.03
    E. 736, 631, 367

Questions 37-38.

DIRECTIONS: Questions 37 and 28 are to be answered on the basis of the following graph.

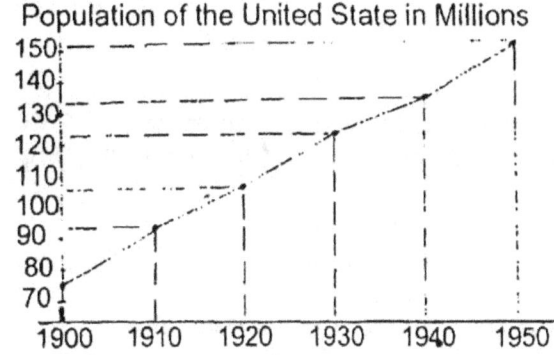

37. According to the above graph, the population of the United States in 1935 was about 37.____
    A. 127,000
    B. 1,270,000
    C. 12,700,000
    D. 127,000,000
    E. 1,270,000,000

38. What was the AVERAGE increase per year between 1900 and 1950? 38.____
    A. 1,500
    B. 15,000
    C. 150,000
    D. 750,000
    E. 1,500,000

39. What is the radio of 2 gallons to 3 quarts? 39.____
    A. 8 to 3   B. 3 to 8   C. 3 to 2   D. 2 to 3   E. 1 to 6

40. What percent of the figure at the right is darkened?
    A. 12
    B. 25
    C. 48
    D. 50
    E. 52

41. A cutting edge .004 inch thick is four times as thick as a second cutting edge. How many inches thick is the second cutting edge?
    A. .001   B. .0032   C. .004   D. .016   E. .04

42. 20% in equal to the fraction $\frac{?}{30}$.
    A. 2/3   B. 6   C. 60   D. 150   E. 600

43. In the figure at the right, the two bars whose lengths have the ratio 2 to 2 are
    A. II and III
    B. IV and I
    C. IV and III
    D. I and III
    E. IV and II

44. The advertisement for a sale reads: *All books reduced more than 20%.* If two books each have the same sale price, which statement MUST be TRUE? The
    A. original prices of both books were the same
    B. original prices of both books were different
    C. percent reduction for both books was the same
    D. sale price of each book is less than 80% of the original price
    E. sale price of each book is more than 80% of the original price.

45. Which of these multiplications will result in an odd number?
    I. 3049   II. 7002   III. 6543   IV. 8765
        ×6431   ×3485   ×3456   ×3497

    The CORRECT answer is:
    A. I and III only
    B. I and IV only
    C. II and IV only
    D. II, III, and IV only
    E. All of the above

46. A movie opened in a theatre on April 6 and was shown every day through April 27.
    On how many days was it shown?
    A. 20
    B. 21
    C. 22
    D. 23
    E. None of the above

47. A student has an average of 80 for three tests.
    What must he score on the next test in order to obtain an average of 84?
    A. 80
    B. 84
    C. 88
    D. 91
    E. 96

48. Of 28 students in a class, 25 contributed to the Junior Red Cross and 16 to the March of Dimes. Every member of the class contributed to AT LEAST one of the two organizations.
    The number who contributed to both is
    A. 3
    B. 12
    C. 14
    D. 16
    E. 25

49. On an arithmetic test, Bill got 32 as an answer to one problem. In working this problem, Bill's only mistake was multiplying by 4 in the last step when he should have divided by 4.
    What is the CORRECT answer to the problem?
    A. 2
    B. 4
    C. 8
    D. 28
    E. It cannot be determined from the information given.

50. Each of two whole numbers is greater than 1. Their product is an odd number. Then, their sum is a(n) _____ their product.
    A. odd number less than
    B. even number less than
    C. odd number greater than
    D. even number greater than
    E. number equal to

KEY (CORRECT ANSWERS)

1.	B	11.	A	21.	B	31.	B	41.	A
2.	B	12.	A	22.	B	32.	B	42.	B
3.	E	13.	D	23.	D	33.	D	43.	A
4.	C	14.	C	24.	A	34.	A	44.	D
5.	E	15.	C	25.	D	35.	C	45.	B
6.	A	16.	C	26.	E	36.	C	46.	C
7.	C	17.	D	27.	A	37.	D	47.	E
8.	C	18.	C	28.	D	38.	E	48.	C
9.	E	19.	D	29.	A	39.	A	49.	A
10.	C	20.	E	30.	B	40.	E	50.	B

9 (#1)

SOLUTIONS TO PROBLEMS

1. 8 and 7 yield 15 by using sum, since 8 + 7 = 15.

2. To average out a group of numbers, add them and divide by the number of numbers. Ex..
The average of 3, 4, 8 = (3+4+8)/3 = 5.

3. 6428 + 974 + 86 + 7280 + 764 + 5407 = 20,938

4. The inverse of division is multiplication. Ex.: To check that 10 ÷ 2 = 5, we note that (5)(2) = 10.

5. 1 in. to 1 yd. = 1 in. to 36 in. = 1 to 36.

6. 6 is not evenly divisible by 8 since whole number.

7. 5.90 ft. = 5 ft. 10.8 in., which is a reasonable man's height.

8. (2+8) ÷ 2 = 5

9. If P is between X and Y, it corresponds to a point between 8 and 12. It would be impossible for W to be between P and X.

10. The greatest common divisor of 24, 40 and 120 is 8 since 24 ÷ 8, 40 ÷ 8, and 120 ÷ 8 all yield whole numbers. No number larger than 8 will divide evenly into each of 24, 40, and 120.

11. $\frac{2}{3} \neq \frac{4}{9}$ because (2)(9) ≠ (3)(4)

12. For addition and subtraction, the rules for placing the decimal point in the answer are alike, namely, to line up the decimal point for each number.

13. $\frac{3}{10} + \frac{1}{5} + \frac{8}{20} = \frac{3}{10} + \frac{2}{10} + \frac{4}{10} = \frac{9}{10}$

14. Let x = missing number. Then, $(\frac{1}{2})(20) = \frac{1}{4}x$. $10 = \frac{1}{4}$, so x = 40

15. 24 is the smallest number which can divide evenly by 4, 6, and 8. This is called the least common multiple.

16. $(\frac{2}{3} \div \frac{1}{2}) \times \frac{1}{2} = \frac{4}{3} \times \frac{1}{2} = \frac{4}{6} = \frac{2}{3}$

10 (#1)

17. $(10{,}003)(\$100) = \$1{,}000{,}300 \approx \$1{,}000{,}000$

18. $\frac{3}{40} = .075$

19. $9\frac{4}{5} + 13\frac{1}{4} = 9\frac{16}{20} + 13\frac{5}{20} = 22\frac{21}{20} = 23\frac{1}{20}$

20. Using 7488, we get $7488 \div 52 = 244$, which is 4 times as large as 36.

21. $2x + 2$ must be even if $x =$ any whole number. The other choices $2x + 1$ and $2x + 3$ must be odd.

22. $407 = (4 \times \text{ten} \times \text{ten}) + (0 \times \text{ten}) + (7 \times \text{one})$.

23. Let $x =$ actual miles. Then, $\frac{4\frac{1}{2}}{72} = \frac{7}{x}$, $4\frac{1}{2}x = 504$, $x = 112$

24. F points to 4, which is in the hundreds place.

25. lies between and . To check convert to decimals, $.\overline{857142}$ is between $.8\overline{3}$ and $.875$

26. $340.292 \div 48.2 = 7.06$

27. From 1:45 PM to 2:15 PM = 30 minutes

28. To completely reduce a fraction, each of numerator and denominator should be divided by the greatest common divisor.

    Ex.: $\frac{18}{30}$ can be reduced to by dividing numerator and denominator by 6. Note: 6 = greatest common divisor of 18 and 30.

29. $3 + \sqrt{64} = 3 + 8 = 11$

30. $-10° + 25° = 15°$ above zero

31. $\$81 \div \$18 = 4.5$. Then, $(4.5)(8) = 36$ weeks

32. When dividing one whole number by another whole number, the remainder must be smaller than the divisor.
    Ex.: $39 \div 17 = 2$ with a remainder of 5, and $5 < 17$.

33. Dividing by 1 or multiplying by 1 will never change the value of a number.

34. $7 \times (3+9) = 84 = (7 \times 3) + (7 \times 9)$

35. $\frac{1}{2}" \div \frac{3}{4}" = (\frac{1}{2})(\frac{4}{3}) = \frac{4}{6} = \frac{2}{3}$

11 (#1)

36. .06, .009, 10 is NOT in descending order. The correct order would be .10, .06, .009.

37. In 1935, the population of the U.S. was about 127,000,000.

38. Average increase = (150,000,000 − 75,000,000) ÷ 50 = 1,500,000.

39. 2 gallons = 8 quarts, so 2 gallons : 3 quarts = 8:3

40. There are 13 darkened boxes out of a total of 25 boxes.
$\frac{13}{25}$ = 52%

41. Second cutting edge = .004" ÷ 4 = .001 in.

42. 20% = $\frac{1}{5} = \frac{6}{30}$

43. Bar II = 3 units, bar III = 1 ½ units, and 3 to 1 ½ = 2 to 1.

44. If a price is reduced by more than 20%, the sales price MUST be less than 80% of the original price. Ex: Original price = $100, reduced by 22%, sales price = $78 = 78% of original price.

45. Since 9×1 = odd and 5×7 = odd, both (3049)(6431) and (8765)(3497) must result in an odd number.

46. 27 − 6 + 1 + 22 days.

47. Let x = score on 4th test. Then, (80)(3) + x = (84)(4). 240 ÷ x = 336. Solving, x = 96

48. Let x = number who contributed to both, 25 − x = number who contributed only to Junior Red Cross, 16 − x = number who contributed only to March of Dimes. Then, x + 25−x+16 −x = 28, so x =13.

49. Since he multiplied by 4, the next to last number = 8. So, 8 ÷ 4 = 2.

50. Since their product is odd, each number must be odd. Their sum is an even number les than their product.
Ex: 3 + 5 = 8 < (3)(5) = 15

ARITHMETIC

EXAMINATION SECTION
TEST 1

DIRECTIONS: Each question or incomplete statement is followed by several suggested answers or completions. Select the one that BEST answers the question or completes the statement. *PRINT THE LETTER OF THE CORRECT ANSWER IN THE SPACE AT THE RIGHT.*

1. 215 x 30 =
   - A. 650
   - B. 6450
   - C. 6500
   - D. None of the above

   1.____

2. How much is saved by buying a $60 bicycle for cash instead of paying $5.25 a month for a year?
   - A. $3.00
   - B. $6.00
   - C. $7.50
   - D. None of the above

   2.____

3. How many square inches are in a square foot?
   - A. 12
   - B. 24
   - C. 144
   - D. None of the above

   3.____

4. What is ten thousand multiplied by one thousand?
   - A. One hundred thousand
   - B. One million
   - C. Ten million
   - D. None of the above

   4.____

5. 4 1/6 + 3 1/12 =
   - A. $7\frac{1}{4}$
   - B. $7\frac{7}{12}$
   - C. $8\frac{1}{4}$
   - D. None of the above

   5.____

6. Tom is awake an average of 15 hours each day. How many hours does he sleep in a week?
   - A. 9
   - B. 45
   - C. 105
   - D. None of the above

   6.____

7. If peppermints costing 70¢ per lb. come in 1 1/2 lb. boxes, what is the cost of 5 boxes?
   - A. $3.50
   - B. $5.25
   - C. $5.75
   - D. None of the above

   7.____

8. What is 349,638 rounded to the nearest hundred?
   - A. 349,600
   - B. 349,640
   - C. 350,000
   - D. None of the above

   8.____

9. 6 1/9 - 3 1/3 =

    A. 2 7/9
    B. 2 8/9
    C. 3 1/2
    D. None of the above

10. Which is less than one-thousandth of an inch?

    A. .025 in.
    B. .004 in.
    C. .0008 in.
    D. None of the above

11. Which is ten million three thousand?

    A. 10,300,000
    B. 10,030,000
    C. 10,003,000
    D. None of the above

12. $\frac{1}{2}+\frac{1}{3}+\frac{1}{6}$

    A. $\frac{1}{11}$
    B. $\frac{5}{6}$
    C. 1
    D. None of the above

13. 2/5 of 20 =

    A. 1/8
    B. 8
    C. 50
    D. None of the above

14. In the following multiplication, N stands for a number.

    4N5
      4
    ―――
    1740

    What is the number?

    A. 3
    B. 6
    C. 8
    D. None of the above

15. 7/8 - 1/2

    A. 3/8
    B. 3/4
    C. 1
    D. None of the above

16. The scale for a house plan is 1/4 in. =1 ft. How long is a hall that is 3 inches long on the plan?

    A. 7 ft.
    B. $12\frac{1}{2}$ ft.
    C. 16 ft.
    D. None of the above

17. 4 1/5 x 1 3/7 =

    A. 5
    B. 5 22/35
    C. 6
    D. None of the above

18. 7/3 - 11/6   18._____

    A. 1/2   B. 1 3/11
    C. 1 1/3   D. None of the above

19. The school pool is 60 feet long.   19._____
    How many lengths must John swim to pass his 100-yard swimming test?

    A. 2   B. 5
    C. 6   D. None of the above

20. A store bought a dozen clocks for $72 and sold each for 50% more than it cost.   20._____
    What was the selling price of one clock?

    A. $6.50   B. $9.00
    C. $26.00   D. None of the above

21. If J stands for John's age and F for his father's age,   21._____
    which shows that John is 26 years younger than his father?

    A. J + F = 26   B. J - 26 = F
    C. J + 26 = F   D. None of the above

22. The board at the right has five equally spaced holes.   22._____
    What is the distance between the centers of holes 2
    and 3?
    A. 8"
    B. 10"
    C. 20"
    D. None of the above

23. $.07 \overline{)51.1} =$ 23._____

    A. 7.3   B. 73
    C. 730   D. None of the above

24. Joe worked from 8:30 A.M. until 4:45 P.M., except for 45 minutes for lunch.   24._____
    How many hours did he work?

    A. $6\frac{1}{2}$ B. $7\frac{1}{2}$

    C. $8\frac{1}{2}$ D. None of the above

25. A highway 150 miles long cost $130 million.   25._____
    What was the AVERAGE cost per mile?

    A. Between $12,000 and $13,000
    B. Between $200,000 and $300,000
    C. Between $800,000 and $900,000
    D. None of the above

KEY (CORRECT ANSWERS)

1. B
2. A
3. C
4. C
5. A

6. D
7. B
8. A
9. A
10. C

11. C
12. C
13. B
14. A
15. A

16. D
17. C
18. A
19. B
20. B

21. C
22. B
23. C
24. B
25. C

SOLUTIONS TO PROBLEMS

1. $(215)(30) = 6450$

2. Savings $= (\$5.25)(12) - \$60 = \$3.00$

3. $(12)(12) = 144$ sq.in. $= 1$ sq.ft.

4. $(10{,}000)(1000) = 10{,}000{,}000 =$ ten million

5. $4\dfrac{1}{6} + 3\dfrac{1}{12} = 4\dfrac{2}{12} + 3\dfrac{1}{12} = 7\dfrac{3}{12} = 7\dfrac{1}{4}$

6. $(9)(7) = 63$ hours of sleep per week

7. $(5)(1\dfrac{1}{2})(.70) = \$5.25$

8. $349{,}638 = 349{,}600$ when rounded to the nearest hundred

9. $6\dfrac{1}{9} - 3\dfrac{1}{3} = 6\dfrac{1}{9} - 3\dfrac{3}{9} = 5\dfrac{10}{9} - 3\dfrac{3}{9} = 2\dfrac{7}{9}$

10. .0008 in. is less than .001 in.

11. $10{,}003{,}000 =$ ten million three thousand

12. $\dfrac{1}{2} + \dfrac{1}{3} + \dfrac{1}{6} = \dfrac{3}{6} + \dfrac{2}{6} + \dfrac{1}{6} = 1$

13. $(\dfrac{2}{5})(\dfrac{20}{1}) = \dfrac{40}{5} = 8$

14. If N = 3, we have $(435)(4) = 1740$. Note: $(5)(4) = 0$ digit and a carry-over of 2 in this multiplication. So, $4 \times N + 2 = 1$ digit Only N = 3 or N = 8 would fit. But note that the final answer of 1740 would eliminate 8 as a choice.

15. $\dfrac{7}{8} - \dfrac{1}{2} = \dfrac{7}{8} - \dfrac{4}{8} = \dfrac{3}{8}$

16. $3" \div \dfrac{1}{4} = 12$. Then, $(12)(1\text{ ft.}) = 12$ ft.

17. $4\dfrac{1}{5} \times 1\dfrac{3}{7} = (\dfrac{21}{5})(\dfrac{10}{7}) = \dfrac{210}{35} = 6$

18. $\dfrac{7}{3} - \dfrac{11}{6} = \dfrac{14}{6} - \dfrac{11}{6} = \dfrac{3}{6} = \dfrac{1}{2}$

19. 100 yds. = 300 ft. Then, 300 ÷ 60 = 5 lengths

20. $72 ÷ 12 = $6.00. Then, ($6.00)(1.50) = $9.00

21. J + 26 = F shows that John is 26 years younger than his father.

22. The distance from hole 1 to hole 5 = 40", so the distance between any two consecutive holes = 40" ÷ 4 = 10"

23. 51.1 ÷ .07 = 730

24. From 8:30 AM to 4:45 PM = 8¼ hrs. Then, hrs. of 3 work. (Note: 45 min. = 3/4 hr.)

25. $130,000,000 ÷ 150 = = $866,666.67 average cost per mile.

    This figure is between $800,000 and $900,000.

TEST 2

DIRECTIONS: Each question or incomplete statement is followed by several suggested answers or completions. Select the one that BEST answers the question or completes the statement. *PRINT THE LETTER OF THE CORRECT ANSWER IN THE SPACE AT THE RIGHT.*

1. What is the volume of the box shown at the right?
   A. 7 cu. ft.
   B. 12 cu. ft.
   C. 14 cu. ft.
   D. None of the above

   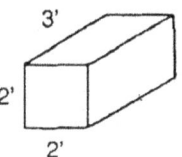

   1.____

2. If lemonade is made by mixing 1 pint of lemon juice with 3 quarts of water, how much lemon juice should be mixed with 3 gallons of water?

   A. 2 quarts
   B. 3 quarts
   C. 1 gallon
   D. None of the above

   2.____

3. What is the area of the figure shown at the right?
   A. 3 sq. in.
   B. 5 sq. in.
   C. 10 sq. in.
   D. None of the above

   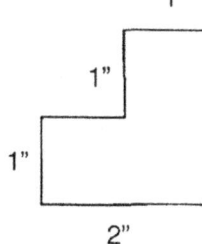

   3.____

4. $\dfrac{21 \times 14 \times 30}{28 \times 15 \times 7} =$

   A. 2
   B. 3
   C. 21
   D. None of the above

   4.____

5. 125% of 60 =

   A. 75
   B. 750
   C. 7500
   D. None of the above

   5.____

6. In the formula I = .05pt, I is the interest due on p dollars borrowed at 5% for t years. What is I if p = $500?

   A. 25t
   B. .10t
   C. .05(500+t)
   D. None of the above

   6.____

7. 4 x 6 = ? x 8. ? =

   A. 3
   B. 24
   C. 192
   D. None of the above

   7.____

8. On a day in January, the temperature in Central City was -18° F. How many degrees below freezing was this?

   A. 14
   B. 18
   C. 50
   D. None of the above

   8.____

9. .875 =

   A. $\dfrac{875}{100}$
   B. $\dfrac{5}{8}$
   C. 7/2
   D. None of the above

10. What is the area of the right triangle shown at the right?
    A. 6 sq. ft.
    B. 12 sq. ft.
    C. 60 sq. ft.
    D. None of the above

11. A United States Savings Bond costs $18.75. How many can be bought for $150?
    A. 6
    B. 8
    C. 12
    D. None of the above

12. One half of a melon was divided equally among 4 boys. What portion of the whole melon did each boy get?
    A. 1/8
    B. 1/6
    C. 1/4
    D. None of the above

13. One third of a foot is what part of a yard?
    A. 1/6
    B. 1/9
    C. 1/12
    D. None of the above

14. What is the sum of XXVIII and XII?
    A. D
    B. XC
    C. XL
    D. None of the above

15. How many people can each have pint of punch from one gallon of punch?
    A. 8
    B. 16
    C. 32
    D. None of the above

16. How much are license plates for a car weighing 3500 lbs. if the cost is $.50 per 100 lbs.?
    A. $17.50
    B. $35.00
    C. $70.00
    D. None of the above

17. What percent of the figure is black?
    A. 20%
    B. 25%
    C. 33 1/3%
    D. None of the above

18. Each week, Bill saves $2 of his own money and $3 given him by his father. When the total is $25, how much of it was from Bill's own money?
    A. $10.00
    B. $12.50
    C. $20.00
    D. None of the above

19. $\dfrac{3}{8} \div \dfrac{1}{4}$

    A. 25   B. .5
    C. 1.5   D. None of the above

20. If the price of a $5 tablecloth is reduced by $1, what is the percent reduction?

    A. 4%   B. 20%
    C. 25%   D. None of the above

KEY (CORRECT ANSWERS)

1.	B	11.	B
2.	A	12.	A
3.	A	13.	B
4.	B	14.	C
5.	A	15.	B
6.	A	16.	A
7.	A	17.	B
8.	C	18.	A
9.	C	19.	C
10.	A	20.	B

SOLUTIONS TO PROBLEMS

1. Volume = (2')(2')(3') = 12 cu.ft.

2. 3 gallons = 12 qts. and 12 qts. 3 qts. = 4.
   Thus, (1 pt)(4) = 4 pts = 2 qts of lemon juice.

3. Area of I = 1" x 1" = 1 sq.in.
   Area of II = 2" x 1" = 2 sq.in.
   Total area = 3 sq.in.

4. $[(21)(14)(30)] \div [(28)(15)(7)] = 8820 \div 2940 = 3$

5. (1.25)(60) = 75

6. I = (.05)($500)(t) = 25t

7. 4 x 6 = 24. Then, 24 ÷ 8 = 3

8. $-18°F = 32° - (-18°) = 50°$ below freezing

9. $.875 = \frac{875}{1000} = \frac{7}{8}$

10. Area = (1/2)(3')(4') = 6 sq.ft.

11. $150 ÷ $18.75 = 8 bonds

12. $\frac{1}{2} \div 4 = \frac{1}{2} \times \frac{1}{4} = \frac{1}{8}$ melon

13. $\frac{1}{3}$ ft = $(\frac{1}{3})(12") = 4"$ and $\frac{4"}{36"} = \frac{1}{9}$ yd.

14. XXVIII + XII = 28 + 12 = 40 = XL

15. 1 gallon = 8 pints. 8 Pints ÷ $\frac{1}{2}$ Pint = 16 servings

16. 3500 ÷ 100 = 35, so (35)($.50) = $17.50

17. $\frac{3}{12}$ = 25% of these boxes are black

18. Let x = Bill's own money. Then, $\frac{2}{5}=\frac{x}{25}$ Solving, x = $10

19. $\frac{3}{8} \div \frac{1}{4} = (\frac{3}{8})(\frac{4}{1}) = \frac{12}{8} = 1.5$

20. $\frac{1}{5}$ = 20% reduction

BASIC MATHEMATICS
EXAMINATION SECTION
TEST 1

DIRECTIONS: Each question or incomplete statement is followed by several suggested answers or completions. Select the one that BEST answers the question or completes the statement. *PRINT THE LETTER OF THE CORRECT ANSWER IN THE SPACE AT THE RIGHT.*

1. Add: 5,796 + 6 + 243 + 24

    A. 6,069   B. 6,079   C. 6,169   D. 6,179

    1.____

2. Subtract: 8,007 - 6,898

    A. 1,109   B. 1,119   C. 1,209   D. 2,109

    2.____

3. Multiply: 3,876 x 904

    A. 364,344
    C. 3,494,904
    B. 3,493,904
    D. 3,503,904

    3.____

4. Divide: $76\sqrt{58,976}$

    A. 775   B. 776   C. 786   D. 876

    4.____

5. Combine: (+4) + (-3) - (-7)

    A. -6   B. +6   C. +8   D. +14

    5.____

6. Simplify: [(-8) x (-6)] ÷ (-3)

    A. -16   B. -14   C. +14   D. +16

    6.____

7. Add: 1 3/5 + 3 7/8

    A. 4 10/40   B. 4 10/13   C. 4 19/40   D. 5 19/40

    7.____

8. Subtract: 4 3/8 - 2 2/3

    A. 1 17/24   B. 2 1/24   C. 2 1/5   D. 2 17/24

    8.____

9. Multiply: 3 2/3 x 5 1/2

    A. 15 1/3   B. 16 1/3   C. 20 1/6   D. 21 1/6

    9.____

10. Divide: $7\frac{1}{2} \div 2\frac{1}{4}$

    A. 3/10   B. 3 1/3   C. 3 1/2   D. 16 7/8

    10.____

11. Add: 434.7 + .04 + 7.107

    A. .441847   B. .442207   C. 441.847   D. 442.207

    11.____

12. Subtract: 986.4 - 34.87

    A. 6.377   B. 63.77   C. 951.53   D. 9,515.3

13. Multiply: 5.96
             x87.4

    A. 51.0904   B. 52.0904   C. 510.904   D. 520.904

14. Divide: $.034\sqrt{6.698}$

    A. 19.2   B. 19.7   C. 192   D. 197

15. Add: $.7 + \frac{1}{2}$

    A. .12   B. 1.2   C. 7/2   D. 15/2

16. What is 5.5% of 75?

    A. 4.125   B. 13.65   C. 41.25   D. 412.5

17. 12 is what percent of 6?

    A. $\frac{1}{2}$%   B. 5%   C. 50%   D. 200%

18. 14 is 28% of _____.

    A. 2   B. 5   C. 50   D. 500

19. A record player sells for $92.00. It is discounted 15% for a special sale. What is the sale price?

    A. $13.80   B. $68.20   C. $77.00   D. $78.20

20. Table A - Acme Mortgage Company
    $320 Loan - 3/4 of 1% Interest

Month	Payment	Principal Paid/Month	Interest Paid/Month
1	$ 27.98	$ 25.58	$ 2.40
2	27.98	25.77	2.21
3	27.98	25.96	2.02
4	27.98	26.15	1.83
5	27.98	26.35	1.63
6	27.98	26.55	1.43
7	27.98	26.75	1.23
8	27.98	26.95	1.03
9	27.98	27.15	.83
10	27.98	27.35	.63
11	27.98	27.56	.42
12	27.93	27.77	.16
Total	$335.82	$ 320.00	$ 15.82

Acme Mortgage Company charges 3/4 of 1% (.0075) on the unpaid balance per month. Bowman Mortgage Company charges 9% per year on the total loan.
Which company charges the LEAST amount of interest on a $320 loan held for one year?

    A. Acme charges the least amount.
    B. Bowman charges the least amount.
    C. Acme and Bowman charge the same.
    D. Insufficient information to determine.

21. Percent of Auto Insurance Discounts for High School Students with Certain Grade Point Averages

Policy Coverage	Grade Point Averages Percent of Discount		
	A	B	C
Liability	33 1/3%	33 1/3%	10%
Comprehensive	20%	10%	-
Collision	25%	20%	-

Frank Verna has a B average. The regular 6-month amounts to be paid for insurance before discount follow:

    Liability $18.00
    Comprehensive $20.00
    Collision $60.00
    Total $98.00

How much does Frank pay for insurance for 6 months?

    A. $20.00   B. $58.00   C. $78.00   D. $156.00

22. Mr. Martinez had a fire in his home. Repairing the damage will cost about $900. His home is valued at $14,000 and is insured for $12,000. Mr. Martinez had paid $32.00 a year for ten years for his insurance. The insurance company has agreed to pay the full amount of the claim ($900).
Which of the following statements are TRUE?
    I. The amount of the claim is more than what has been paid to the company.
    II. The insurance company should pay $14,000 for this claim.
    III. If the house had been completely burned, the insurance company would pay $14,000.
    IV. The maximum claim Mr. Martinez could collect is $12,000
The CORRECT answer is:

    A. I, II   B. I, III   C. II, III   D. I, IV

23. When two coins are tossed, what is the chance that both will be heads?
1 in

    A. 1   B. 2   C. 3   D. 4

24. If 4 teams are in a football league, how many games are necessary to allow each team to play every team one time? _____ games.

    A. 6   B. 9   C. 12   D. 16

25. Five people donated money to the Red Cross. The donations were: $52.00, $76.00, $18.00, $94.00, and $120.00.
What was the AVERAGE donation?

   A. $70   B. $72   C. $76   D. $360

26. From the following statements, determine the CORRECT conclusion.
   I. If Lauraine is a red-head, then Lauraine is hot-tempered.
   II. Lauraine is not hot-tempered.
   The CORRECT answer is:

   A. Lauraine is a red-head.
   B. Lauraine is not a red-head.
   C. Lauraine could be a red-head.
   D. All red-heads are hot-tempered.

27. The graph represents the way the Jones family spends its money (budget). What is the monthly income if they are spending $4080 per year for food?
   A. $1,020
   B. $1,360
   C. $4,080
   D. $16,320

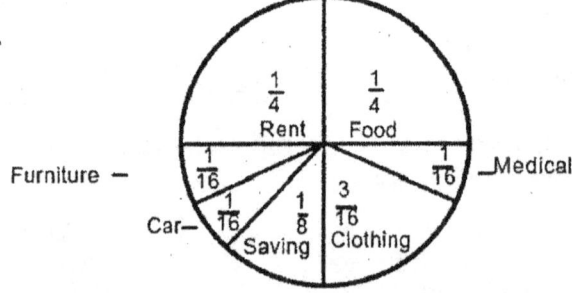

28.

	S	M	T	W	T	F	S
Charlie Simms	?	8	8	8	8	8	3
Jim Chow	2	9	8	8	9	9	4

Time and one-half is paid on Saturdays and for hours worked beyond 8 hours each day. Double-time is paid for Sunday work.
Mr. Simms would have to work how many hours on Sunday to earn as much as Mr. Chow?

   Regular time - $2.00/hour
   Time and one-half - $3.00/hour
   Double time - $4.00/hour

   _____ hours.

   A. 2   B. 5   C. 6   D. 20

29. Jane Gunther wrote checks for these items:
   $16.95 for a hair dryer
   $125.50 for a car payment
   $33.68 for television repair
   $21.59 for a dress
Jane had a beginning check balance (before she wrote the checks) of $351.76. She also deposited $41.50 into her account.
After the checks were written and the deposit made, what was her new balance?

   A. $154.04   B. $195.54   C. $196.54   D. $239.22

30. Given the formula I = PRT:
    If I = 24, R = .05, T = 3, find P.

    A. .00625   B. 1.6   C. 3.6   D. 160.0

    30.____

31. Fencing is needed to enclose a piece of land 26 meters on a side.
    How much fencing is needed?
    _____ meters.
    A. 52
    B. 98
    C. 104
    D. 676

    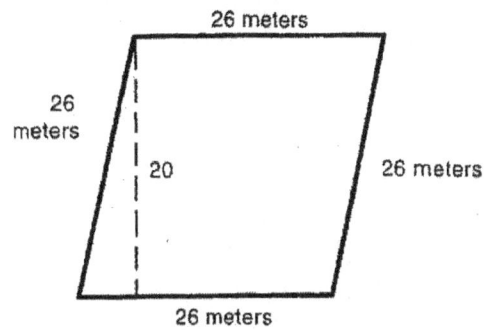

    31.____

32. The area of figure A is 12 square units, and the area of B is 18 square units.
    What is the area of figure C?
    _____ square units.
    A. 16
    B. 16 1/2
    C. 17
    D. 17 1/2

    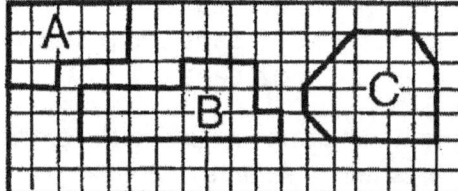

    32.____

33. Using a 3 gallon spray can with a mixture rate of 1 teaspoon of insecticide per quart of water and an application rate of 1 gallon of mixture per 100 square feet, how much water and how much insecticide will be needed to spray an 85 feet by 10 feet lawn?
    _____ teaspoons of insecticide and _____ gallons of water.

    A. 34; 8 1/2   B. 34; 11   C. 17; 8 1/2   D. 24; 6

    33.____

34. Bill Mata will carpet his living room which has the following dimensions. If Bill pays $6.00 per square yard for the carpet, how much will it cost to carpet his living room?
    (9 square feet = 1 square yard)
    A. $192
    B. $216
    C. $1,728
    D. $1,944

    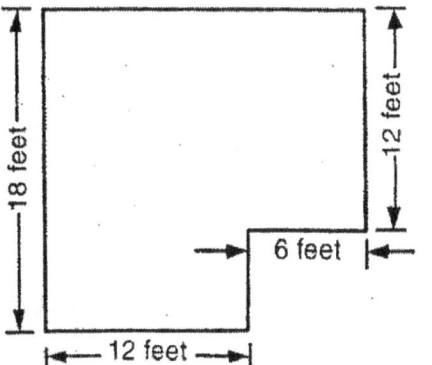

    34.____

35. A cube is painted red and then divided into 27 smaller cubes.
    How many of the smaller cubes are painted on one side only?
    A. 4
    B. 6
    C. 8
    D. 10

    35.____

36. John and Frank wish to pour a cement walk 108 feet long, 4 feet wide, and 3 inches deep.
    If ready-mix concrete can be delivered on weekdays for $19.50 a cubic yard and on weekends for $22.50 a cubic yard, how much would they save on the complete job if they decide on Thursday rather than on the weekend? (1 cubic yard = 27 cubic feet)

    A. $3.00   B. $12.00   C. $36.00   D. $78.00

36.____

37. Antifreeze may be purchased in different size containers for different prices:
    8 oz. can - 43¢
    10 oz. can - 51¢
    12 oz. can - 62¢
    If exactly 15 pints of antifreeze are needed, how many cans of each size are needed for the cost to be minimum? (16 oz. = 1 pint)

    A. 12 - 10 oz. cans and 10 - 12 oz. cans
    B. 24 - 10 oz. cans
    C. 18 - 12 oz. cans and 3-8 oz. cans
    D. 20 - 12 oz. cans

37.____

38. From the graph, assuming the growth rate in the senior class is constant, how many students will be seniors in 2006?

    A. 225
    B. 250
    C. 300
    D. 375

38.____

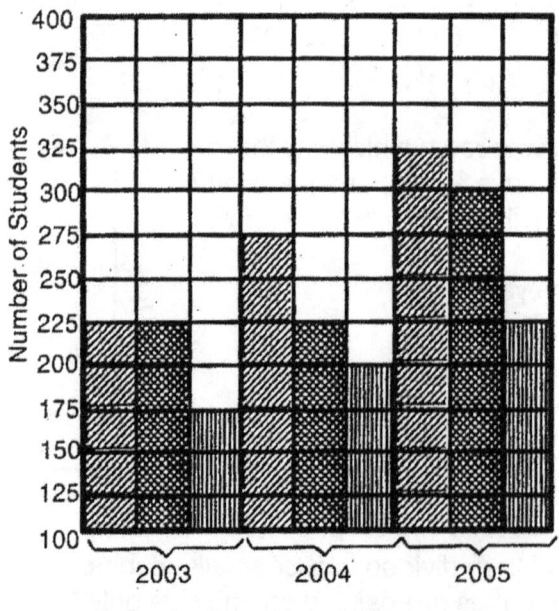

39.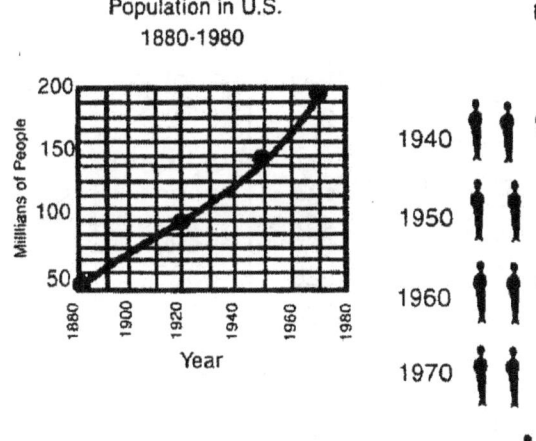

In looking at the two graphs, which of the following conclusions are TRUE?
  I. Both graphs show population growth.
  II. Both graphs cover exactly the same time period.
  III. The percentage of *over 65* population remains the same over the 1940 to 1970 period.
  IV. If you were in the retail business, you might expect greater sales to the *over 65* population in 1970 than in 1940.
  V. In the general population of about 200 million people in 1970, 24 million were over 65.
  VI. In 1920, there were only about 7 million people *over 65* out of about 100 million people.

The CORRECT answer is:

  A. I, III, IV   B. II, IV, V
  C. II, III, VI   D. I, IV, V

40. Jerry Martin owns a home with a market value of $180,000. Its assessed value is 25% of the market value. The tax rate is $5.00 per $100 of assessed value.
What is the amount of his tax?

  A. $225.00   B. $2,250.00   C. $4,500.00   D. $6,750.00

41. You are governor of the state and you need an additional 500 million dollars in tax money. To raise the money, an increase in sales tax is required.
What information would be MOST helpful in determining the new tax rate?
  I. Average income per person in the state
  II. Number of people out of work
  III. Population of the state over 18 years of age
  IV. Birth rate in the state
  V. Percent of income spent on taxable goods
  VI. Percent of income spent on non-taxable goods
  VII. Number of people filing income tax returns

The CORRECT answer is:

  A. I, IV, VI   B. II, III, VII
  C. V, VI   D. I, V

42.

Income Tax Table

If adjusted gross income is-		And the number of exemptions is -					
		1	2	3	4	5	6
At least	But less than			Your tax is -			
$24,500	$24,750	$2360	$1240	$230	$0	$0	$0
24,750	25,000	2400	1280	260	0	0	0
25,000	25,250	2440	1320	300	0	0	0
25,250	25.500	2480	1360	330	0	0	0
25,500	25,750	2530	1390	370	0	0	0
25,750	26,000	2570	1430	400	0	0	0
26,000	26,250	2610	1470	440	0	0	0
26,250	26,500	2650	1510	470	0	0	0
26,500	26,750	2700	1550	510	0	0	0
26,750	27,000	2740	1590	540	0	0	0
27,000	27,250	2780	1630	580	0	0	0
27,250	27,500	2820	1670	610	0	0	0
27,500	27,750	2870	1710	650	0	0	0
27,750	28 000	2910	1750	680	0	0	0
28,000	28,250	2950	1790	720	0	0	0
28,250	28,500	2990	1830	760	0	0	0
28,500	28,750	3040	1870	790	0	0	0

Jerry Ladd earned $28,390.00 during the year. To find his adjusted gross income, he must reduce the amount earned by the standard 10% deduction. He had only one exemption, himself.
How much tax did Jerry pay?

A. $1390   B. $1830   C. $2530   D. $2990

43.

Weight in Ounces	2 oz.	4 oz.	12 oz.	21 oz.
Price	5¢	7¢	15¢	24¢

Using the above table, predict the price if the weight is 32 ounces.

A. 27¢   B. 28¢   C. 29¢   D. 35¢

44. Given [(0,2), (1,4), (2,6),...(5,y)].
What is the value of y?

A. 8   B. 10   C. 12   D. 14

45. If the larger of two numbers is two and one-half times the smaller number, what fraction is the smaller of the larger?

A. 3/4   B. 4/5   C. 5/8   D. 2/5

46. John can save 75¢ a week. He has $3.75 in the bank now. How many weeks will it take him to have a total deposit of $12?

A. 16   B. 9   C. 11   D. 17

47. Using the approximation of 3.14 for pi, find the area of a circle whose diameter is 20 inches.
    _____ square inches.
    A. 31.4 B. 314 C. 628 D. 1256

48. Express .045 as a percent.
    A. 45% B. 4.5% C. .45% D. .045%

49. Twenty is what percent of 50?
    A. 40 B. 60 C. 25 D. 16 2/3

50. Two hundred twenty-five percent of 160 is
    A. 80 B. 350 C. 360 D. 440

KEY (CORRECT ANSWERS)

1. A	11. C	21. C	31. C	41. C
2. A	12. C	22. D	32. C	42. C
3. D	13. D	23. D	33. A	43. D
4. B	14. D	24. A	34. A	44. C
5. C	15. B	25. B	35. B	45. D
6. A	16. A	26. B	36. B	46. C
7. D	17. D	27. D	37. B	47. B
8. A	18. C	28. B	38. B	48. B
9. C	19. D	29. B	39. D	49. A
10. B	20. A	30. D	40. B	50. C

SOLUTIONS TO PROBLEMS

1. $5796 + 6 + 243 + 24 = 6069$

2. $8007 - 6898 = 1109$

3. $(3876)(904) = 3,503,904$

4. $58,976 \div 76 = 776$

5. $(+4) + (-3) - (-7) = 4 - 3 + 7 = +8$

6. $[(-8)(-6)] \div -3 = 48 \div -3 = -16$

7. $1\frac{3}{5} + 3\frac{7}{8} = 1\frac{24}{40} + 3\frac{35}{40} = 4\frac{59}{40} = 5\frac{19}{40}$

8. $4\frac{3}{8} - 2\frac{2}{3} = 4\frac{9}{24} - 2\frac{16}{24} = 3\frac{33}{24} - 2\frac{16}{24} = 1\frac{17}{24}$

9. $(3\frac{2}{3})(5\frac{1}{2}) = (\frac{11}{3})(\frac{11}{2}) = \frac{121}{6} = 20\frac{1}{6}$

10. $7\frac{1}{2} \div 2\frac{1}{4} = \frac{15}{2} \div \frac{9}{4} = (\frac{15}{2})(\frac{4}{9}) = \frac{60}{18} = 3\frac{1}{3}$

11. $434.7 + .04 + 7.107 = 441.847$

12. $986.4 - 34.87 = 951.53$

13. $(5.96)(87.4) = 520.904$

14. $6.698 \div .034 = 197$

15. $.7 + \frac{1}{2} = .7 + .5 = 1.2$

16. $(.055)(75) = 4.125$

17. $\frac{12}{6} = 2 = 200\%$

18. $14 \div .28 = 50$

19. $\$92 - (.15)(\$92) = \$78.20$

20. Acme's interest charge = $\$15.82$, whereas Bowman's interest charge = $(.09)(\$320) = \$28.80$. Thus, Acme charges less.

11 (#1)

21. $(\$18.00)(66\frac{2}{3}\%) + (\$20.00)(90\%) + (\$60.00)(80\%) = \$78.00$

22. Statements I and IV are correct. For 10 years, he has paid $320, but collected $900 on his claim. Also, since the insured value of the home is $12,000, he could not collect more than that amount on any claim.

23. Probability of 2 heads = (1/2)(1/2) = 1/4, which means 1 in 4.

24. The number of required games = (4)(3) ÷ 2 = 6

25. Average donation = ($52.00 + $76.00 + $18.00 + $94.00 + $120.00) ÷ 5 = $72

26. The correct conclusion is B: Lauraine is not a redhead. Let p = Lauraine is a redhead, q = Lauraine is hot-tempered. The given statement says: *If p, then q*. The contrapositive, which is also true, says, *If not q, then not p.* This corresponds to statement B.

27. Let x = monthly income. Then, $4080 = Solving, x = $16,320.

28. Mr. Chow's earnings = (2)($4) + (40)($2) + (7)($3) = $109.
For Monday through Saturday, Mr. Simms' earnings =
(40)($2) + (3)($3) = $89. Thus, Mr. Simms would need to earn
109 - 89 = $20 on Sunday. This means Sunday's time =
$20 ÷ $4 = 5 hours.

29. New balance = $351.76 + $41.50 - $16.95 - $125.50 - $33.68 - $21.59 = $195.54.

30. 24 = (P)(.05)(3), 24 = .15P, so P = 160

31. Fencing: (26)(4) = 104 meters.

32. Area of $C = (4)(5) - (\frac{1}{2})(1)(1) - (\frac{1}{2})(2)(2) - (\frac{1}{2})(1)(1) = 17$

33. (85)(10) = 850 sq.ft. = 8.5 gallons of water. Now, 8.5 gallons = 34 quarts, so 34 teaspoons of insecticide are needed.

34. Area = (12)(6) + (12)(18) = 288 sq.ft. = 32 sq.yds. Total cost = (32)($6) = $192

35. There are 6 cubes painted red on only one side. They are found in the center of each face of the original cube.

36. $(108)(4)(\frac{1}{4}) = 108$ cu.ft. = 4 cu.yds. Savings would be ($22.50)(4) - ($19.50)(4) = $12.00

37. 15 pints = 240 oz. The costs for each selection are:
For A: (12)(.51) + (10)(.62) = $12.32; for B: (24)(.51) = $12.24; for
C: (18)(.62) + (3)(.43) = $12.45; for D: (20)(.62) = $12.40.
So, selection B is the minimum cost.

38. The number of seniors in 2003, 2004, 2005 are 175, 200, and 225, respectively. If growth is constant, the number of seniors in 2006 is 250.

39. Statements I, IV, V are correct. Statement II is wrong because the 1st graph covers 1800-1970, whereas the 2nd graph covers 1940-1970. Statement III is wrong because the *over 65* population increases in percent from 7% in 1940 to 12% in 1970.

40. (25%)($180,000) = $45,000 assessed value. Amount of tax =
    ($5.00)($45,000 ÷ $100) = $2,250

41. For increasing sales tax, it would be helpful in knowing the respective percent of incor spent on taxable vs. non-taxable goods.

42. Adjusted gross income = ($28390)(.90) = $25551.00. On the tax chart, this figure lies between $25500 and $25750. Using the column for 1 exemption, the tax is $2530.

43. Using 2 oz. = .05, note that each additional oz. = 1 cent more. So, 32 oz. = .05 + .30 = .35.

44. (5,y) represents the sixth point in this sequence. Thus, the corresponding y value = (2)(6) = 12

45. Let x = smaller number, 2.5x = larger number.
    Then, $\dfrac{X}{2.5X} = \dfrac{1}{2.5} = \dfrac{10}{25} = \dfrac{2}{5}$

46. $12 - $3.75 = $8.25. Then, $8.25 ÷ .75 = 11 weeks

47. Radius = 10 in. Area = (3.14)(10^2) = 314 sq.in.

48. .045 = 4.5%

49. $\dfrac{20}{50} = 40\%$

50. (225%) (160) = (2.25) (160) = 360

BASIC MATHEMATICS

EXAMINATION SECTION

TEST 1

DIRECTIONS: Each question or incomplete statement is followed by several suggested answers or completions. Select the one that BEST answers the question or completes the statement. *PRINT THE LETTER OF THE CORRECT ANSWER IN THE SPACE AT THE RIGHT.*

1. 534
    18
    +1291

    A. 1733   B. 1743   C. 1833   D. 1843   E. 1853

    1._____

2. (17×23) − 16 + 20 =
    A. 459   B. 427   C. 411   D. 395   E. 355

    2._____

3. 3/7 + 5/11 =
    A. 33/35   B. 4/9   C. 8/18   D. 68/77   E. 15/77

    3._____

4. 4832 ÷ 6 =
    A. 905 1/3   B. 805 1/3   C. 95 1/3   D. 95   E. 85 1/3

    4._____

5. 62.3 − 4.9 =
    A. 5.74   B. 7.4   C. 57.4   D. 58.4   E. 67.4

    5._____

6. 3/5 × 4/9 =
    A. 4/15   B. 7/45   C. 27/20   D. 12/14   E. 15/4

    6._____

7. 14/16 − 5/16 =
    A. 8/16   B. 9/16   C. 11/16   D. 8   E. 9

    7._____

8. 5.03 + 2.7 + 40 =
    A. .570   B. 4.773   C. 5.70   D. 11.73   E. 47.73

    8._____

9. 5.37 × 21.4 =
    A. 11491.8   B. 1149.18   C. 114.918
    D. 11,4918   E. 1.14918

    9._____

10. 5 1/4 + 2 7/8 =
    A. 8 1/4   B. 8 1/8   C. 7 2/3   D. 7 1/4   E. 7 1/8

    10._____

11. −14 + 5 =
    A. −19   B. −9   C. 9   D. 19   E. 70

    11._____

12. 2/7 of 28 =
    A. 98   B. 16   C. 14   D. 8   E. 4

13. 2/5 =
    A. .10   B. .20   C. .25   D. .40   E. .52

14. 20% of _____ is 38.
    A. 7.6   B. 19   C. 76   D. 190   E. 760

15. $\frac{8.4}{400}$ =
    A. .0021   B. .021   C. .21   D. 2.1   E. 21

16. $\frac{4}{5} = \frac{?}{60}$
    A. 240   B. 48   C. 20   D. 15   E. 12

17. What is the area of the rectangle shown at the right?
    A. 47 mm²
    B. 94 mm²
    C. 240 mm²
    D. 480 mm²
    E. 960 mm²

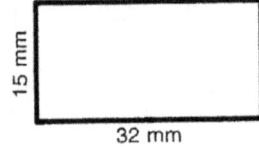

18. What number does ☐ represent in the following equation: 25 - ☐ - ☐ - ☐ - ☐ = 13?
    A. 13   B. 12   C. 7   D. 4   E. 3

19. Approximate lengths are given in the right triangles shown at the right.
    What does length x equal?
    A. 48
    B. 39
    C. 37
    D. 35
    E. 32

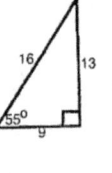

20. What is the perimeter of the triangle shown at the right?
    A. 10 × 15 × 17
    B. 10 + 15 + 17
    C. 1/2 × 10 × 15
    D. 1/2 × 10 × 17
    E. 1/2(10+15+17)

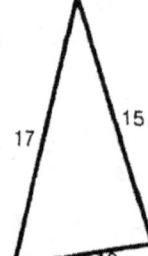

21. Which of the following expressions will give the same answer as 45 × 9?
    A. 5 × 3³   B. (4×9)+(5×9)   C. (40+9) × 5
    D. (45×3) + (45×3)   E. (45×10) − (45×1)

22. Find the average of 19, 21, 21, 22, and 27.
    A. 23   B. 22   C. 21   D. 20   E. 19

22.____

23. In the triangle at the right, how many degrees is <T?
    A. 75°
    B. 85°
    C. 95°
    D. 114°
    E. 180°

23.____

24. About how long is the paper clip?
    A. 5 cm   B. 4 cm   C. 3 cm   D. 2 cm   E. 1 cm

24.____

25. Five stores sell the same size cans of tomato soup. Their prices are listed below.
    Which sells the soup for the LOWEST price per can? _____ cans for _____.
    A. 6; 99¢   B. 6; 90¢   C. 5; 93¢   D. 3; 56¢   E. 3; 50¢

25.____

26. Rock star Peter Giles receives $1.97 royalty on each of his albums that is sold. 14,127 albums are sold.
    Estimate how much Peter Giles will receive.
    A. $7,000   B. $14,000   C. $20,000   D. $26,000   E. $28,000

26.____

27. An amplifier is advertised for 20% off the list price of $430.
    What is the sale price?
    A. $516   B. $454   C. $354   D. $344   E. $215

27.____

28. If 9 dozen eggs cost $3.60, what do 25 dozen eggs cost?
    A. $90.00   B. $10.00   C. $9.00   D. $2.54   E. $40

28.____

29. The distance between New York State and San Antonio is 1,860 miles. If a jet averages 465 miles per hour, how many hours will it take to travel the distance?
    A. 9   B. 5   C. 4   D. 3   E. 2

29.____

30. In a high school homeroom of 32 students, 24 are girls.
    What percent are girls?
    A. 3/4%   B. 24%   C. 25%   D. 75%   E. 80%

30.____

31. Which problem could give the answer shown on the calculator?
    A. 2 + .3
    B. 2 × 3/10
    C. 2 × 1/3
    D. 33333 + .2
    E. 7 ÷ 3

31.____

32.

Cost of Eating at Home
(One Week)

Age	Male	Female
6-11 yrs.	$14	$14
12-19 yrs.	$19	$15
20-54 yrs.	$20	$16
55 and Up	$14	$14

According to the above table, how much will it cost in a typical week for the 3 members of the Wright family to eat at home? Mr. Wright is 56 years old; Mrs. Wright, 52; and their son, Harry, 17.
A. $125   B. $52   C. $49   D. $42   E. $40

32.____

33. According to the above table shown in Question 32, how much does it cost in a typical four-week month to feed a 12-year-old girl?
A. $4   B. $16   C. $48   D. $64   E. $78

33.____

34. Reverend Whilhite jogs for 1½ hours each day, 6 days a week. If he burns 800 calories per hour of jogging, how many calories does he burn in a week?
A. 4800   B. 5600   C. 7200   D. 8400   E. 9000

34.____

35. Ground meat costs 90¢ per pound.
How much does the meat on the scale cost?
    A. $1.80
    B. $1.60
    C. $1.54
    D. $1.44
    E. $.90

35.____

36. According to the graph at the right, about when did the weekly wages for a minimum wage worker go over $100?
    A. 2005
    B. 2010
    C. 2014
    D. 2019
    E. 2020

36.____

37. According to the bar graph at the right, what is the approximate height of the Crystal Beach Comet?
    A. 40 ft.
    B. 90 ft.
    C. 92 ft.
    D. 94 ft.
    E. 98 ft.

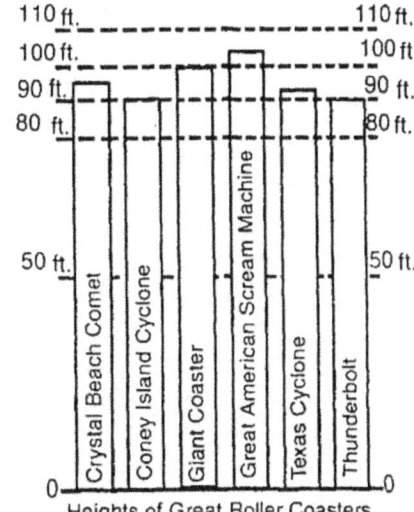

37.____

38. According to the bar graph shown in Question 37, what is the difference in height between the tallest and shortest roller coasters? _____ feet.
    A. 5   B. 10   C. 15   D. 20   E. 50

38.____

39. How much change will you receive from a $10 bill when you buy 4 grapefruits at 90¢ each and 3 apples at 40¢ each?
    A. $6.20   B. $5.20   C. $4.80   D. $4.20   E. $4.00

39.____

40. A medical supplier packages medicine in boxes. The cost of packaging is computed with the flow chart at the right.
What is the cost of packaging medicine in a box that is 30 cm long, 20 cm wide, and 20 cm high?
   A. $.20
   B. $.24
   C. $2.00
   D. $2.40
   E. $3.00

40._____

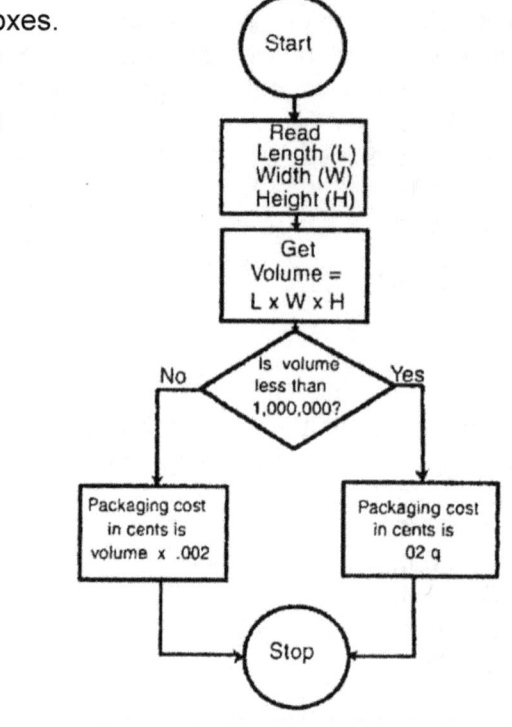

KEY (CORRECT ANSWERS)

1.	D	11.	B	21.	E	31.	E
2.	D	12.	D	22.	B	32.	C
3.	D	13.	D	23.	B	33.	D
4.	B	14.	D	24.	C	34.	C
5.	C	15.	B	25.	B	35.	D
6.	A	16.	B	26.	E	36.	C
7.	B	17.	D	27.	D	37.	D
8.	E	18.	E	28.	B	38.	C
9.	C	19.	A	29.	C	39.	B
10.	B	20.	B	30.	D	40.	A

SOLUTIONS TO PROBLEMS

1. $534 + 18 + 1291 = 1843$

2. $(17 \times 23) - 16 + 20 = 391 - 16 + 20 = 395$

3. $\frac{3}{7} + \frac{5}{11} = \frac{33}{77} + \frac{35}{77} = \frac{68}{77}$

4. $4832 \div 6 = 805\frac{1}{3}$

5. $62.3 - 4.9 = 57.4$

6. $\frac{3}{5} \times \frac{4}{9} = \frac{12}{45} = \frac{4}{15}$

7. $\frac{14}{16} \cdot \frac{5}{16} = \frac{9}{16}$

8. $5.03 + 2.7 + 40 = 47.73$

9. $5.37 \times 21.4 = 114.918$

10. $5\frac{1}{4} + 2\frac{7}{8} = 7\frac{9}{8} = 8\frac{1}{8}$

11. $-14 + 5 = -9$

12. $\frac{2}{7}$ of $28 = (\frac{2}{7})(\frac{28}{1}) = 8$

13. $\frac{2}{5} = .40$ as a decimal

14. Let x = missing number. Then, $.20x = 38$. Solving, $x = 190$

15. $\frac{84}{400} = .021$

16. Let x = missing number. Then, $\frac{4}{5} = \frac{x}{60}$. $5x = 240$, so $x = 48$

17. Area = $(15)(32) = 480 mm^2$

18. Let x = □. Then, $25 - 4x = 13$. So, $-4x = -12$. Solving, $x = 3$.

19. $\frac{9}{27} = \frac{16}{x}$. Then, $9x = 432$. Solving, $x = 48$.

20. Perimeter = $17 + 10 + 15 = 42$

21. $45 \times 9 = 405 = (45 \times 10) - (45 \times 1)$

8 (#1)

22. 19 + 21 + 21 + 22 + 27 = 110. Then, 110 ÷ 5 = 22

23. ∠T = 180° - 50° - 45° = 85°

24. The paper clip's length is about 5 – 2 = 3 cm.

25. For A: price per can = $\frac{.99}{6}$ = .165
    For B: price per can = $\frac{.90}{6}$ = .15
    For C: price per can = $\frac{.93}{5}$ = 186
    For D: price per can = $\frac{.56}{3}$ = .18$\overline{6}$
    For E: price per can = $\frac{.50}{3}$ = .1$\overline{6}$

    Lowest price is for B.

26. $1.97 = $2.00. Then, ($2.00)(14,127) = $28,254 = $28,000

27. Sale price = ($430)(.80) = $344

28. Let x = cost. Then, 9x = $90, so x = $10.00

29. $\frac{1860}{465}$ = 4 hours

30. $\frac{24}{32}$ = 75%

31. $\frac{7}{3}$ = 2.$\overline{3}$ = 2.33333 on the calculator shown

32. Total cost = $14 + $16 + $19 = $49

33. Cost = ($16)(4) = $64

34. (800)(1$\frac{1}{2}$)(6) = 7200 calories

35. (.90)(1.6) = $1.44

36. Around 2015, the minimum weekly wages exceeded $100.

37. The Crystal Beach Comet's height is about 94 ft.

38. Tallest = 105 ft. and the shortest = 90 ft. Difference = 15 ft.

39. $10 – (3)(.90) – (3)(.40) = $5.20 change.

40. (30)(20)(20) = 12,000 cm³. Since 12,000 < 1,000,000, the price is 20 cents.

EXAMINATION SECTION
TEST 1

DIRECTIONS: Each question or incomplete statement is followed by several suggested answers or completions. Select the one that BEST answers the question or completes the statement. *PRINT THE LETTER OF THE CORRECT ANSWER IN THE SPACE AT THE RIGHT.*

1. Which of the following fractions is the SMALLEST?
   A. 2/3　　B. 4/5　　C. 5/7　　D. 5/11

2. 40% is equivalent to which of the following?
   A. 4/5　　B. 4/6　　C. 2/5　　D. 4/100

3. How many 100's are in 10,000?
   A. 10　　B. 100　　C. 10,000　　D. 100,000

4. $\frac{6}{7} + \frac{11}{12}$ is approximately
   A. 1　　B. 2　　C. 17　　D. 19

5. The time required to heat water to a certain temperature is directly proportional to the volume of water being heated.
   If it takes 12 minutes to heat 1 ½ gallons of water, how many minutes will it take to heat 2 gallons of water?
   A. 12　　B. 16　　C. 18　　D. 24

6. The cost of an item increased by 25%.
   If the original cost was C dollars, identify the expression which gives the new cost of that item.
   A. C + 0.25　　B. 1/4 C　　C. 25C　　D. 1.25C

7. Given the formula PV = nRT, all of the following are true EXCEPT
   A. T = PV/nR　　B. P = nRTN　　C. V = P/nRT　　D. n = PV/RT

8. If a Fahrenheit (F) temperature reading is 104, find its Celsius (C) equivalent, given that C = i(F-32).
   A. 36　　B. 40　　C. 72　　D. 76

9. If 40% of a graduating class plans to go directly to work after graduation, which of the following must be TRUE?
   A. Less than half of the class plans to go directly to work.
   B. Forty members of the class plan to enter the job market.
   C. Most of the class plans to go directly to work.
   D. Six in ten members of the class are expected not to graduate.

10. Given a multiple-choice test item which has 5 choices, what is the probability of guessing the correct answer if you know nothing about the item content?
   A. 5%   B. 10%   C. 20%   D. 25%

11.
S	T
0	80
5	75
10	65
15	50
20	30
25	5

Which graph BEST represents the data shown in the above table?

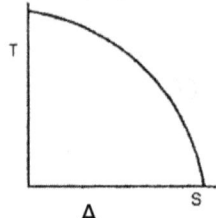
A
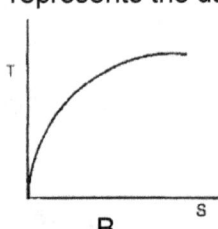
B
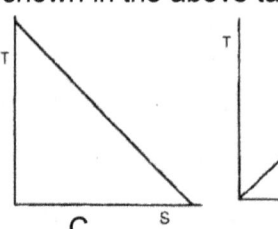
C
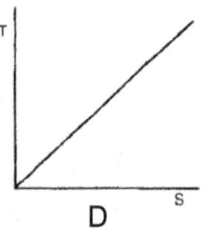
D

12. If 3(x+5y) = 24, find y when x = 3.
   A. 1   B. 3   C. 33/5   D. 7

13. The payroll of a grocery store for its 23 clerks is $395,421. Which expression below shows the average salary of a clerk?
   A. 395,421 × 23
   B. 23 ÷ 395,421
   C. (395,421 × 23
   D. 395,421 ÷ 23

14. If 12.8 pounds of coffee cost $50.80, what is the APPROXIMATE price per pound?
   A. $2.00   B. $3.00   C. $4.00   D. $5.00

15. A road map has a scale where 1 inch corresponds to 150 miles. A distance of 3 3/4 inches on the map corresponds to what actual distance? ____ miles.
   A. 153.75   B. 375   C. 525   D. 562.5

16. How many square feet of plywood are needed to construct the back and 4 adjacent sides of the box shown at the right?
   A. 63
   B. 90
   C. 96
   D. 126

17. One thirty-pound bag of lawn fertilizer costs $20.00 and will cover 600 square feet of lawn. Terry's lawn is a 96 foot by 75 foot rectangle. How much will it cost Terry to buy enough bags of fertilizer for her lawn?
Which of the following do you NOT need in order to solve this problem? The
   A. product of 96 and 75
   B. fact that one bag weighs 30 pounds
   C. fact that one bag covers 600 square feet
   D. fact that one bag costs $20.00

17.____

18. On the graph shown at the right, between which hours was the drop in temperature GREATEST?
   A. 11:00 – Noon
   B. Noon – 1:00
   C. 1:00 – 2:00
   D. 2:00 – 3:00

18.____

19. If on a typical railroad track the distance from the center of one railroad tie to the next is 30 inches, approximately how many ties would be needed for one mile of track?
   A. 180   B. 2,110   C. 6,340   D. 63,360

19.____

20. Which of the following is MOST likely to be the volume of a wine bottle?
   A. 750 milliliters   B. 7 kilograms
   C. 7 milligrams   D. 7 liters

20.____

21. What is the reading on the gauge shown at the right?
   A. -7
   B. -3
   C. 1
   D. 3

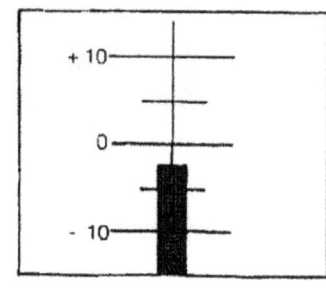

21.____

22. Which statement below disproves the assertion, *All students in Mrs. Marino's 10th grade geometry class are planning to go to college?*
   A. Albert is in Mrs. Marino's class, but he is not planning to take mathematics next year.
   B. Jorge is not in Mrs. Marino's class, but he is still planning to go to college.
   C. Pierre is in Mrs. Marino's class but says he will not be attending school anymore after this year.
   D. Crystal is in Mrs. Marino's class and plans to attend Yale University when she graduates.

22.____

23. A store advertisement reads, *Buy not while our prices are low. There will never be a better time to buy.*
    The customer reading this advertisement should assume that
    A. the prices at the store will probably never be lower
    B. right now, this store has the best prices in town
    C. prices are higher at other stores
    D. prices are always lowest at this store

24. *Given any positive integer, there is always a positive number B such that A × B is less than 1.*
    Which statement below supports this generalization?
    A. 8 × 1/16 = 1/2
    B. 8 × 1/2 = 4
    C. 5/2 × 1/10 = 1/4
    D. 1/2 × 1/2 = 1/2

25. Of the following expressions, which is equivalent to 4C + D = 12E?
    A. C = 4(12E-D)
    B. 4 + D = 12E − C
    C. 4C + 12E = -D
    D. $C = \frac{12E-D}{4}$

KEY (CORRECT ANSWERS)

1.	D	11.	A
2.	C	12.	A
3.	B	13.	D
4.	B	14.	C
5.	B	15.	D
6.	D	16.	C
7.	C	17.	B
8.	B	18.	D
9.	A	19.	B
10.	C	20.	A

21.	B
22.	C
23.	A
24.	A
25.	D

SOLUTIONS TO PROBLEMS

1. Converting to decimals, we get $.\overline{6}$, $.8$, $.714$ (approx..), $.\overline{45}$. The smallest is $.\overline{45}$ corresponding to 5/11.

2. 40% = 40/100 = 2/5

3. 10,000 ÷ 100 = 100

4. $\frac{6}{7} + \frac{11}{12} = (72+77) \div 84 = \frac{149}{84} \approx 1.77 \approx 2$

5. Let x = required minutes. Then, 12/1 ½ = x². This reduces to 1 1/2x = 24. Solving, x = 16.

6. New cost is C + .25C = 1.25C

7. For PV = nRT, V = nRT/P

8. C = 5/9 (104-32) = 5/9(72) = 40

9. Since 40% is less than 50% (or half), we conclude that less than half of the class plans to go to work directly after graduation.

10. The probability of guessing right is 1/5 or 20%

11. Curve A is most accurate since as S increases, we see that T decreases. Note, however, that the relationship is NOT linear. Although S increases in equal amounts, the decrease in T is NOT in equal amounts.

12. 3(3+5y) = 24. This simplifies to 9 + 15y = 24. Solving, y = 1

13. The average salary is $395,421 ÷ 23

14. The price per pound is $50.80 ÷ 12.8 = $3,96875 or approximately $4.

15. Actual distance is (3 3/4)(150) = 562.5 miles.

16. The area of the back = (6)(5) = 30 sq. ft. The combined area of the two vertical sides is (2)(6)(3) = 36 sq. ft. The combined area of the horizontal sides is (2)(5)(3) = 30 sq. ft. Total area = 30 + 36 30 = 96 square feet.

17. Choice B is not relevant to solving the problem since the cost will be [(96)(75)/600][$20] = $240. So, the weight per bag is not needed.

18. For the graph, the largest temperature drop was from 2:00 P.M. to 3:00 P.M. The temperature dropped 20 – 10 = 10 degrees.

19. 1 mile = 5280 feet = 63,360 inches. Then, 63,360 ÷ 30 = 2112 or about 2110 ties are needed.

20. Since 1 liter = 1.06 quarts, 750 milliliters = (750/1000)(1.06) = .795 quarts. This is a reasonable volume for a wine bottle.

21. The reading is -3.

22. Statement C contradicts the given information, since Pierre is in Mrs. Marino's class. Then he should plan to go to college.

23. Since there will never be a better time to buy at this particular store, the customer can assume the current prices will probably never be lower.

24. Statement A illustrates this concept. Note that in general, if n is a positive integer. then $(n)(\frac{1}{n-1}) < 1$

25.

TEST 2

DIRECTIONS: Each question or incomplete statement is followed by several suggested answers or completions. Select the one that BEST answers the question or completes the statement. *PRINT THE LETTER OF THE CORRECT ANSWER IN THE SPACE AT THE RIGHT.*

1. Which of the following lists numbers in INCREASING order?
   A. 0.4, 0.04, 0.004
   B. 2.71, 3.15, 2.996
   C. 0.7, 0.77, 0.777
   D. 0.06, 0.5, 0.073

   1._____

2. $\dfrac{4}{10}+\dfrac{7}{100}+\dfrac{5}{1000}=$
   A. 4.75
   B. 0.475
   C. 0.0475
   D. 0.00475

   2._____

3. 700 times what number equals 7?
   A. 10
   B. 0.1
   C. 0.01
   D. 0.001

   3._____

4. 943-251 is approximately
   A. 600
   B. 650
   C. 700
   D. 1200

   4._____

5. The time needed to set up a complicated piece of machinery is inversely proportional to the number of years' experience of the worker.
   If a worker with 10 years' experience needs 6 hours to do the job, how long will it take a worker with 15 years' experience?
   A. 4
   B. 5
   C. 9
   D. 25

   5._____

6. Let W represent the number of waiters and D, the number of diners in a particular restaurant.
   Identify the expression which represents the statement: There are 10 times as many diners as waiters.
   A. 10W = D
   B. 10D = W
   C. 10D + 10W
   D. 10 = D + W

   6._____

7. Which of the following is equivalent to the formula F = XC + Y?
   A. F – C = X + Y
   B. Y = F + XC
   C. $C = \dfrac{FY}{X}$
   D. $C = \dfrac{FX}{Y}$

   7._____

8. Given the formula A = BC/D, if A = 12, B = 6, and D = 3, what is the value of C?
   A. 2/3
   B. 6
   C. 18
   D. 24

   8._____

9. 5 is to 7 as X is to 35. X =
   A. 7
   B. 12
   C. 24
   D. 49

   9._____

10. Kramer Middle School has 5 seventh grade mathematics teachers: two of the math teachers are women and three are men.
    If you are assigned a teacher at random, what is the probability of getting a female teacher?
    A. 0.2
    B. 0.4
    C. 0.6
    D. 0.8

    10._____

11. Which statement BEST describes the graph shown at the right?
    Temperature
    A. and time decrease at the same rate
    B. and time increase at the same rate
    C. increases over time
    D. decreases over time

12. If $3x + 4 = 22y$, find y when $x = 2$.
    A. 0   B. 3   C. 4 1/2   D. 5

13. A car goes 243 miles on 8.7 gallons of gas.
    Which numeric expression should be used to determine the car's miles per gallon?
    A. 243 × 87   B. 8.7 ÷ 243   C. 243 ÷ 8.7   D. 243 − 8.7

14. What is the average cost per book if you buy six books at $4.00 each and four books at $5.00 each?
    A. $4.40   B. $4.50   C. $4.60   D. $5.40

15. A publisher's sale offers a 15% discount to anyone buying more than 100 workbooks.
    What will be the discount on 200 workbooks selling at $2.25 each?
    A. $15.00   B. $30.00   C. $33.75   D. $67.50

16. A road crew erects 125 meters of fencing in one workday.
    How many workdays are required to erect a kilometer of fencing?
    A. 0.8   B. 8   C. 80   D. 800

17. Last month Kim made several telephone calls to New York City totaling 45 minutes in all.
    What does Kim need in order to calculate the average duration of her New York City calls?
    The
    A. total number of calls she made to New York City
    B. cost per minute of a call to New York City
    C. total cost of her telephone bill last month
    D. days of the week on which the calls are made

18.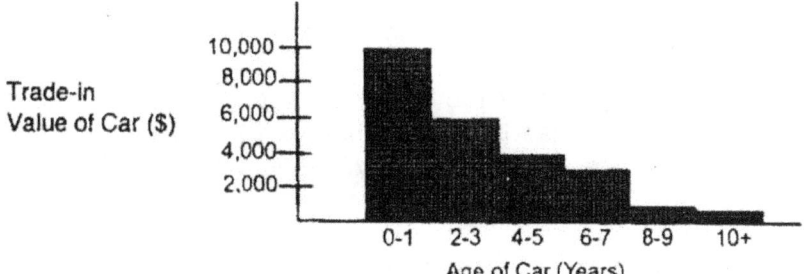

    The above chart relates a car's age to its trade-in value.
    Based on the chart, which of the following is TRUE?
    A. A 4- to 5-year old car has a trade-in value of about $2,000
    B. The trade-in vale of an 8- to 9-year old car is about 1/3 that of a 2- to 3-year old car.
    C. A 6- to 7-year old car has no trade-in value.
    D. A 4- to 5-year old car's trade-in value is about $2,000 less than that of a 2- to 3-year old car.

19. Which of the following expressions could be used to determine how many seconds are in a 24-hour day?
    A. 60 × 60 × 24
    B. 60 × 12 × 24
    C. 60 × 2 × 24
    D. 60 × 24

20. For measuring milk, we could use each of the following EXCEPT
    A. liters
    B. kilograms
    C. millimeters
    D. cubic centimeters

21. What is the reading on the gauge shown at the right?
    A. 51
    B. 60
    C. 62.5
    D. 70

    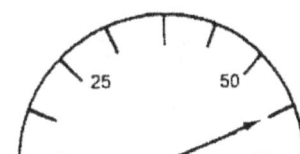

22. Bill is taller than Yvonne. Yvonne is shorter than Sue. Sue is 5' tall.
    Which of the following conclusions must be TRUE?
    A. Bill is taller than Sue.
    B. Yvonne is taller than 5'4".
    C. Sue is taller than Bill.
    D. Yvonne is the shortest.

23. The Bass family traveled 268 miles during the first day of their vacation and another 300 miles on the next day. Maria Bass said they were 568 miles from home.
    Which of the following facts did Maria assume?
    A. They traveled faster on the first day and slower on the second.
    B. If she plotted the vacation route on a map, it would be a straight line.
    C. Their car used more gasoline on the second day.
    D. They traveled faster on the second day than they did on the first day.

24. *The word LEFT in a mathematics problem indicate that it is a subtraction problem.*
   Which of the following mathematics problems prove this statement FALSE?
   A. I want to put 150 bottles into cartons which hold 8 bottles each. After I completely fill as many cartons as I can, how many bottles will be left?
   B. Sarah has 5 books but gave one to John. How many books did Sarah have left?
   C. Carlos had $4.25 but spent $3.75. How much did he have left?
   D. We had 38 models in stock but after yesterday's sale, only 12 are left. How many did we sell?

24.____

25. *Let Q represent the number of miles Dave can jog in 15 minutes.*
   Identify the expression which represents the number of miles Dave can jog between 3:00 P.M. and 4:45 P.M.
   A. 1 3/4 Q   B. 7Q   C. 15 × 1 3/4xQ   D. Q/7

25.____

KEY (CORRECT ANSWERS)

1.	C		11.	D
2.	B		12.	D
3.	C		13.	C
4.	C		14.	A
5.	A		15.	D
6.	A		16.	B
7.	C		17.	A
8.	B		18.	D
9.	C		19.	A
10.	B		20.	C

21.	C
22.	D
23.	B
24.	A
25.	B

5 (#2)

SOLUTIONS TO PROBLEMS

1. Choice C is in ascending order since .y < .77 < .777

2. Rewrite in decimal form: .4 + .07 + .005 = .475

3. Let x = missing number. Then, 700x = 7. Solving, x = 7/700 = .01

4. 943 – 251 = 692 ≈ 700

5. Let x = hours needed. Then, 10/15 = x/6. Solving, x = 4

6. The number of diners (D) is 10 times as many waiters (10W). So, D = 10W, or 10W = D

7. Given F = XC + Y, subtract Y from each side to get F – Y = XC. Finally, dividing by X, we get (F-Y)/X = C

8. 12 = 6C/3. Then, 12 = 2C, so C = 6

9. 5/7 = x/35. Then, 7x = 175, so x = 25

10. Probability of a female teacher = 2/5 = .4

11. Statement D is best, since as time increases, the temperature decreases.

12. (3)(2) + 4 = 2y. Then, 10 = 2y, so y = 5.

13. Miles per gallon = 243/8.7

14. Total purchase is (6)($4) + (4)($5) = $44. The average cost per book is $44 ÷ 10 = $4.40

15. (220)($2.25) = $450. The discount is (.15)($450) = $67.50

16. The number of workdays is 1000 ÷ 125 = 8

17. Choice A is correct because the average duration of the phone calls = total time ÷ total number of calls.

18. Statement D is correct since a 4-5 year old car's value is $4,000, whereas a 2-3 year-old car's value is $6000.

19. 60 seconds = 1 minute and 60 minutes = 1 hour. Thus, 24 hours = (24)(60)(60) or (60)(60)(24) seconds.

20. We can't use millimeters in measuring milk since millimeters is a linear measurement.

21. The reading shows the average of 50 and 75 = 62.5

22. Since Yvonne is shorter than both Bill and Sue, Yvonne is the shortest.

23. Statement B is assumed correct since 568 = 269 + 300 could only be true if the mileage traveled represents a straight line.

24. To find the number of bottles left, we look only for the remainder when 150 is divided b 8 (which happens to be 6).

25. 3:00 P.M. to 4:45 P.M. = 1 hour and 45 minutes = 105 minutes
    Let Q = 15 minutes
    105 / 15 = 7
    7(15) = 105 = 7Q

EXAMINATION SECTION
TEST 1

DIRECTIONS: Each question or incomplete statement is followed by several suggested answers or completions. Select the one that BEST answers the question or completes the statement. *PRINT THE LETTER OF THE CORRECT ANSWER IN THE SPACE AT THE RIGHT.*

1. 2/3 × 12 equals
   A. 4
   B. 6
   C. 8
   D. 18
   E. None of the above

   1.____

2. 83.97
   1.78
   14.36
   9.03
   The sum of the above column is
   A. 99.13
   B. 99.24
   C. 109.14
   D. 109.23
   E. 109.24

   2.____

3. The value of x in the equation 5x = 75 is
   A. 13
   B. 15
   C. 70
   D. 80
   E. None of the above

   3.____

4. 65 ÷ .13 equals
   A. .501
   B. 5.01
   C. 50.1
   D. 501
   E. None of the above

   4.____

5. The sum of 6 feet 8 inches and 3 feet 4 inches is
   A. 2 ft. 2 in.
   B. 9 ft.
   C. 10 ft.
   D. 10 ft. 12 in.
   E. None of the above

   5.____

6. 3/4 − 1/2 + 1/8 equals
   A. 3/10
   B. 3/8
   C. 5/8
   D. 1 3/8
   E. None of the above

   6.____

7. 4 5/16 − 2 3/8 equals
   A. 1 15/16
   B. 2 1/16
   C. 2 ¼
   D. 2 15/16
   E. None of the above

   7.____

8. (−12)+(−3) equals
   A. −9
   B. +15
   C. +9
   D. −15
   E. None of the above

   8.____

9. The ratio of the lengths of two lines is 5 to 3. The length of the shorter line is 30 inches. The length of the longer line is _____ inches.
   A. 18
   B. 48
   C. 50
   D. 140
   E. None of the above

   9.____

10. .025 written as a common fraction is
    A. 25/10   B. 25/100   C. 25/1000
    D. 25/10,000   E. None of the above

11. In the proportion 5/2 = 9/x the value of x is
    A. 1.8   B. 3.6   C. 22.5
    D. 36   E. None of the above

12. 33 1/3 percent of 3 equals
    A. 1   B. 10   C. 100/3
    D. 100   E. None of the above

13. $\sqrt{233}$ equals
    A. 15   B. 20.5   C. 25
    D. 112.5   E. None of the above

14. On the portion of the scale shown at the right, the reading to which the arrow points is _____ units.
    A. 6 3/16
    B. 6 3/5
    C. 6 3/4
    D. 7 5/8
    E. None of the above

15. If 4x/5 – 6 = 10, then x equals
    A. 15 1/5   B. 5   C. 4
    D. 3 1/5   E. None of the above

16. The difference between 8 hours 0 minutes 6 seconds and 6 hours 4 minutes 15 seconds is _____ hr. _____ min. _____ seconds.
    A. 0; 54; 51   B. 1; 54; 51   C. 2; 4; 9
    D. 2; 54; 45   E. None of the above

17. The scores made by nine pupils on a science test are: 2, 4, 6, 6, 8, 10, 12, 14, 19.
    The MEAN score is
    A. 6   B. 8   C. 9
    D. 81   E. None of the above

18. A certain cost formula is represented graphically in the figure at the right. From the graph, when n = 7, the value of C is about
    A. 140
    B. 120
    C. 110
    D. 102
    E. None of the above

19. A simplified form of the expression A = 1/2 bh + 1/2 ah is 19.____
    A. A = ½ h(b+a) B. bh + ah C. A = abh
    D. $\frac{A}{1/2bh}$ = 1/2 ah E. None of the above

20. The ratio of 6 inches to 3 feet is 20.____
    A. 6/1 B. 2/1 C. 1/2
    D. 1/18 E. None of the above

21. The value of s in the equation 3s = 12 – s is 21.____
    A. 6 B. 4 C. 3 2/3
    D. 3 E. None of the above

22. 16 2/3 percent of what number is 30? 22.____
    A. 5 B. 18 C. 160
    D. 180 E. None of the above

23. The line graph shown at the right represents the temperature readings in Albany, New York, at two-hour intervals from 4 A.M. to 10 P.M. on a certain day in February. The APPROXIMATE change in temperature between 7 A.M. and 9 A.M. is _____ degrees. 23.____
    A. 3.5
    B. 3.0
    C. 2.5
    D. 2.0
    E. None of the above

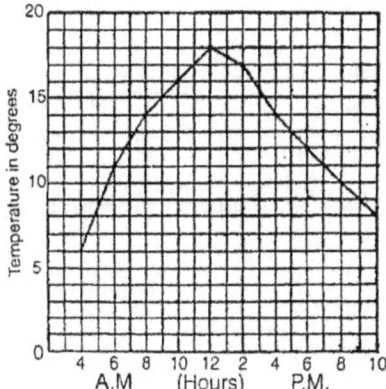

Questions 24-25.

DIRECTIONS: Questions 24 and 25 are to be answered on the basis of the following figure and information.

In the figure below, a square whose side is b is cut from a square whose side is a.

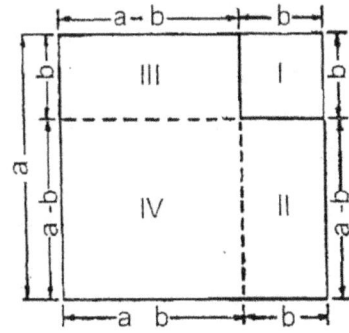

24. The sum of the perimeters of Section I and Section III can be represented by 24.____
    A. b^2 　　　　　　B. $4a - 2b$ 　　　　　　C. $2a + 3b$
    D. $a(a-b)$ 　　　　E. None of the above

25. The sum of the areas of Section II and Section IV can be represented by 25.____
    A. b^2 　　　　　　B. $4a - 2b$ 　　　　　　C. $2a + 3b$
    D. $a(a-b)$ 　　　　E. None of the above

26. The temperature reading (F) on the Fahrenheit scale equals 32 more than 9/5 of the Centigrade reading (C). 26.____
    This rule when translated into symbols is expressed by
    A. $F = 9/5C + 32$ 　　B. $F = 9/5(C+32)$ 　　C. $F = 9/5 + 32C$
    D. $F + 32 = 9/5C$ 　　E. None of the above

27. In the equation $6x - 114 = .3x$, the value of x is 27.____
    A. 38 　　　　　　　B. 20 　　　　　　　　　C. 12 2/3
    D. 2 　　　　　　　　E. None of the above

28. What percent of 42 is 84? 28.____
    A. 4% 　　　　　　　B. 2% 　　　　　　　　　C. 50%
    D. 200% 　　　　　　E. None of the above

29. The CORRECT name of the solid figure at the right is 29.____
    A. semicircle
    B. circle
    C. sphere
    D. cone
    E. cylinder

30. Which of these fractions has the LARGEST value? 30.____
    A. 1/2 　　　　　　　B. 5/9 　　　　　　　　　C. 7/12
    D. 2/3 　　　　　　　E. 3/4

31. The formula for the area of a circle is A = 31.____
    A. π^2 　　　　　　B. $2/3 \pi^2$ 　　　　　　C. $2\pi r$
    D. bh 　　　　　　　E. None of the above

32. The CORRECT name of the figure at the right is 32.____
    A. pentagon
    B. hexagon
    C. rectangle
    D. trapezoid
    E. square

33. The figure at the right is a
    A. rectangle
    B. square
    C. pentagon
    D. trapezoid
    E. parallelogram

33.____

34. If x = -18, y = 3, and z = -2, then x – y + z equals
    A. 3   B. -3   C. -23   D. -52   E. -56

34.____

35. The number 335,560 rounded off to the nearest thousand is
    A. 335,000   B. 335,500   C. 336,000
    D. 340,000   E. None of the above

35.____

36. In the triangle ABC at the right, the sum of the angles is _____ degrees.
    A. 360
    B. 180
    C. 90
    D. 35
    E. None of the above

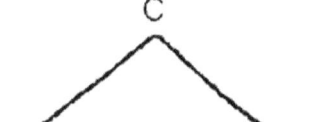

36.____

37. According to the map shown at the right, the APPROXIMATE distance between the southern point of New York City and Albany is _____ miles.
    A. 50
    B. 75
    C. 130
    D. 180
    E. 200

37.____

38. If 6 is added to a certain number n, the result is 1. An equation which expresses this relationship is
    A. n + 6 = 1   B. n – 1 = 6   C. 6 – n = 1
    D. n + 1 = 6   E. None of the above

38.____

39. In the expression $2n^3$, the 3 is called a(n)
    A. coefficient   B. factor   C. exponent
    D. multiplicand   E. None of the above

39.____

40. The number of inches in n feet is represented by
    A. 12n   B. 3n   C. n/3
    D. n/12   E. None of the above

40.____

41. The simple interest on $600 for 3 months at 4 percent per year is represented by 600 × .04x
    A. 1/4
    B. 1/3
    C. 3
    D. 4
    E. None of the above

41.____

42. The circle graph shown at the right indicates how a family's annual budget of $3,000 was planned.
    Food   40 percent
    Shelter   25 percent
    Clothes   15 percent
    Operating Expenses   10 percent
    Insurance & Savings   10 percent
    The part of the circle representing Shelter is _____ degrees.
    A. 25
    B. 45
    C. 90
    D. 250
    E. None of the above

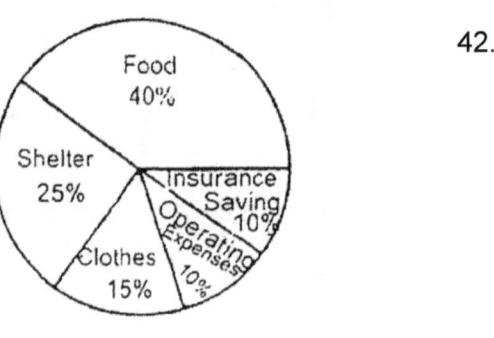

42.____

43. In the parallelogram ABCD shown at the right, each small square represents 4 square inches. The area of the right triangle AED represents _____ square inches.
    A. 3
    B. 12
    C. 24
    D. 48
    E. None of the above

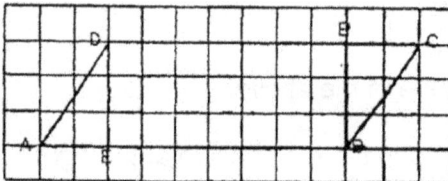

45.____

44. A surveyor measured angle x with a transit. (See figure at the right.) Angle x is called
    A. the angle of depression B from A
    B. an obtuse angle
    C. the supplement of angle
    D. the angle of elevation of B from A
    E. none of the above

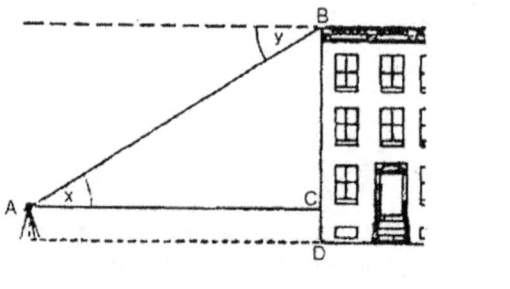

44.____

45. In the figure at the right, AOB is a straight line. An equation showing the relationship between u and v is
    A. u = 1/2v
    B. u = 180 – v
    C. u + v = 90
    D. v = 3u
    E. None of the above

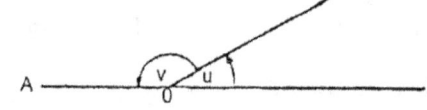

45.____

46. If x = 4 when y = 6 and x varies directly as y, then when y = 15, x equals
    A. 20   B. 10   C. 1 3/5
    D. 1 1/3   E. None of the above

47. A discount of 15 percent from a marked price produces a net price which is _____ of the marked price.
    A. .15%   B. .85%   C. 15%   D. 85%   E. 115%

48. When the formula A = P + Prt is solved for t, t equals
    A. A − P − Pr   B. $\frac{A-Pr}{P}$ C. $\frac{A-P}{I+r}$
    D. $\frac{A-P}{Pr}$ E. None of the above

49. The Greek letter π
    A. was assigned the value 3.1416 by the International Court of Law
    B. was given an arbitrary value of 22/7 by a famous mathematician
    C. was discovered to be exactly 3.142
    D. when multiplied by the radius of a circle equals the area
    E. is used as a symbol for the ratio of the circumference of a circle to its diameter

50. If the base and altitude of a triangle are doubled, the area
    A. remains constant   B. is multiplied by 4   C. is doubled
    D. is divided by 4   E. is none of the above

51. Each side of the equilateral triangle in the figure at the right is s inches long. The length of an altitude of the triangle is represented as
    A. s in.
    B. S√2
    C. S√3
    D. $\frac{S\sqrt{3}}{2}$ in.
    E. None of the above

52. The length of a meter is about _____ inches.
    A. 1   B. 6   C. 12   D. 40   E. 100

53. A point which lies on the straight-line graph of the equation 2x − 3y = 12 is
    A. (3,-2)   B. (2,-3)   C. (-4,0)
    D. (0,6)   E. None of the above

54. If the two parallel lines AB and CD in the figure at the right are cut by a third line, EF, then the FALSE statement is
   A. ∠r + ∠s = ∠s + ∠y
   B. ∠y + ∠w = ∠t + ∠s
   C. ∠u + ∠w = ∠s + ∠x
   D. ∠r + ∠x = ∠t + ∠w
   E. ∠s + ∠u = ∠r + ∠t

54._____

55. The product of n^4 and n^2 equals
   A. $2n^8$ B. $2n^6$ C. n^8
   D. n^2 E. None of the above

55._____

56. The volume of the rectangular solid shown at the right is
   A. 12 cu. in.
   B. 44 sq. in.
   C. 48 cu. in.
   D. 88 sq. in.
   E. None of the above

56._____

57. Baseball bats listed at twenty-one dollars per dozen are sold to schools at a discount of 20 percent.
   How much do they cost the schools per dozen?
   A. $4.20   B. $16.80   C. $20.80
   D. $25.20   E. None of the above

57._____

58. Last year a Chicago merchant's total business amounted to $30,000. For the goods sold, he paid $12,000, for rent he paid $2,500, for clerk services $4,742, and for other expenses $1,058.
   His average monthly net profit was
   A. $676.67   B. $891.67   C. $2,500.00
   D. $9,700.00   E. None of the above

58._____

59. If the marked price of an article is $100 and the first discount is 10 percent and the second discount 2 percent, the sale price is
   A. $78.20   B. $88.00   C. $88.20
   D. $88.80   E. None of the above

59._____

60. Mr. Smith agreed to pay an automobile agency a commission of 18 percent of the selling price of his car.
   If the selling price was $1,250, Mr. Smith would receive
   A. $225.00   B. $1,025.00   C. $1,227.50
   D. $1,475.00   E. None of the above

60._____

61. Mr. Browne receives $30.45 per year on an investment of $870.
   At this rate, if his total investment was $1,500, his annual interest would be
   A. $52.50   B. $62.50   C. $625.00
   D. $655.45   E. None of the above

61._____

62. The Ephrata National Bank discounted a 60-day note for $3,500 at 3½ percent per year.
    The proceeds of the note were
    A. $3,377.50   B. $3,479.58   C. $3,520.42
    D. $3,622.50   E. None of the above

    62.____

63. The normal weight of an adult can be found by using the formula w = 5.5(20+d), where w represents the weight in pounds and d the number of inches one's height exceeds 5 feet.
    By this formula, the normal weight of an adult who is 5'6" tall is _____ pounds.
    A. 134   B. 140.25   C. 140.8
    D. 143.0   E. None of the above

    63.____

64. In the figure at the right, triangles ACB and ADE are similar triangles. The length of side DE is _____ feet.
    A. 30
    B. 32
    C. 48
    D. 50
    E. None of the above

    64.____

65. A square piece of tin shown in the figure at the right is used to make an open box. One-inch squares are cut from each corner of the piece of tin and the sides then turned up, to form a box containing 49 cubic inches.
    The length of a side of the original square piece of tin required to make this box is _____ inches.
    A. 5
    B. 7
    C. 8
    D. 9
    E. None of the above

    65.____

KEY (CORRECT ANSWERS)

1.	C	11.	B	21.	D	31.	A	41.	A	51.	D	61.	A
2.	C	12.	A	22.	D	32.	A	42.	C	52.	D	62.	B
3.	B	13.	A	23.	C	33.	E	43.	B	53.	A	63.	D
4.	D	14.	E	24.	E	34.	C	44.	D	54.	E	64.	B
5.	C	15.	E	25.	D	35.	C	45.	B	55.	E	65.	D
6.	B	16.	E	26.	A	36.	B	46.	B	56.	C		
7.	A	17.	C	27.	B	37.	C	47.	D	57.	B		
8.	D	18.	A	28.	D	38.	A	48.	D	58.	E		
9.	C	19.	A	29.	E	39.	C	49.	E	59.	C		
10.	C	20.	E	30.	E	40.	A	50.	B	60.	B		

11 (#1)

SOLUTIONS TO PROBLEMS

1. $2/3 \times 12 = \frac{12}{1} = \frac{24}{3} = 8$

2. Adding, we get 109.14

3. If 5x = 75, x = 75/5 = 15

4. 65.13 ÷ 13 = 501

5. 6 ft. 8 in. + 3 ft. 4 in. = 9 ft. 12 in. = 10 ft.

6. 3/4 – 1/2 + 1/8 = 6/8 – 4/8 + 1/8 = 3/8

7. 4 15/16 – 2 3/8 = 3 21/16 – 2 6/16 = 1 15/16

8. (-12) + (-3) = -15

9. Let x = length of longer line. Then, 5:3 = x:30. Solving, x = 50

10. .025 = 25/1000 (Can also be reduced to 1/40)

11. Cross-multiplying, 5x = 18. Thus, 18/5 = 3.6

12. 33 1/3% of 3 = (1/3)(3) = 1

13. $\sqrt{225}$ = 15, since 15^2 = 225

14. The arrow points to 6 3/8

15. 4x/5 – 6 = 10. Adding 6, 4x/5 = 16. Then, x = 16 ÷ 4/5 = 20

16. 8 hrs. 0 min. 6 sec. – 6 hrs. 4 min. 15 sec. can be written as 7 hrs. 59 min. 66 sec. – 6 hrs. 4 min. 15 sec. to get 1 hr. 55 min. 51 sec.

17. Mean = (2+4+6+8+10+12+14+19) ÷ 9 = 9

18. When n = 0, c = 0. When n = 5, c = 100. Thus, c = 20n. Finally, for n = 7, c = (20)(7) = 140

19. A = 1/2 bh + 1/2 h(b+a)

20. 6 inches : 3 feet = 6 inches : 36 inches = 1/6

21. Add 5 to both sides to get 4s = 12, so s = 3

22. 16 2/3% of x is 30. Then, 1/6 x = 30. Then, 1/6 x = 180

12 (#1)

23. At 7:00 A.M. the temperature was 12.5, while at 9:00 A.M. the temperature was 15. The change was 2.5 degrees.

24. Perimeter of Section I is 4b and the perimeter of Section III is $2b + 2a - 2b = 2a$. The sum of the perimeters is $4b + 2a$,

25. Area of Section II is $b(a-b) = ab - b^2$ and the area of Section IV is $(a-b)^2 = a^2 - 2ab + b^2$. The sum of the areas is $a^2 - ab = a(a-b)$.

26. Direct translation of words to symbols yields $F = 9/5C + 32$

27. Subtract 6x to get $-114 = 5.7x$. Solving, $x = 20$

28. $(84/42)(100)\% = 200\%$

29. The figure is a cylinder.

30. Converting each choice to a decimal, we get $.5, .\overline{5}, .58\overline{3}, .6, .75$. The largest is .75 corresponding to 3/4.

31. For a circle, $A = \pi r^2$

32. A five-sided enclosed figure with straight sides is called a pentagon.

33. A quadrilateral with opposite sides parallel is called a parallelogram. Rectangles and squares are parallelograms with 90° angles.

34. $x - y + z = 18 - 3 - 2 = 23$

35. Since the digit in the hundreds place is 5 or greater, the answer is 336,000.

36. The sum of the angles of any triangle is 180°.

37. The scale difference is about 2 inches, and since 50 miles corresponds to 3/4 inch, the actual distance is about $(50)(2 \div 3/4) = 133\ 1/3$ mi. Closest answer given s 130 mi.

38. 6 added to n means $6 + n$. Thus, $6 + n = 1$ or $n + 6 = 1$.

39. 3 is an exponent for $2n^3$.

40. 12 inches in 1 foot means 12n inches in n feet.

41. 3 months = 1/4 year

42. 25% of 360 degrees = 90 degrees.

43. Area of $\triangle AED = (1/2)(2)(3) = 3$ square units = 12 sq. inches.

44. Angle X is the angle of elevation to B from A.

13 (#1)

45. Since u + v = 180, we can also write u = 180 – v

46. 4/x = 6/15 Cross-multiplying, 6x = 60. Solving, x = 10

47. 100% - 15% = 85%

48. A = P + Prt becomes A – P = Prt. Dividing by Pr, we get: t = (A-P)/Pr

49. π = ratio of circumference to diameter of a circle.

50. Let B = base, H = altitude. Original area of triangle = 1/2BH. If new base and altitude are 2B and 2H, new area = ½(2B)(2H) = 2BH, which is 4 times the value of 1/2BH.

51. Let x = altitude. Then, $x^2 + (s/2)^2 = s2$. This becomes $3/4s^2 = x^2$. Solving, x = s √3 /2

52. 1 meter ≈ 39.37 inches ≈ 40 inches.

53. Substituting (3,-2), 2(3) – 3(-2) = 12. The other points do not lie on 2x – 3y = 12.

54. The false statement is ∠2 + ∠u = ∠r + ∠t. It is only true that ∠x = ∠u and∠ r = ∠t).

55. $n^4 • n^2 = n^6$, since exponents are added in multiplication.

56. Volume = (6)(4)(2) = 48 cu. in.

57. ($21)(.80) = $16.80

58. $30,000 - $12,000 - $2,500 - $4,742 - $1,058 = $9,700. The monthly amount is $9,700 ÷ 12 = $808.33

59. ($100)(.90) = $90. Then, ($90)(.98) = $88.20

60. 1,250 – (1,250)(.18) = $1,025

61. $30.45/$870 = 3.5%. Then, 3.5% of $1,500 = $52.50

62. (.035)(60/360) = .00583̄ = discount for 60 days.
    The value of the note = (1 - .00583̄)($3500) = $3,479.58.

63. W = 5.5(20+6) = (5.5)(26) = 143

64. x/80 = 40/100. Solving, x = 32. Note that AD:AC = DE:BC

65. When folded, each new side is √49 = 7

EXAMINATION SECTION
TEST 1

DIRECTIONS: Each question or incomplete statement is followed by several suggested answers or completions. Select the one that BEST answers the question or completes the statement. *PRINT THE LETTER OF THE CORRECT ANSWER IN THE SPACE AT THE RIGHT.*

1. A solid which has a point at one end and a circle at the other end is a
    A. cone   B. sphere   C. cylinder   D. prism

    1.____

2. $(5 \times 10^2) + (3 \times 10^1) + (4 \times 1) =$
    A. 84   B. 534   C. 5034   D. $(5+3-4)10$

    2.____

3. All members of R are members of T, but no members of T are members of V. Therefore, you know that
    A. some members of R are members of V
    B. no members of V are members of R
    C. some members of V are members of T
    D. no members of T are members of R

    3.____

4. The multiplication of 6x48 can be distributed as
    A. (6x40) + (8x8)
    B. (6x20) + (20x8)
    C. (6x20) + (6x20) + (6x8)
    D. (6x6) + (6x8)

    4.____

5. Which of these could be used as a divisor and NOT change a dividend?
    A. 0
    B. 1
    C. The dividend itself
    D. There is no such number

    5.____

6. Through any one point, there can be
    A. an unlimited number of lines
    B. only one line
    C. only one set of parallel lines
    D. only two lines

    6.____

7. Ten girls have an average of 25 points on a test. If 5 points are added to each girl's number, what will the average then be?
    A. 3   B. 25.5   C. 27   D. 30

    7.____

8. E + A =
    A. 2EA   B. AE   C. A+E   D. A-E

    8.____

9. A number that indicates how many times a base number is used as a factor is a(n)
    A. prime number
    B. rational number
    C. reciprocal
    D. exponent

    9.____

10. Some of the multiples of a certain number are w, k, m, p, and z. Some of the multiples of another number are k, p, z, and r.
    A common multiple of the two numbers is

    A. r   B. w   C. m   D. k

11. Which is another way to multiply axbxc?

    A. (a+b)xc   B. cxaxb
    C. bx(a+c)   D. (axb) + (axc)

12. The set of any two points on a line and all points between them is a

    A. ray   B. bisector of an angle
    C. half line   D. line segment

13. What is the area of this rectangular region?
    A. 12 sq. ft.
    B. 20 sq. ft.
    C. 24 sq. ft.
    D. 36 sq. ft.

    (rectangle: 6 ft. by 4 ft.)

14. In the numeral (6568, the 6 that is underlined stands for how many times as many as the other 6?

    A. 10   B. 100   C. 1000   D. the same

15. According to the distributive principle, one third of 6 ft. 9 in. would be

    A. 23 in.   B. 3 ft. 3 in.
    C. 2 ft. + 3 in. D. 1 yd. + 3 in.

16. Two names for the same thing are USUALLY indicated by which sign?

    A. ε B. =   C. ~   D. u

17. Mary has 60¢ saved to buy three hairbows which cost 25¢ each.
    Which sentence can be used to find out how many cents more (n) she needs?

    A. $60 \div n = 3 \times 25$ B. $3 \times 25 = 60n$
    C. $60 \div 3 - n = 25$ D. $3 \times 25 = 60 - n$

18. Which of these is a prime number?

    A. 43   B. 68   C. 87   D. 165

19. Which means 24 divided by a number equals twice the number?

    A. $\dfrac{24}{n} = \dfrac{2n}{24}$ B. $24 \div n = \dfrac{n}{2}$

    C. $2 \times \dfrac{24}{n} = n$ D. $\dfrac{24}{n} = 2n$

20. Which of these numerals can you be sure is NOT correctly written?   20._____

   A. 257 $_{eight}$ B. 362 $_{seven}$ C. 421 $_{four}$ D. 453 $_{six}$

21. What is 3754 rounded to the nearest 500?   21._____

   A. 3500   B. 3700   C. 3750   D. 4000

22. When a person measures, he ALWAYS   22._____

   A. tallies   B. compares   C. marks   D. weighs

23. Four is what percent of 37?   23._____
    To find the percent, a person may use the equation

   A. $\dfrac{4}{37} = \dfrac{n}{100}$ B. $\dfrac{4}{100} = \dfrac{37}{n}$

   C. $\dfrac{(100 \times 37)}{4} = n$ D. $\dfrac{37}{100} = \dfrac{n}{4}$

24. Angle a is a right angle.   24._____
    Therefore, the sum of the measurements of angles b and c is

   A. 45°
   B. 90°
   C. 180°
   D. 270°

   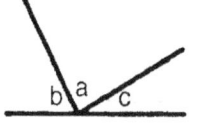

25. If 2 pencils cost 5¢, how many cents will 6 pencils cost at the same rate?   25._____
    The solution equation is

   A. $\dfrac{2}{6} = \dfrac{n}{5}$ B. $\dfrac{2}{5} = \dfrac{n}{6}$ C. $\dfrac{2}{5} = \dfrac{6}{n}$ D. $\dfrac{2}{n} = \dfrac{5}{6}$

26. a(b+c) = ab + ac illustrates the _____ principle.   26._____

   A. commutative   B. associative
   C. distributive   D. binary

27. If the measurement of angle a is 130°, the measurement of angle b is   27._____

   A. 30°
   B. 40°
   C. 50°
   D. 70°

   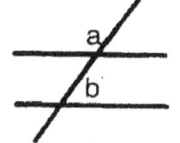

28. In which of these will the product be LESS than m when m is a positive number and not 0?   28._____

   A. $m \times \dfrac{2}{3}$ B. $1\dfrac{1}{4} \times m$ C. $1.0 \times m$ D. $m \times \dfrac{5}{4}$

333

29. 15.94 x 0.5 is APPROXIMATELY

    A. 0.08   B. 0.8   C. 8   D. 80

30. If X = |2, 4, 6, 8| and Y = |3, 6, 9, 12|, then

    A.   X ∩ Y = |2,3,4,6,8,9,12| B.   X ∪ Y = |6|
    C.   X ∪ Y = |2,3,4,6,8,9,12| D.   X ∩ Y = |2,3|

31. If the measurement of angle b is 65 and of angle c is also 65, then the measurement of angle a is

    A. 60°
    B. 50°
    C. 40°
    D. 20°

32. What is the area within triangle JKL? _____ sq. ft.
    A. 48
    B. 50
    C. 95
    D. 100

33. The place holder, or the unknown, in an equation is called

    A.   the empty set   B.   a variable
    C.   an equality   D.   an inequality

34. If part of K is all of W, and all of K is part of M, you can be sure that

    A.   all of W is part of M
    B.   all of K is all of W
    C.   K is less than M - W
    D.   W + K is less than M

35. On the number line above, all points to the right of zero, whether marked or not, represent numbers that are

    A.   positive   B.   whole
    C.   fractions (rationals)   D.   in base ten

36. $\sqrt{5^6}$

    A. 5^2 B. 5^3 C. 5^4 D. 5^{12}

37. Identify the rational number or numbers among the expressions 1/4, 3/4, 4/4, and 5/4.

    A.   1/4, 3/4   B.   1/4 *only*
    C.   5/4   D.   all of them

38. The MOST precise of these measurements of length is

    A. 2 ft. B. 3.25 ft. C. 4 1/2 ft. D. 29 in.

39. A circle graph showing that a person spends 25 percent of his budget for clothes will have an angle whose measurement is

    A. 22 1/2° B. 25° C. 45° D. 90°

40. In Figure _____ , you do NOT see a vertex.

    A.   B.   C.   D.

41. The chart at the right demonstrates
    A. addition facts for the binary base
    B. addition facts for base three
    C. multiplication facts in a non-decimal base
    D. a magic square

	0	1	2
0	0	1	2
1	1	2	10
2	2	10	11

42. Which of these numerals indicates that 4 has been used as a factor twice?

    A. 4 + 4 B. 4/2 C. 4 x 2 D. 16

43. All the pupils in an elementary class who are each over 7 ft. 8 in. tall may be described as the

    A. odd numbers   B. solution set
    C. empty set   D. unique domain

44. 6784.65 is APPROXIMATELY 6.8 x

    A. 10^4 B. 10^2 C. 10^1 D. 10^3

45. If X is less than Y, and Z is greater than Y, then

    A. $\frac{z}{2} > \frac{y}{2}$ B. X+Y < Z

    C. Y > Z   D. $X = \frac{1}{2}y = \frac{1}{2}z$

46. If the length of each side of a square is doubled, the area of the square would be multiplied by

    A. 1 B. 2 C. 4 D. 8

47. -2 x -3 =

    A. 6 B. -1 C. -3 D. -6

48. Bob has laid out these right triangles to measure the distance across the river at AB. How wide is the river at AB?
    A. 60'
    B. 67 1/2'
    C. 75'
    D. 90'

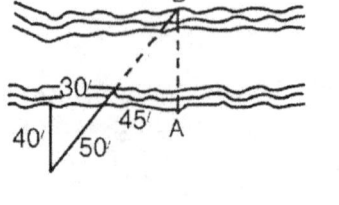

49. Which mathematical sentence below would you use to find the rate of interest earned on an investment of $1000 which earns $45 annually?

    A. $45 \div 1000 = \dfrac{100}{n}$

    B. $\dfrac{45}{100} = \dfrac{n}{1000}$

    C. $1000 \div 45 = \dfrac{100}{n}$

    D. $\dfrac{n}{100} = \dfrac{45}{1000}$

50. $5^6 \div 5^2 =$

    A. 1^3 B. 5^3 C. 5^4 D. 5^{12}

51. Suppose you were taking the 5 marbles from this box one at a time without looking until they are all gone. You draw one which is black. Now, what are the chances that you will draw a black marble the second time?

    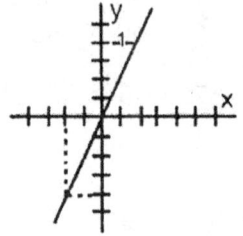

    A. 1/3   B. 1/4   C. 1/5   D. 2/5

52. This is a graph of the solution set for
    A. y = 2 + x
    B. x = 2 + y
    C. y = 2x
    D. x = 2y

53. A square, a rhombus, a rectangle, and a trapezoid are ALL
    A. pentagons   B. prisms
    C. parallelograms D. quadrilaterals

54. A multiple of a number is
    A. a common denominator of that number and a greater number
    B. a multiplier
    C. one of two factors in a multiplication
    D. a product of that number and another factor

55. $\sqrt{13} \times \sqrt{13} =$

    A. 3.4   B. 13   C. $\sqrt{13}$ D. $\sqrt{26}$

56. ←•—•—•—•—•→
      P Q R S T

    $\overline{PR} \cap \overline{ST} =$

    A. ∅ B. $\overline{RS}$ C. $\overline{PT}$ D. $\overline{RT}$

57. In this group of symbols (⊥ , = , + , ~ , ≅ , ≡), there is no symbol that means

    A. plus or minus
    B. is equal to
    C. is similar to
    D. is perpendicular to

58. The numeral in base ten for a certain number has four digits.
    The numeral in base four for the same number will have _____ digits.

    A. four
    B. more than four
    C. less than 4
    D. One can't tell without knowing what the number is

59. Some integers are positive numbers and some integers are negative numbers, but no positive numbers are negative numbers.
    Which diagram illustrates these facts?

    a   b   c   d

60. If A < B - C and all three are positive whole numbers greater than zero, then

    A. A < B
    B. A + C > B
    C. $A < \frac{B+C}{2}$
    D. B < C

61. If the sum of the digits of a numeral is 36, you can be sure that the number is divisible, without a remainder, by

    A. 2 B. 4 C. 6 D. 9

62. A car goes one mile in 75 seconds.
    To find the equivalent speed in miles per hour, which equation can be used?

    A. $\frac{60}{75} = \frac{60}{n}$
    B. $\frac{n}{60} = \frac{75}{60}$
    C. $\frac{1}{75} = \frac{n}{60 \times 60}$
    D. $75 \div 60 \times 60 = n$

63. The prime factors of three numbers are, respectively, |2,2,3,5|, |2,3,3|, and |3,3,2,5|.
    The GREATEST common factor of the three numbers is

    A. 6 B. 12 C. 30 D. 90

8 (#1)

64. Each square represents a digit in the numeral 3 ☐ ☐ ☐ 144. Even though you do NOT know what digits the squares represent, you can be sure that 3 ☐ ☐ ☐ 144 is divisible by

    A. 3   B. 6   C. 8   D. 9

64.___

65. Which fraction is the LARGEST?

    A. 9/8   B. 7/8   C. 6/7   D. 5/4

65.___

KEY (CORRECT ANSWERS)

1. A	16. B	31. B	46. C	61. D
2. B	17. A	32. A	47. A	62. C
3. B	18. A	33. B	48. A	63. A
4. C	19. D	34. A	49. D	64. C
5. B	20. C	35. A	50. C	65. D
6. A	21. D	36. B	51. B	
7. D	22. B	37. D	52. C	
8. C	23. A	38. B	53. D	
9. D	24. B	39. D	54. D	
10. D	25. C	40. C	55. B	
11. B	26. C	41. B	56. A	
12. D	27. C	42. D	57. A	
13. C	28. A	43. C	58. B	
14. B	29. C	44. D	59. C	
15. C	30. C	45. A	60. A	

SOLUTIONS TO PROBLEMS

1. A cone has a point at one end and a circle at the other end.

2. $5 \times 10^2 + 3 \times 10^1 + 4 \times 1 = 500 + 30 + 4 = 534$

3. The appropriate diagram would look like this:

   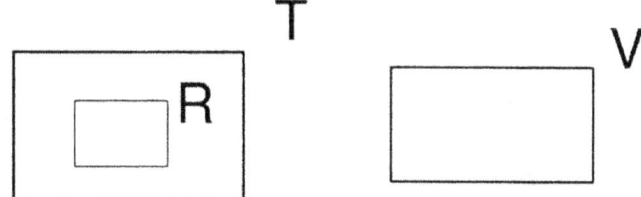

   Thus, no members of V are members of R.

4. Since $40 = 20 + 20 + 8$, $6 \times 48 = (6 \times 20) + (6 \times 20) + (6 \times 8)$

5. Any number divided by 1 remains unchanged.

6. An unlimited number of lines can pass through a given point.

7. Adding 5 points to each score will also raise the average 5 points to a new average of 30.

8. $E + A = A + E$ by the commutative law in algebra.

9. An exponent describes the number of times a base is used as a factor. Example, $n^3 = n \cdot n \cdot n$

10. A multiple in both lists is K (p,z were also in both lists)

11. $a \times b \times c = c \times a \times b$ always

12. A line segment is a portion of a line with endpoints.

13. Area = $(6)(4) = 24$ sq.ft.

14. The underlined 6 means thousands whereas the other 6 means tens. The first 6 is 100 times the other 6.

15. $\frac{1}{3}$ (6 ft. 9 in.) = 2 ft. 3 in. or 2 ft. + 3 in.

16. = means two things are the same.

17. Let n = additional cents needed. Then, $60 + n = (3)(25)$

18. 43 is a prime since it can only be divided evenly by itself and 1 (negative numbers excluded).

19. Let n = number. Then, $\frac{24}{n} = 2n$

20. 421$_{four}$ has no meaning since only 0, 1, 2, 3 may be used in base four.

21. 3754 is closer to 4000 than to 3500, so rounded to the nearest 500, 3754 becomes 4000.

22. Measuring means comparing with some reference like a scale or a ruler, for example.

23. $\frac{4}{37} = \frac{n}{100}$ will yield what percent of 37 is 4.

24. $\angle a + \angle b + \angle c = 180°$. Since $\angle a = 90°$, $\angle b + \angle c = 90°$

25. Using a proportion, 2/5 = 6/n will yield the correct cost.

26. a(b+c) = ab + ac is the distributive property.

27. $\angle a + \angle b = 180°$. If $\angle a = 130°$, Then $\angle b = 50°$

28. $m \times \frac{2}{3} = \frac{2}{3}m$ which is less than m if m > 0.

29. (15.94)(.5) = 7.975 ≈ 8

30. X∨Y means the set of elements in X or Y or both = |2, 3, 4, 6, 8, 9, 12].

31. $\angle a + 65° + 65° = 180°$. Thus, $\angle a = 50°$

32. Area = ($\frac{1}{2}$)(16)(6) = 48 sq.ft.

33. A variable will represent the unknown in an equation.

34. The appropriate diagram appears as:

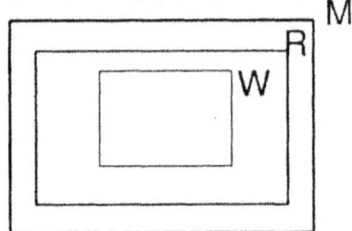

Thus, all of W is part of M.

35. All points to the right of zero represent positive numbers.

36. $\sqrt{5^6} = 5^3$ since $5^3 \cdot 5^3 = 5^6$

37. Any fraction with an integer in both numerator and denominator is a rational number.

38. 3.25 ft. is more precise than the other choices because the accuracy is in hundredths, and the others are whole numbers or contain accuracy only to one decimal place.

39. $(.25)(360°) = 90°$

40. A sphere does not contain a vertex, since there does not exist an intersection of line segments.

41. The given chart shows addition for base 3, where the only allowable digits are 0, 1, 2.

42. Since $16 = 4 \times 4$, the number 4 is a factor twice.

43. A set with no elements is called an empty set.

44. $6784.65 = 6.78465 \times 10^3$ or about 6.8×10^3

45. Since Z is greater than Y, then dividing by 2 yields Z/2 is greater than Y/2. Symbolically, $Z/2 > Y/2$.

46. Let x = original side of a square so that area = x^2.
Doubling each side to 2x makes the area $(2x)^2 = 4x^2$.
Now, $4x^2$ is 4 times as big as x^2.

47. $(-2) \times (-3) = 6$. Two negatives multiplied yield a positive.

48. By similar triangles, 45'/AB = 30'/40'. Solving, AB = 60'

49. $45/1000 = n/100$ will yield the annual rate of interest.

50. $5^6 \div 5^2 = 5^4$. When dividing, subtract exponents.
Note   Bases must be the same.

51. Since only 1 black marble exists out of 4 marbles, the probability is 1/4.

52. The line contains the points (0,0) and (2,4). The related equation is $y = 2x$.

53. A quadrilateral is any enclosed 4-sided figure.

54. A multiple of a number includes a product of that number and another factor. Example: 8 is a multiple of 4, since $8 = 4 \times 2$.

55. $\sqrt{13} \times \sqrt{13} = \sqrt{169} = 13$

56. $\overline{PR} \cap \overline{ST} = \emptyset$ since there are no points in common.

57. The missing symbol is $\pm$, which means plus or minus.

58. In base four, the placeholders are 1, 4, 16, 64, 256, 1024, 4096, etc. If the number is 1000 in base ten, it would correspond to a 5-digit number in base four. If the number is 9999 in base ten, it would correspond to a 7-digit number in base four. Thus, any 4-digit number in base ten would require more than 4 digits in base four.

59. Diagram C is correct, where the 2 smaller circles represent positive and negative numbers, respectively.

60. Since A < B - C, A + C < B. Now, A < A + C because A, B, C are all positive. Finally, A < A + C < B, so A < B.

61. The rule for divisibility of 9 is that the sum of the digits must divide (with no remainder) by 9. Of course, 36 is one such number.

62. 1 mile in 75 seconds = n miles in 3600 seconds.
    This can also be written as 1/75 = n/60 X 60.

63. The factors in common are 2 and 3 and (2)(3) = 6

64. For a number to be divisible by 8, the portion of the number named by the last three digits (on the right) must be divisible by 8. Of course, 144 ÷ 8 = 18, which is a whole number.

65. Converting each fraction to a decimal, we get: 1.125, .875, .857 (approx.), 1.25. By inspection, 1.25 = 5/4 is the largest in this group.

www.ingramcontent.com/pod-product-compliance
Lightning Source LLC
Chambersburg PA
CBHW081757300426
44116CB00014B/2151